DUANE THOMAS
AND THE FALL OF
AMERICA'S TEAM

DUANE THOMAS
AND THE FALL OF
AMERICA'S TEAM

DUANE THOMAS
AND
PAUL ZIMMERMAN

WARNER BOOKS

A Warner Communications Company

W A Warner Communications Company

Printed in the United States of America
First printing October 1988
10 9 8 7 6 5 4 3 2 1

Library of Congress Cataloging-in-Publication Data

Thomas, Duane.
  Duane Thomas and the fall of America's team.

  1. Thomas, Duane.   2. Football players—United
States—Biography.   3. Dallas Cowboys (Football team)
I. Zimmerman, Paul Lionel.   II. Title.
GV939.T46A3   1988   796.332′092′4   [B]   88-40083
ISBN 0-446-51404-7

Book design: H. Roberts

To my parents, John F. Thomas and Lauretta Thomas, who never saw me play pro ball, and to my children: Hisani, Idris, Aisha, Jamila, Niema, and Duane II.

D.T.

Special thanks to Arthur and Richard Pine, Shatemar Thomas, Ron Gabler, Claxton Welch, Ray May, Pettis Norman, Rayfield Wright, Malcolm Brockman, Inge Drechsler, Guy Draper, Howard Cosell, and Wayne Morris and family.

Very special thanks to Muhammud Ali, The Greatest; Miles Davis; Jim Brown; Jessie Jackson, America's Fair Voice; Jim Campbell; Abner Haynes; Clarence Derken; Aunt Madie; Bob Jones; Mansfield Collins; Tody Smith, Bubba Smith, Willie Rae Smith and parents; Floyd Gaston and family; Harold and Claudia Stuart; Baba Ishanghi; Earth, Wind, & Fire and Maurice White; Tom Jr.; Dr. Wenefrett Conner; Marvin Gaye; Calvin Hill, my Cowboy mate and brother, and Bob Lilly and Jethro Pugh, awesome Cowboy teammates.

These are the people who supported me during and after my stand with the Cowboys and believed in truth, and the real American way.

D.T.

CONTENTS

DUANE THOMAS
AND THE FALL OF
AMERICA'S TEAM

★
SUPER BOWL 1972

A writer speaks . . .

I've been to a lot of strange and unusual Super Bowl press conferences. I've covered twenty-one years of them. I remember the warmth and friendliness of the Oakland Raiders before their first Super Bowl, Number Two—excuse me, II—in Miami, Ben Davidson and Tom Keating sitting around the patio with a couple of writers, signing for the drinks and laying out the game plan for us . . . "Now here's what we're gonna do, but you can't write it, okay?" I remember the Raiders' old coach, Johnny Rauch, droning on in a monotone, piling one platitude on top of another until we wanted to scream, and finally Jimmy Cannon, the great old New York columnist, snapping in that machine-gun voice of his, "Okay, you've got a gun to your head and you've got to answer the question. The question is, do you run more or pass more? . . . Now remember, there's a gun to your head. . . . What do you say?"

"I try to balance my offense," Rauch droned.

"Bang!" we yelled.

I was at the dinner the night Joe Namath promised everyone that the Jets would beat the Colts in Super Bowl III ("I guarantee it"), and I sat in on a lot of whacky press conferences with Jets players at poolside, with wives chasing screaming kids in an atmosphere so hectic that the bookies took one look and raised the 17-point spread to 19½ by kickoff.

I listened to the Steelers' Fats Holmes talk nonstop for half an hour at Picture Day for Super Bowl IX—without understanding one word of what he was saying. I recorded, with numb fingers, the wisdom of Kansas City coach Hank Stram, in the frozen ballroom of New Orleans' Fountainbleu Hotel at Super Bowl IV, and I remember the most valuable Super Bowl press conference of all—the Raiders' Phil Villapiano telling a select group of writers, "Do your family a favor and bet the mortgage on us . . . there's no way we won't cover 6½ against the Vikings."

Yep, I've seen a million of 'em, but the strangest one of all, the one I still have nightmares about, was Duane Thomas in Tulane Stadium in New Orleans, January 10, 1972. Picture Day, they called it, later changed to Picture and Interview Day, because that's what it was supposed to be, an interview session. In reality it was twenty minutes of silence. Nothing. Not a word. Just Thomas, the leading running back for the Dallas Cowboys, on a bench in the far corner of the crumbling, decaying stadium, and fifteen or so writers, locked in this overwhelming silence.

The first few questions had petered out when it was obvious that they wouldn't be answered, but no one would leave. Perhaps we should have . . . yes, I know we should have left . . . but it was mesmerizing, like the hypnotic effect of a cobra. Also there was the traditional newspaperman's terror of being someplace while something important was going on elsewhere, and what if he did say something?

Actually he did. After fifteen minutes or so he asked the man directly in front of him, Will Grimsley of the AP, "What time is it?" And Grimsley was so nervous that he studied his naked wrist for perhaps ten seconds, as if he expected a watch to sprout miraculously, before he murmured, "I don't know . . . I don't have a watch." And later a few writers angrily accosted poor Grimsley . . . "Why didn't you tell him? He might have said something."

And while that weird, embarrassing pseudo–press conference was going on, I studied this person, Duane Thomas, who was staring off into the wide, sunny Louisiana sky, and wondered what private hell had enfolded him so completely, because, you see, we already knew that he wouldn't say anything. He had spent a year without hardly talking to his teammates or coaches, except on the field, where it was absolutely necessary. His silence was complete.

Duane Thomas, twenty-four years old, 6-1, 220 pounds, light brown skin, deep, brooding eyes, shockingly handsome; his features bore the look of something ancient, something classical—African, yes, but maybe touched with a Grecian strain. In his running style you saw traces of Jim Brown, perhaps the greatest runner of all time, the same combination of grace and power, the control, explosive power, but always under control. There was something of the jungle in Thomas's running, the lope of one of the great cats, then the burst as it closed for the kill. And in his countenance there was also something of the jungle, the deep, unrelenting stare. "Exotic" was the first impression of Elizabeth Malone, who married Thomas when he was a junior in high school.

But then he smiles and a different world opens up, a world of sunshine and light, the South Dallas street kid who could run like the wind and only wanted to run, to run, faster . . . farther. I didn't see that smile until almost fifteen years later when I got to know Duane Thomas and learned of the strange, troubled life that turned a ferociously driven athlete, whose greatest desire was to excel, to produce, into a lonely, withdrawn, puzzling human being. I learned it from the person himself and from a 200-page journal that he kept, a chronicle of a man's loss of faith, not in his God . . . that always remained steady . . . but in people he had come to trust, and finally a retreat into silence.

JOURNAL: Out of all the conflict and fear in this world, silence was my way of creating a perfect place within myself.

What had happened? In the mid-1960s Thomas emerged as a 215-pound superstar of the black high school leagues in Dallas—the schools weren't integrated then—and then became an equally gifted fullback at West Texas State in Canyon, Texas. His coach was a Southwest legend: Joe Kerbel, 5-9, 300 pounds, an ex-Marine sergeant with a voice that could shake the trees. Tough, given to violent rages, Kerbel was always fair with his players, and in his sternness Thomas saw the image of his own father, who had died when Duane was a sophomore in college, ten months before his mother died.

The Dallas Cowboys drafted Thomas in the first round in 1970—no West Texas State player had ever gone that high until then—and he repaid them with a brilliant season in which he was named Rookie of the Year by three publications or wire services. In Tom Landry, the Cowboys' coach, he had another image of his dead father, different in style from Kerbel—Landry was unemotional and always under control—but the same firmness was there, the sense of command.

The situation seemed perfect for the rookie running back, but there was trouble underneath the surface. Thomas's contract had been minimal, in line with Dallas's rather frugal scale but below the standard for the rest of the NFL. A New York–based agent had skinned him, had taken a ten percent bite of his entire package, including the playoff money, and under the power of attorney that Thomas had signed over to him, had promised to take care of all bills. He never did. The IRS was closing in, Thomas's now-estranged wife was demanding support payments for their two children, the young man's world was collapsing, but every time he picked up a paper he read glowing words of praise from the press or Landry or Tex Schramm, the president and general manager, or Gil Brandt, the player personnel director, who had a file on Thomas going back to high school. The irony of the situation was not lost on him.

He asked for more money. He had clearly outperformed a contract that had him locked in for another two years. Yes, we'll redo it, they told him, but another year would have to be added on, which meant that his salary would be set for four years, total, that even if he should shine brighter than the biggest star in the league, which was quite possible, he would not be paid like a star. For the Cowboys it was business as usual, a deal's a deal, but for Thomas, drowning in a financial whirlpool, it was the ultimate hypocrisy. They praise me, they say they're my family, why won't they pay me what I'm really worth, why won't they help me get out of this nightmare? Look at me, I'm your child and I'm drowning. When Landry refused to step in and help resolve the conflict, when the club left him to get out of his own entanglements, Thomas felt the underside of his dedication—betrayal—and his energy turned inward, to hatred, and then silence. What we found in Tulane Stadium that January day was the product of a rage that had been building for almost a year.

An eccentric, people figured, an oddball whose behavior was to become even odder when he was traded one season later to San Diego, a team he was never to play for. Then came the slide, two less-than-brilliant seasons in Washington, a nondescript period with Hawaii of the World Football League, hints of drug involvement, two unsuccessful tries at a comeback, a succession of business ventures that failed, but finally a sort of inner peace and reflection that allowed him to go back to the Cowboys' training camp in the summer of 1987 and take a clearer look at an organization that had been his family for two years but was now experiencing its own brand of turmoil, which was failure.

An expansion baby in its first few seasons, and then a brilliant, dominating force in the NFL for almost twenty—Thomas saw the first manifestation of that true greatness; he was a key figure on Dallas's first championship team—the Cowboys had sunk to mediocrity by 1987. With the flow of talent drying up and injuries claiming some of the more critical performers, the Cowboys floundered and submerged. There was none of that inner strength to draw on, the kind of emotional strength that sometimes propels teams beyond the level of mere athletic ability. The Cowboys were always known as a cold organization, but now that coldness was translated into performance; it reached the field. The scouting ingenuity that had found a Duane Thomas at West Texas State and made him the number one draft choice was being ridiculed. The coaching staff was filled with indecision, and even Landry himself finally came under intense fire, something that hadn't happened in more than two decades.

They ran parallel courses, Duane Thomas and the Dallas Cowboys, separated by the years but going in the same downward direction. Except that at the end the roles were reversed, and it was the athlete who looked on as the organization struggled.

2

THOUSAND OAKS

JOURNAL: The Dallas Cowboys have control of the media. Anything that a player wants to say has to be approved by the Cowboys, which is Tom Landry.

We are sitting on a grassy slope overlooking the practice field—Duane Thomas, myself, and Tony Dorsett. This is the Cowboys' training camp at California Lutheran College in Thousand Oaks, thirty miles northwest of Los Angeles in the Conejo Valley. Duane is visiting, I'm taking notes for my 1987 preseason scouting reports for *Sports Illustrated,* and on this breezy July day Dorsett is giving us his views on what it's like to be phased out, after ten straight years of leading the Cowboys' running attack. I'm not aware that this is an official Tom Landry–approved interview, but what the hell, a lot of things change in sixteen years, including perceptions.

"They brought in Herschel Walker to replace me, okay, that's their privilege, but it could have been handled better," Dorsett says. Walker, the record-breaking runner for the USFL, was a fifth-round draft choice steal. In 1986 the Cowboys signed him to a $5-million, five-year contract.

His base salary of $350,000 was the same as Dorsett's, but the pot was sweetened by a $1.4-million bonus. The Cowboys never had parted with this kind of money for a player.

Dorsett outgained Walker by 11 yards in '86, but Walker's 76 pass receptions set a team record. Now the talk is of a running attack built around the 6-1, 225-pound world class sprinter.

"You've got to look at what I've done over the years, what I've brought to the picnic," Dorsett says. "They could have called me in and said, 'Hey, Tony, we're doing this or that.' I felt I was owed a conversation. A guy shouldn't have to read in the paper that he's gonna be demoted."

"It's always been the Cowboys' way," Thomas says.

"Yeah, but we're people, we're human beings," Dorsett says. "Landry or the general manager owes it to us. We should hear it first from a coach or the front office."

It's Thomas's second or third visit to camp. Management's feelings about his return are mixed, happiness at the idea of the prodigal son returning, undercut by a slight sense of uneasiness—what's he up to now? Tom Landry is genuinely happy to see him. You get the impression that this man, who believes so strongly in orderliness, feels that with Thomas's return some kind of order has been restored, a tilted painting on the wall has been righted.

A few of the veteran players with a sense of history seem genuinely impressed by the idea of meeting Thomas.

"Hey, man, you paved the way for all of us," says cornerback Everson Walls, grasping Thomas's hand warmly. Walls, who was a Dallas grade school youngster when Thomas was playing for the Cowboys, is one of the more outspoken black players on the team, along with Dorsett.

"Sometimes you can look in a guy's eyes and see if there's remorse," Walls was to say a few months later, after he had gone through his own ordeal during the players' strike. "I didn't exactly see remorse in Duane's eyes. What I saw was . . . well, he looked weathered, like he'd really been through it."

There are the usual jokes about staying in shape. Thomas, his playing weight of 220 trimmed to 200 through daily long-distance runs and a vegetarian diet, looks sleek and fit.

"Some of those guys couldn't believe my physical condition," he said later. "You see most of the guys I played with, and now they look like East Texas truck drivers on a Saturday night."

The media's reaction to Thomas was interesting: awe at first, then relief when they saw him laughing on the sidelines during practice, finally the cautious approach when they realized he wouldn't bite.

"I couldn't believe this was the same fierce guy I'd read about," said NBC-TV's Bill Macatee. "He actually came over to me and introduced himself and said, 'If there are any guys you want to meet, I'd be happy to set it up for you.' I mean, the guy was like a PR man or something."

The round of newspaper stories came out on the same day, July 22. "No More Silent Treatment" was the headline in the *Dallas Morning News*. "Thomas Reverses His Field," in the *Times Herald*. "Thomas in Touch With the Past," in the *Fort Worth Star-Telegram*.

JOURNAL: Tex Schramm: A horse-trading mentality. Big ego. His own sports show. Conservative dresser. PR specialist. He and Pete Rozelle entered the NFL through the realm of public relations. High visibility. Objective is to be the most knowledgeable person in the business. Became president and general manager of the Cowboys. A closet racist. Crusty.

Gil Brandt: The player personnel director. Has the mentality of a street pimp. No integrity and no alliance to anything but power and money. Tex's hatchet man. Supplier of vices ... the Vice Man. Excellent negotiator. Very shrewd and cunning with in-depth knowledge about each player. A pro. A liar.

Tom Landry: Head coach. An illusionist who used Christianity for his own vanity, greed, and power. A John Birch mentality. Used the computer to create Landry's Humanoids and recruited predominantly southern players, both black and white, to keep separation active and maintain total control (because of the southern conditioning of his men). Large ego. White supremacist mentality. His philosophy was intimidation, intimidation, intimidation, of the mind and body.

The July 1987 stories touched on the main issue of Thomas's seething resentment but never really got into it. How could they? Time was limited. There were other things to write about, the opening of camp, the rookies. Everything was upbeat—Thomas sitting between Landry and Schramm at lunch, Thomas walking out of the dining room arm in arm with Dick Mansberger, a scout who'd been on the West Texas State staff when Duane was there. Thomas went through a tough period, but he's over it now, thank God, was the tenor of Schramm's

THOUSAND OAKS ★ 9

and Landry's quotes. "I survived it," Thomas said. "I know some guys who went through some of the same things and they are dead."

Old quotes were hauled back, including Thomas's most famous line of all, when CBS's Tom Brookshier asked him in a locker room interview after Duane had run for 95 yards against the Dolphins in the Super Bowl, "Are you really that fast?" And Thomas replied, "Evidently." And of course, the nastiest quotes, during the off-season of '70–'71 when Thomas had called Gil Brandt "a liar," and Schramm, "sick, demented, and totally dishonest" (and of course, Schramm's classic reply, "He got two out of three"), and when he'd called Landry, "a plastic man."

"Maybe I'll have a plastic chapter in his book," Landry joked on that July day in Thousand Oaks.

"I know what I would have asked you," I told Thomas as we were walking past the Cal Lutheran dormitory area, which now housed the players.

"What's that?"

"I'd have asked you what was going through your mind during that Picture Day session in Tulane Stadium."

"You people were studying me, and I was studying you, too," he said. We stopped, and Thomas looked up at the sign over an entrance to one of the dorms and read it aloud.

" 'Cal Lutheran, Home of the Kingsmen,' " he said. "The violet and white. A clean, cool training camp. Never too hot. Nice fresh Pacific breezes. At our camp at West Texas State it used to get up to 114 degrees, 120 sometimes. Every other day a linesman would go down.

"Cal Lutheran. See that dorm? See that window up there? That was my room my rookie year. I remember looking out that window, down into the courtyard, and seeing Lance Rentzel and Joey Heatherton kissing good-bye, and I remember thinking, 'Wow, that's a fine-looking woman.' "

A fan came up to Thomas, an old-timer.

"St. Louis Cards, 1971," he said. "Three touchdowns, 77 yards around right end."

"Yeah, and Bob Hayes running sideways alongside me," Thomas said, "cutting left, cutting right. I told him, 'Don't you ever do that again.' "

"Yeah, man," the guy said. "You guys was something."

Thomas watched him leave.

"Good fan, bad memory," he said. "The run was 53 yards."

Earlier, when we were talking to Dorsett, a slim man in Levi's and a striped shirt came up to Thomas. A small crowd hung behind him.

"Arthur Smith, Beaumont, Texas, Hebert High, class of '68," he said. "Warren Wells, six years before me; Jerry LeVias, before me; Floyd Hodge, after me; Alvin Maxson and Dwight Houston, my teammates. You remember all those guys?"

"Of course I remember them. We beat all those Beaumont and Galveston guys in the North-South High School game."

"I ran a 4.4," Arthur Smith said. "You want to test your skills?" Someone in the back chuckled. Thomas studied the man, reached down, and slowly took off his street shoes and socks.

The race was from sideline to sideline. It was a race for, maybe, twenty yards, and then Thomas, running without much apparent effort, slowly pulled away. When he hit the finish he was gliding, his face and body totally relaxed.

"Hey, man, gimme five," Arthur Smith said. "Now come take a picture with me and my wife."

3

CHILDHOOD

JOURNAL: I was not into football but I was into running. I'd run two miles every night. I would not miss a workout. I would work on my sprints and starts, do 200 sit-ups, 100 pull-ups, and ask God for strength so I could do more.

He ran, but when he first started, he took part in no organized program, no track team. Running was his thing, his escape, and he didn't want adults messing it up. This was in Los Angeles; he lived in West L.A., Sixtieth Place between Budlong and Vermont, a mile or so south of the L.A. Coliseum, where the big track meets were held.

His parents had sent him out from Dallas to live with his mother's sister, Madie Daniels. The year was 1957. Duane was ten, a fourth grader. He would live there until he was fifteen, with one interim return in the sixth grade, and then he would come back to Dallas to stay.

There were five children in the family, Johnetta, the oldest; Franklin, nicknamed Sonny, two years older than Duane; Bertrand, his younger brother by three years; and Jocelyn, the baby. His father had lost the funeral home that he owned, his mother had gone into domestic service.

"The decision to send me out to live with my aunt was basically a mathematical one," Thomas says, "based on how much food five kids consumed and how much money was coming into the house."

John Franklin Thomas, Duane's father, was born in Marshall, Texas, "where George Foreman is from," Duane says. The population was predominantly black, mostly field hands and factory workers. There were two black colleges there at the time, Wylie and Bishop. Bishop is now in Dallas. "My dad went to Wylie for a year and a half, played the trumpet in the band, and then dropped out," Thomas says. "Had to work."

His mother, Lauretta Jones, was from Little Rock, Arkansas. A gentle, studious person, she concentrated on history, Latin, and religion in high school, applied to Wylie College but never went.

"She believed in two things," Thomas says, "education and faith. She made all the kids in the family take music lessons. She was active in the PTA in school, she was always dropping in to see the teachers and check up on us. My mother was a historian. She'd tell us about persecution, not only of blacks but all people, the Jersey Indians, the persecutions in the Old and New Testaments. She'd talk about faith, the faith involved in any struggle, and about persecution through ignorance. That's the way we were brought up.

"She was firm with us, but if there were any serious punishments to be handed out, my father would take over. She handled the whippings, but we knew she couldn't really hurt us, and if my father would sense a certain attitude being taken on, he'd step in. No more infantry. It was time for the heavy artillery.

"He was quiet and tremendously strong, very powerful with his hands. They said he had to leave Marshall and come to Dallas because he'd killed a man when he was young, maybe twenty-one or twenty-two."

"Once me and Duane's brother Bertrand were changing a tire on their station wagon," says Harold Chambers, who lived next door. "The car fell off the jack. Duane's daddy came out of the house and lifted the car up and put it back on, that's how strong he was."

Duane Julius Thomas was born June 21, 1947.

"A charmer," says his cousin, Dr. Wenefrett Conner, a Los Angeles chiropractor. "A very lovable child. His mother always used to say he was going to be an actor because he had such a beautiful expression."

His father had a funeral home on Spring Avenue in South Dallas, eight blocks from the Cotton Bowl. The family lived in East Dallas. Duane's first memories are of fields and the animals they had.

"We had a cocker spaniel that used to babysit us when my mother went to the store," he says. "I had a pet billy goat, and once it butted me and my mother told my father, 'We've got to get rid of that goat, it's killing my baby.'

"My father said, 'Don't worry, they're just boys.'

"Both my aunts were right next door. On the other side was a huge field. We controlled the entire corridor. Then the government came in and bought the land and built these huge housing projects. That's one of the early things I remember, moving to Baldwin Street in South Dallas.

"I was a biter when I was really little. Then one day my uncle bit me, to show me what it was like. That ended my biting days.

"What else do I remember? I remember sometimes meeting my father at the funeral parlor and getting glimpses of the bodies. For some reason it didn't bother me. I figured people had to live, they had to die. My father used to tell us he never knew anybody yet who left this world alive. We'd hear the usual jokes . . . 'How's the funeral business?' 'It's dead, man . . .' "

Summers, until the fourth grade, were spent in Marshall, working on the farm of his grandfather, his father's father. He was something of a local legend, old even when Duane was a child, fiercely driven by the idea of work.

"He died supposedly when he was ninety-eight," says Dr. Wenefrett Conner, whose mother was the sister of Duane's father, "but he was really older, older than one hundred. You know how old people bend, especially in the shoulder? Well, his shoulders were never bent, even when he was very old. My grandmother had a picture of him with a whole tree across his back."

"Snapped a snake's head off one time by swinging it," Duane says. "Punched a horse and buckled him. I'll never forget that farm. Five Notch Road, Marshall, Texas. Sonny and I would go there together, and he had a complete program for us. You think the NFL was organized? He knew exactly what we were going to do, every minute. There was no place to breathe, unless you were breathing on some work.

"Wenefrett would come in and wake us at four-thirty A.M. She'd say in this high-pitched voice, 'Boys, boys, time to get up and slop the hogs.' I'd pull the curtain back. It would be pitch-black outside. I'd heard stories of wildcats running around there. I'd say, 'I'm not hungry. I know those hogs aren't hungry.' My grandfather wouldn't spend much time arguing. It would take time away from work."

"They'd slop the hogs, feed the cows, feed the horses and chickens, draw water from the well," Dr. Conner says. "When I was living there year-round I'd have to get up at three to milk eight cows before I went to school. Our grandfather didn't believe in anyone having an idle hour. The sight of someone relaxing drove him wild. If you were sitting down he'd find something for you to do, shucking corn, shelling peas, there was always something. There was a syrup mill where we made our own syrup, there was sorghum and sugarcane."

"It made me realize why he had so many kids," Duane says. "A built-in labor force. He loved for you to eat. More energy to work. The food was so well prepared there. There was love in it. It tasted completely different . . . I remember fried corn every morning, fresh biscuits, everything cooked on a wood stove. By the time we were called in for breakfast we'd already fed the animals and chopped wood. After breakfast we'd move out to the fields . . . we'd take our lunch with us. We'd pick cucumbers and corn, cotton, sugarcane, watermelons, alfalfa, maize, you name it. Everything was done manually.

"Sonny and I would see the Santa Fe Railroad run by. I'd say, 'Wonder where it's going to?' My brother would say, 'Well, not to work.'

"Sonny wrote a letter to my father. He said, 'They're killing us with work.' My father drove down. He didn't say a word. It was Sunday around five o'clock and I was thinking, 'When's my old man going to tell us to pack our clothes?' Finally he said, 'Well, y'all gonna be all right,' and he left. I couldn't believe it. I was really mad at the old man because he didn't take us home.

"I decided to run away one time. I walked about five miles and changed my mind. I started thinking about those wildcats. Another time, when I was really little, I threw a goat in the pond. I thought it could swim. All you could see were bubbles. My grandfather told my grandmother, 'Honey, they're tougher than me. They're killing my livestock.'

"Anyway, I worked on that farm every summer. Then I got the chance to go to L.A. and it was bye-bye."

"We all still own the farm," Dr. Conner says, "but nobody tends it anymore. There was a fire there, all the fruit orchards are overgrown now, there are a couple of oil wells on the place. A couple of weeks ago I passed by it. It was just wild trees and scrub."

The home the Thomas family found when they moved out of East Dallas was a yellow, wood-frame two-story just east of the Cotton Bowl . . . "4527 Baldwin Street," Duane Thomas says. "I even remember the phone number, Hamilton 8–6266."

Behind the house was a four-foot chain link fence. Harold Chambers, a Dallas fireman now, remembers Duane clearing it and announcing that he was going to be a hurdler.

"He liked to practice jumping the fence and he liked to climb trees," Chambers says. "Sometimes we'd climb the big pear tree in back, just to get away from people and talk things over, sometimes we'd go up in those trees for fruit. Mr. Bell had a peach tree and a plum, Miss Lilton had the pear tree in front and fig in back. We used to make the rounds."

"He liked to race people, but he always had to win," says Larry Jefferson, who lived a few houses down the block and is now an ordained minister. "If you'd beat him from that post to here, he had to make it longer. If you beat him longer, then it was, 'Let's race around the block.' So Sonny would race him around the block and win, and Duane would say, 'Let's go around twice.'

"One time he was getting his hair cut inside his house, and he ran outside with half his hair off. This kid, Governor Anderson, started taunting him. He was older but not bigger. Duane ran inside and got a hammer and ran at him, and Governor hit him in the mouth and dropped him. Duane wasn't much of a fighter. I started giving him boxing lessons after that. I had eight brothers and they all lived in those boxing gyms around South Dallas, like Curtis Cokes's gyms, and they knew boxing. They taught me, I taught Duane."

"Yeah, I remember that fight with Governor," Thomas says. "The first thing I did was try to get Sonny to help me, but my father said, 'You'd better go back out there and fight. We're not going to help you out.'"

Duane's father lost the funeral home. He worked in a sheet-metal plant for a while, then he did odd jobs, and finally he started his own painting business. Money was hard to come by. Lauretta Thomas, who had once dreamed of becoming a teacher, went to work cleaning houses.

"It bothered me, sure it bothered me," Duane says. "I think of how brilliant she was, how she could speak Latin and how much she cared about education. She had started studying to be a teacher, but her education was cut off. She had to support her family. We were planned kids, my brothers and sisters and I, but my mother's two younger sisters and brother weren't. She was the oldest. She had to help in their support.

"When I was little, Sonny and I would go with her to some wealthy person's house she was cleaning. The size of some of those houses got me . . . we're talking about seven and eight bedrooms. Me and Sonny, we'd sit behind one of those big desks in the study and pretend we were making some deal.

"I would think about the unfairness of it. How could someone be so good and so God-fearing and righteous and not have that kind of life? One of my objects was to provide for my parents. Then they died so suddenly when I was in college.

"My older sister was a prodigy on the piano. She started when she was five, playing classical music. When my mother died, she just gave it up. I told her, 'Do you realize how dynamic you are, how you can excel if you want to?' She said, 'Duane, I just don't care. I don't care about music anymore.' "

Duane's father always had been a quiet person, but his business failures turned everything inward. The silence that would later become Duane Thomas's public image had appeared a generation earlier.

"His father and his father's brother would visit each other," Dr. Conner says, "and they'd say, 'Hi, how are you?' and then they'd have nothing to say to each other. They'd just sit there."

"I saw my father changing," Duane says. "He would hold things to a point and then he'd just explode. He'd break down in tears. It was his family, his family's welfare that troubled him. He'd see something, maybe a program on TV, and it would set him off. Who knew what was going through his mind?

"I'd see my father cry, but it wasn't embarrassment I'd feel. I wanted to show some support, to say something, but I didn't know how. I was a kid. What could I say? I'd ask him, 'Is there anything I can do?' and he'd say no."

So his parents sent him to Los Angeles to live with his aunt Madie, who worked for L.A. General Hospital. For the first time he met white kids, got to know them.

"I couldn't get over the freedom of it," he said. "You could actually go up to a white lady and talk to her without everybody looking at you funny."

He set up his own workout schedule; he ran, gradually lengthening the distance as he grew older and stronger. He liked to dress well, slacks instead of jeans, knitted shirts and sweaters.

"I was what they called a sugar dude, not a tough guy," he says. "The few times I got into fights it was because of my clothes. I loved L.A., but by the time I was finishing up the eighth grade, I had outgrown it. I had a big argument with my aunt. She wanted me in by nine o'clock, I wanted to stay out till ten. She called my mother. 'He needs to come home,' she said. 'He needs to be with his father.'

"I felt real good about going back to Dallas, seeing my brothers and sisters, seeing how tall everyone had grown. I saw that I was as tall as Sonny. We'd gotten into fights when we were kids. I never liked fighting. Every time I had to fight I'd be shaking and trembling. I told him, 'Sonny, the ass-kicking days are over. From now on we're going to get along.' "

"What kind of a person was Duane when he came back?" says Larry Jefferson. "Likable, honest, straightforward. He didn't go around Jericho to get to Jerusalem when he wanted to tell you something. But he was basically a loner. I guess he always had that in him."

4

LINCOLN HIGH

We'd hear it every year in training camp. Every year Coach
Landry would make the same speech. We'd call it his Duane
Thomas speech and we used to try to guess what day he'd
make it. He'd say, "Duane Thomas used to sit in the meeting
room and he'd never look up and he'd never open his
playbook, but come Sunday he was perfect. He didn't make a
mistake, ever. He knew his assignment and everyone else's."
Some of the veterans got a little tired of that speech.

Everson Walls

The system at Lincoln High School in South Dallas was unique.
There were no playbooks handed out, very little blackboard work. The
teaching and visualizing were done on the field, and the brain was the
playbook. Lincoln was a preintegration black high school and funds were
limited, and facilities certainly lagged behind the high school counter-
parts in white Dallas, but the football system, starting in the ninth
grade, was the ultimate in sophistication.

"I wouldn't let them have playbooks," says Robert (Rabbit) Thomas, who coached Duane as a ninth grader. "I used to tell them, 'If you get it up here, in your head, then it can't be taken away from you.' If they write it all down, then the next thing they know it could be gone. They lose it, look for it, can't find it, and panic. Their mind goes blank. If it's in their heads to begin with, then it can't be lost."

Thomas was the ninth-grade coach and varsity assistant under Floyd Iglehart. They'd been teammates at Wylie College in Marshall, Thomas a 6-2, 210-pound offensive and defensive end; Iglehart, an all-purpose back and sixth-round draft choice of the Los Angeles Rams in 1950—as a defensive back.

"He had it all, he was going to be a great player," says Gil Brandt, a Rams' scout at the time. "He was going to be another Night Train Lane. Then he tore up a knee and that was the end of his career. But he became a great coach."

"The players had to know every assignment," Rabbit Thomas says, "what everybody did on each play. The things we did in junior high were more complicated than a lot of NFL offenses today. We ran a pro attack, shifting, motion in all directions."

"The backs had to understand," Duane Thomas says, "that if the linebackers made a deeper drop, they had to go under, a shallower drop, then go over."

"On that whole team," Rabbit Thomas says, "we only had two guys who couldn't grasp what we were doing, offensively. So we took them out and put them on defense . . . just go for the ball.

"Kids were always dropping in to talk football. I had a science class and the football players would wait for it to finish and then talk football during the break. They'd drop by during different periods. Duane would pop in during his lunch period.

"The first thing I noticed about Duane was his speed . . . he always could run . . . but he had an explosion, too, whether he was on offense or defense. Plus he was a nice-looking kid, and that helped catch your eye."

Duane had a reputation before he even arrived at Lincoln, but not in football. Track was his thing. In his last year in Los Angeles he'd started to make a name for himself in the schoolboy meets, and he'd send clippings back to Richard Adams, who'd been one of his teachers during his brief return in the sixth grade.

"I'd read those clippings," Adams said, "and I'd always send word back to Duane, 'You can do better.' "

When he arrived at Lincoln in the fall, his brother Sonny was a varsity regular as a 210-pound offensive guard and defensive middle guard. A year later, as a senior, he would win several all-city and all-district awards.

"I wanted to run track, Sonny wanted me to play football," Duane says, "so I said, 'Look, I'll make a deal with you. I'll go out for football if you go out for track, so we can spend some time together.' We hadn't really seen much of each other for five years. So he went out for track and became an outstanding hurdler. I went out for football and the rest is history."

The first day Duane showed up for practice he was wearing slacks, a Ban-Lon stretch shirt, and tennis shoes from the gym. He asked for a tryout.

"You have to wait for a uniform," Coach Thomas told him.

"I can play just like I am," Duane said.

"Your momma's not gonna like that, getting your nice clothes messed up."

Charles Ray Henderson, the quarterback, "Hotfoot" Henderson, who would later become Duane Thomas's best friend and travel with him to West Texas State, asked him what position he played.

"I only knew one position," Duane says. "End. That's what I told him. He said, 'Offense or defense?' I said it didn't make any difference."

"All right, get over there with the defensive group," Coach Thomas said.

"We went through drills at first, and they're all looking at me and laughing," Duane says. "Then we lined up on defense and I was at end. Charles Ray said, 'If they go around end, get the man.'

"They ran a sweep. I've always been strong, but I didn't understand anything I was doing. A guy tried to block me and I slapped him out of the way. The runner threw the stiff-arm at me. I grabbed his arm and swung him 360 degrees into a fence and he got mad. It was a weird feeling.

"There was silence on the field. Finally someone said, 'Coach, that's a strong sumbitch there.' "

It took two days for him to get a uniform.

"Next day I came out in another Ban-Lon shirt. I tore my pants up. Guys were apologizing . . . 'That's okay, you're from L.A. You've got plenty of clothes.' People started acting friendly. I'd be friendly, too. I'd stick out my hand . . . 'Hi, I'm Duane Thomas.' There was no pressure on me. If I made it, fine. If I didn't, fine. It didn't mean anything. In two weeks I was starting both ways for the ninth-grade team. I loved defense, but I knew I could catch a long pass, too."

Professional players were a familiar sight around Lincoln High.

Abner Haynes, the all-AFL halfback for the Dallas Texans, which would later become the Kansas City Chiefs, was a Lincoln grad. He'd bring over teammates such as Curtis McClinton and Stone Johnson to help the kids. Football was beginning to take hold of fifteen-year-old Duane Thomas. He became a Texans fan because of Haynes. He liked the Giants in the NFL because there was something he found appealing in the image of their bald-headed quarterback, Y. A. Tittle. He began to study some of the professional receivers in the pros, the ones whose style he liked: Lenny Moore of the Colts, Charley Taylor of Arizona State and the Redskins. From Chris Burford, the Texans' all-pro wide-out, he learned the art of relaxation in going for the deep one.

"I first found out that I could catch the long pass against our big rival, Booker T. Washington, the Bulldogs," Thomas says. "I caught an 80-yard touchdown pass, 40 in the air, 40 on the run. It was just a concentration thing."

"Our freshman team was undefeated that year," Rabbit Thomas says. "The last game of the season, I never will forget it, we were playing Sequoia for the championship, and we were behind, and we had time for one more play. Now this is for the championship, don't forget. Coach King, my assistant, looked at me and called time-out. The man came over and informed us, 'No more time-outs.'

"I told one of the kids, 'Phillip, tell Duane to go as far as he can, right between the goalposts.' That was the name of the play, 'Far as You Can.' Well, Duane caught it between three guys as the clock ran out. We won the championship and everyone said I was a hell of a coach."

Football had become a serious sport for Duane Thomas, but the sunshine sport was still track. You met the enemy, face-to-face, you traded one-liners, there was psych and double-psych. It was fun. Washington was the local power, with an awe-inspiring array of talent. The black Texas high school track circuit in those days was something unique in sports. The meets were held in rickety stadiums on patched-up tracks. The only thing big-time was the collection of athletes, whose names would become famous, who would go on the world class lists, and here they were, going against each other before a loose, hip crowd, most of whom knew the athletes personally. Admission was free, or maybe a dollar or two, to see one of the best shows in sports.

"I always loved to run against Washington," Duane Thomas says. "I knew a lot of their guys from football—Emmett Richey, who'd been a big star, a Mister Everything guy like Charley Taylor . . . he passed, he ran, he caught the ball, he played defense. A big heart, too. He used to run the quarter mile. They had Bo Lyndon Johnson, who'd been a halfback. He'd run 45- and 46-second quarters; he beat the Olympic quarter miler, Ray Saddler, in high school. He ran all three relays, too, and they had a cheer when he took the stick: 'Bo got the bone and gone, woo, woo, woo . . . Bo got the bone and gone, woo, woo, woo.'

"In the spring I'm running varsity and junior high, both, just changing shirts, and we're running against Booker T., and they had this guy who was faster than Bo in the sprints . . . Bo wasn't a 100-yard-dash guy. His name was Adam Woods and he looked like a little Martian—round face and head, big, bright eyes, about 5-8, and explosive.

"Well, I thought I was pretty fast, 9.8 in the hundred, 22-flat in the 220, and I'm running second leg against Adam Woods in the 440 relay. My man brought me the baton three yards in front of him, I beat him on the exchange. When I got about fifty yards down the track I started hearing something behind me . . . 'Dit-dit-dit-dit.' I didn't want to look. I could feel the force coming up. I looked anyway. Couldn't help it. And there he was. He came by me so fast I almost stopped running. No one ever passed me so fast.

"Everyone was partying after the meet. I went home. My mother asked me, 'How did you do?' and I said, 'All right.' I always said that. I took a nice, hot bath, changed clothes, and I went back on the street, down to the railroad tracks, to do more roadwork. No one's ever going to pass me like that again.

"The hundred never was my race, though. Too fast. I took a lot of thirds and fourths that spring. I'd get down in the blocks, boom, the race was gone. Hey, wait a minute . . . sorry, Bo, it's gone. I never did get my legs under me. I just didn't have that kind of muscle twitch. So I got out of the 100 and into the 220."

In his sophomore year Thomas first ran into authority at the whacko level, and that's when the problems started.

"The varsity backfield coach and the man I came into contact with most was Lendolph Blakely," Thomas says, "and he was nuts. He'd do things like making the backs run through the line blindfolded, with live tackling. He'd say, 'You have to have a second sense. You must not know fear. When you flinch, that's projecting fear.' The man nearly got some people killed."

"Duane must have quit five times," says his younger brother, Bertrand, a geophysicist who's in the oil exploration business now. "One of those coaches would raise too much hell with him, he'd just walk out. People kept talking him into coming back; they wouldn't let him quit."

The star of the team was a different Thomas, Franklin, who had by now established himself as a formidable hurdler on the track team.

"In the spring of my sophomore year Sonny said he was going to make a hurdler out of me," Duane says. "He tried to teach me, and I kept knocking them down. I said, 'How the hell do you run these sumbitches?' He said, 'It's all stride and technique. You can't get out of your stride.' So I devised my own workout schedule and it paid off. I'd run fifteen flights of high hurdles, back-to-back. I was tired of getting my ass beat.

"In the city track meet my brother and I and a guy from Booker T., Tommy Johnson, were the favorites. I told my brother I was going to win. I got in the blocks, and I could hear all these girls on the sidelines yelling, 'C'mon, Tommy, c'mon, Tommy,' and I thought, 'I'm gonna kick this guy's ass, too.' The gun sounded. I had a great take-off . . . that's where I got 'em, on the takeoff. I could hear everything during the race, my steps, everything. I knew I couldn't be beat. When I won, my brother couldn't believe it. But he was happy, too. At least it was still in the family. From that time on I was one of the top two hurdlers in the city.

"I didn't win 'em all, though. In the district meet a guy named Bruce Washington came over to me and said, 'I heard about you, brother. I hope you get a good second place today.'

"I said, 'If you beat me, you're gonna have to break a record.' Well, he beat me and broke the record. I felt good about the loss, though. He beat me on speed. I had to stride and pick the speed up. It wasn't technique that had beaten me."

By his junior year Thomas was a varsity regular on the football team. He was still an offensive end, but his greatest skill was defense. He played everywhere: end, tackle, linebacker, safety . . . "They moved me wherever they needed to stabilize a position," he says.

He had established his own training program, which included a lot of running and a self-styled form of weight training.

"One of my teammates, Bobby Turner, had this friend named Lorenzo Goosby who went to Madison," Thomas says. "Lorenzo had all these weights in the back of his garage. He had a weight room, a sweat room. Bobby was into gymnastics and tumbling. He'd work on every muscle you could think of. He'd keep a chart.

"Lorenzo's whole family were gymnasts. His nephew became an

acrobat for Barnum & Bailey. The guys at Madison at that time were more into that kind of training. They looked like athletes. They always had an excellent track program. So we used to work out at Lorenzo's garage. That's the thing about black ballplayers in those days. They'd try to help each other. It didn't matter if you were from different schools or you were in the same school, competing for the same position. They'd lend a helping hand to one another.

"Kids nowadays, I don't know if they're into that so much, or into self-motivated training. They miss out on a lot by having cars. Maybe if they walked more and ran, and rode bikes more, like we did, there would be fewer leg injuries. We were into the idea of being in shape just to be in shape, to walk down the street and look good. There were no cars. Anytime you got ready to move you had to move your feet."

After supper Duane would walk over to his friend Charles Ray Henderson's house on Pine Street, a couple of miles away. Then he'd run the two miles home. Occasionally he'd stop off to visit his girlfriend, Elizabeth Malone, who also lived on Pine Street.

"I'd run track myself at Lincoln," says Elizabeth Malone, who has changed her name to Imani Pamoja. "That's where I first noticed Duane, on the track. He was tall and, well, exotic looking. He had the mystique of coming here from another state. We started going together when he was in the ninth grade and I was in the tenth."

One night in the fall of 1964, Duane's junior year, Elizabeth Malone told him she was pregnant.

"Duane didn't want to marry her, but he wanted to do what was right," his aunt Mary Weller said. "The girl's mama promised him that if he'd give the baby a name, she'd have the marriage annulled. Remember now, Duane was just a junior in high school."

In October 1964 they were married. The annulment never happened. They lived together, on and off, for almost twenty-two years, a strange love-hate relationship that produced two divorces, six children, and innumerable heartbreaks and reconciliations.

"At the time not many people knew they were married," Bertrand Thomas said. "If they had, Duane never would have been allowed to play his last two years of football at Lincoln."

Floyd Iglehart was shock therapy for the troubled sixteen-year-old. A graduate of Lincoln High, where he'd run on a championship quarter-mile relay team, a veteran of the Texas black college circuit and the L.A. Rams, Iglehart was a fire-breather, rough as a Texas cactus but well suited to coach in South Dallas.

"He was tall and slim with funny-looking eyes, cat's eyes," Thomas says. "He had a funny way of talking. If a kid would give him back talk he'd yell at him, 'Hey, nigger, fuck with me and I'll get my knife and cut your throat!' He told me that his coach at Wylie had said that a guy who didn't curse, who said 'yessir' and 'nosir,' wasn't mean enough to play football. He'd say, 'What the hell's wrong with you, boy? There are no goody-goodies at black schools.'

"The greatest thing about Coach Iglehart and Coach Thomas, though, was that they were part of the community. They weren't people you put up on a platform, and you had to pray to them so they could ordain you."

"I knew Duane's family," Rabbit Thomas says. "I taught his brothers and sisters. Hell, I knew all the parents. I was born in Dallas, went to Lincoln High. I knew all the neighborhood trouble spots, all the hoods that hung around the street corners. I knew Bonton and Roosevelt Heights, the rough areas, and I wasn't afraid to go there. You weren't just a coach at Lincoln. You were involved in the entire life of the community."

"When a kid needed a pair of track shoes, and the budget was short, you pulled the money out of your pocket, no big deal," says John E. Kincaide, who coached Washington in those days and is now the athletic administrator for the Dallas Independent School District.

"You see, the thing about the South Dallas black high school community was that everybody knew each other. A PTA was a real PTA."

Duane Thomas was moved to fullback as a senior. His weight was up to 215. "He didn't look as fast as he really was," Rabbit Thomas said in the winter of 1987, echoing Tommy Brookshier's fifteen-year-old remark in the Super Bowl locker room. "We had 9.4 and 9.5 sprinters on the team, but Duane was the guy the opposing coaches were always devising defenses to stop. I noticed that when he first came into the NFL they called him a glider, but he ran with power, too. He could break tackles, run fluid, juke, anything you wanted. And he blocked like a maniac."

It was quite a team, Duane and Hotfoot Henderson, who could play quarterback or halfback, and Ralph Anderson, who later played defensive back for the Steelers. But Thomas was the one who caught the scouts' eye.

"There was plenty of talent in those black schools," says Clarence Dierking, who recruited Duane for West Texas State and is now a scout for the Detroit Lions. "You just had to go find it. The black schools didn't get much exposure.

"I was at some games where I was the only white person in the crowd. It didn't bother anybody. They knew why I was there."

"The high schools in Dallas didn't really integrate until 1967," Duane says. "We always wanted to see how we'd do against the white schools. Sometimes I'd go over and watch them. It was three yards and a cloud of dust.

"Black players in those days were into showmanship. You not only had to play well, but you had to perform, or you might as well get off the field. I once saw Bubba Smith's brother, Willie Ray, Jr., play for Charlton Pollard in Beaumont, and he was like that. Not a big guy, 5-11 or so, but every run he made was kind of amazing, he'd give it some little personal signature, and the crowd ate it up.

"I saw Otis Taylor play at Prairie View and he was like that, too. Every time he touched the ball something happened. When I was a senior, I saw him make one play for the Chiefs I'll never forget. He was going across the end zone and Len Dawson threw the ball behind him; Otis is galloping like a stallion and I'm thinking, 'He's gonna overrun the ball.' He was like a machine, one-two-three-four. One . . . pass, two . . . reach, three . . . stab, four . . . spike. That smooth. I started yelling, 'Isn't he great! Isn't he great!'

"There was a flashy type and there was a flat-out playing type. I was just a player."

On Thanksgiving Day, 1965, Lincoln beat Washington, 14–13, for the black City Championship. Thomas, who had changed his jersey number from 32, Jim Brown's old number, to 38, before the game, had perhaps the most brilliant day of his career, 232 yards on 27 carries. It was almost a one-man show. He had carried five straight times for the first touchdown, ripping off runs of 13, 22, 22, and 10 yards, and finally the 3-yard score. On the winning drive, when Washington bunched to stop him, he powered inside for gains of 4, 3, 3, and 6 yards, setting up Henderson's touchdown.

Lincoln's final game was for the District Championship against I. M. Terrill of Fort Worth.

"It was a rough, vicious game in front of twenty thousand fans in Cobb Stadium in Fort Worth," Thomas says. "A grudge game. Lots of fistfights. I remember coming to the sideline one time with my nose gushing blood and someone yelled, 'Coach, Coach Iglehart, Duane's hurt!'

" 'What wrong with him?' Iglehart said.

" 'His nose is bleeding.'

" 'Hey, I'll tell you when Duane's hurt,' Iglehart said. 'He can't afford to get hurt today.'

"Anyway, they beat us on a 90-yard run by Don Johnson, who wound up going to West Texas State."

There was one game remaining for Thomas, who had gained 1,443 yards for Lincoln, the North-South Black High School All-Star game, with Thomas leading the North.

"We won the game, we dominated," he said. "But you know, it was kind of fun meeting all those guys from Galveston and Beaumont and Houston and places like that. I met Tody Smith, who was drafted number one by Dallas the year after I was. I met a lot of the people I'd been hearing about. Texas is great for legends. Warren Wells was a legend around Beaumont and Galveston. You remember him, the great wide receiver for the Raiders who wound up in prison.

"Once I met Earl Campbell, who'd played at Tyler, and our relationship was so natural. It was like we'd known each other all our lives. Texas guys have that kind of relationship with each other."

The smaller Texas schools were interested in Thomas. The Southwest Conference, which had just broken the color line with Jerry LeVias at SMU, was mildly interested. The omnipresent Gil Brandt had tipped off his old school, Wisconsin, about Thomas, and Missouri was also showing interest. West Texas State, which had tried to recruit Franklin Thomas two years earlier, was the most interested of all.

Duane had made black all-city in Dallas and one combined black-white team. He was mentioned on several schoolboy all-Americans.

"I could have gone to Wisconsin, Missouri, or Texas," Thomas says. "I almost went to Wisconsin. I didn't want to go to the SWC. I was not interested in being another Jerry LeVias. I'd talked to him . . . he told me of the abuse he had to go through just being at SMU. Also, the conference schools were limited. Freshmen played two, three games. At West Texas freshmen could play on the varsity. The traveling was limited, too, in the SWC. West Texas traveled around the entire country.

"I visited Wisconsin. It was frigid when they brought us in. The activities usually centered around a basketball game. I remember seeing Michigan's Cazzie Russell play against Wisconsin. They took us to dinner, and next day the alumni association set up a grand tour of the campus. I was interested in business, so they introduced me to the dean of that school. I loved it. I enjoyed the people; very hospitable, genuine people. I was tempted to go there, and I almost did, but the reason I didn't was they didn't accept one of my teammates, a guy who played tailback for us . . . Redderick (Bay Bay) Price. There was a problem with grades. West Texas accepted him. Plus I noticed that a lot of running backs had been injured at Wisconsin.

"I visited Missouri and had a chance to meet Johnny Roland and Francis Peay, who had been the Giants' number one draft choice. I was impressed with that, with the big money he'd made. I met Charlie Brown, a track guy; they had a good track program at the time. They toured us around. It was a little more loose in terms of black brothers; Wisconsin had been more conservative in terms of blacks. They got us dates at Missouri. I had a Saturday night date. They made sure we weren't hurting for money. I don't remember how much, but I never ran out.

"I'm sorry I never got to meet Woody Hayes. He was the kind of coach I'd have loved to play for. If he'd have been my coach in the pros, I'd have had a long career. He was really into it, my kind of guy. But at the time I didn't know much about him or Ohio State, and they never tried to recruit me.

"North Texas State offered Coach Thomas two thousand dollars if he would deliver me. I pleaded with him to take it. I said I'd go. I loved Coach Thomas. He said, 'No, Duane, I'm not about to be selling my players to anybody.' "

Finally Joe Kerbel paid a personal visit to the Thomas house on Baldwin Street and the hunt was over.

5

WEST TEXAS STATE

If you could recruit at that place, you could recruit anywhere.
Bobby Beathard, General Manager, Washington Redskins

The Thomas family was out in the backyard, barbecuing, when Joe Kerbel's car pulled up. The West Texas State coach hoisted his 300 pounds out of the driver's seat, his wife and family following behind. That was his first master stroke in the psychology of dealing with the parents of a recruit. Bring your family along.

He'd already gotten a full report from his defensive coach, Clarence Dierking, who'd been assigned the Dallas–Fort Worth area. The words "Can't Miss" were written across the top of it. And also this notation —"Best-conditioned high school athlete I've ever seen."

"I'd been following Duane around, going to his track meets, getting to know him," Dierking says. "I explained to him that West Texas was a good place for running backs, because Kerbel would help a guy's statistics if he could. It started with Pistol Pete Pedro in '62. He ended up sixth-leading rusher in the country."

Kerbel's approach was different. He aimed his pitch at the family.

"As soon as Kerbel sat down, my father said, 'What are you offering?' " says Franklin Thomas, who was home on leave from the service at the time.

"That was my daddy's way, full of surprises," Duane says. "I guess he was expecting to hear some big money deal, and then he would have thrown him out."

"Kerbel said, 'Well, Mr. Thomas, we don't give out cars,' " Franklin Thomas says, " 'we don't give money, and we don't give out special favors. But I guarantee you two things. One, we'll give him an education'—he made sure to put that one first; he should have been a psychology teacher—'and two, he'll have the opportunity to play football. That's all we're offering at West Texas.'

"My father said, 'Good. Not only will you have Duane, but the other two as well.' "

Franklin, after a year at Los Angeles City College, went into the service and eventually did end up at West Texas on the GI Bill, where he played briefly with Duane as a second-string guard and linebacker. His career ended with a series of severe kidney disorders. Bertrand followed Duane to West Texas and became a trainer.

"Duane finally made up his mind that he wanted to come, but his mother wasn't sure," Kerbel said in an interview shortly before his death in 1972. "Five times he got ready to sign the grant-in-aid, and five times she put her hand on his arm and said, 'Honey, I don't know. Are you sure this is the best thing for you?' Finally his father had to tell her to shut up and let the boy sign if he wanted to."

"I still remember that ride to West Texas," Duane says. "We drove down in Coach Dierking's blue Lincoln. Coach Dierking later became my favorite assistant coach at West Texas, but that day I was impressed with his stereo system."

West Texas State, affiliated with no conference, was in Canyon, a quiet Panhandle town eighteen miles south of Amarillo. In Kerbel's six seasons before Thomas arrived, the Buffalos finished above .500 three times. In Thomas's four years they had winning records every season, including an 8-2 record when he was a junior. A year before Thomas enrolled, Kerbel had gone as far north as Pennsylvania to recruit Eugene (Mercury) Morris, a quick and elusive halfback, and Morris became the NCAA's leading career rusher of all time. It represented a new thrust in the recruiting focus. Athletically, West Texas had been practically all white, but Kerbel wanted to win. He brought in black prospects, he tapped the junior colleges.

Black West Texas State players of Thomas's era began appearing on NFL rosters—Raymond Brown, drafted in the sixth round by Atlanta, an eight-year starter at strong safety; Ralph Anderson, number five by the Steelers and a cornerback on their first playoff squad; Morris, third round by the Dolphins and a standout on their two winning Super Bowl teams; Thomas and halfback Rocky Thompson, first-round picks by the Cowboys and Giants, respectively; A. Z. Drones, a sixth-round choice by the Rams, his career cut short by a knee injury.

"Utah State's Phil Olsen, the guy who was drafted number one by the Patriots, was the only guy who ever gave A.Z. trouble," Dierking says. "I remember going down to Cameron JC in Lawton, Oklahoma, to recruit A.Z. I went up to his dorm and all these guys were in the room, sleeping, with the lights on. A.Z. loved to sleep. On the way up to West Texas I told him, 'You know, your sleeping days are over now.'"

The black migration didn't sit well with some members of the administration.

"When I first went there, there were maybe fifteen or so male black students, mostly all of them playing football or some other sport," Thomas said. "When I left, maybe forty percent of the football team was black. They had this terribly racist dean there, Dean T. Paige Carruth, the dean of student activities. I'll never forget him. He had called Kerbel in and asked him why he didn't recruit more white players from the area.

"Kerbel told me about it one time. He said, 'Duane, I told that son of a bitch I want to win and you can't win with this shit around here.' He told me, 'I recruited black players because you guys will make us a winner, and as long as I keep winning these sons of bitches can't say anything to me.'

"He even called a team meeting about it once. He said, 'If black players will win for us, we're gonna keep recruiting 'em and no damn dean is gonna tell me what to do. I run this show.' It worked. Everything Kerbel told us worked. Everyone was fired up.

"That's one of the things I liked about Kerbel. He had command of things. He was in control. That's one of the reasons I went to West Texas. In Canyon he was king. He used to be speeding down the freeway and pass a highway patrolman and just wave to him and the guy would wave back. He'd go to a store and never get out of the car. They'd bring everything out. He'd say, 'Put it all on my bill.' Sometimes they wouldn't even charge him. I'll tell you, he had those people hopping around like grasshoppers."

There was one area, though, that was even too touchy for Kerbel to handle, the relationship of black male students to white coeds.

"Coach Kerbel tried to avoid any problem that would disrupt his football team," Thomas says, "and when he talked to me about it, it made sense. I was more into athletics at that point than girls, anyway. I remember at sixteen my sex drive hit me so fast I said, 'Wow, what's happening to me?' I felt the isolated environment of West Texas State would be a good thing.

"When I got to West Texas there were maybe half a dozen black girls, not terribly attractive. They all had this brown stuff on their teeth from the fluorides in the water. They were friendly. They'd say 'Hi' to you in this kind of screech; the white girls would say 'Howdy.'

"The authorities were terrified with the idea of the black players fraternizing with white girls. Let's say they noticed a black guy walking to class with a white girl, and believe me, it didn't have to be an attractive girl . . . well, if they saw this on a consistent basis, the people involved would be called in to see Dean Carruth.

"A lot of students were there on some kind of grant, government or something, and Dean Carruth would tell these girls that if they didn't stop walking up and down the street with those niggers they'd lose their grant. When Franklin arrived—he was already an army vet, he'd seen something of the world—he became a regular in Dean Carruth's office. Franklin told me what the meetings were like.

"He said Dean Carruth told him one time, 'You know, Franklin, there aren't too many girls up here'—he meant black girls—'but we're thinking of bringing more in.'

"Franklin said, 'There are over two thousand girls here,' and Dean Carruth turned red as the shirt I'm wearing."

Franklin Thomas was a bitter young man by the time he got to West Texas. He had gone to LACC with the hope of training to be an Olympic hurdler; the best he'd done was a third-place finish in the Long Beach Relays. He'd quit and gone into the army. Then he had driven a tow truck. When his father died, he was the one who took over the paint business and tried to keep it going, tried to keep the family together. Already he was suffering the first twinges of the renal failure that would put him in the hospital and nearly cost him his life.

"You have to understand that West Texas State was still a primitive place when I got there," Franklin said. "Advanced athletically, yes, thanks to Kerbel, but primitive, socially, with heavy racist overtones."

He was sitting in his office of Enercon Group, Inc., the construction engineering firm he owns in the mostly black Dallas suburb of South Oak Crest, a tall, lightly bearded man with deep, searching eyes. Enercon, Inc. is the outgrowth of his father's old paint business. Newspaper stories during Duane's troubles with Dallas would occasionally refer to his "militant" brother Franklin, mentioning his West Texas State days. One story called him "the closest thing to a militant to be found in Canyon, Texas."

"They had this tradition at West Texas called Old South Day," Franklin said, "run by the Kappa Alpha fraternity. It was a march with Confederate flags, white folks living in the past. Once they had hung a black man in effigy on Old South Day. It was their attempt to maintain as much tradition as they could without considering how repulsive it was to some people, namely black people, like the swastika is to Jews. It was amazing, amusing, and very stupid . . . but it was an unusual thing.

"I helped organize a protest of Old South Day. Before I got there the blacks in the school had been apathetic. We filed a petition. Most of the black students signed it and some of the whites, athletes mostly, football players. It received national publicity. Garrett Puckering, who publishes the *Smithsonian Review* now, was a freshman and he was active. Harper Lee, the author of *To Kill a Mockingbird*, came down and spoke.

"The authorities accepted the petition. Our demonstration was basically peaceful. Maybe a rock or two was thrown, but there were no fights. Mostly debates. Next year Old South Day was gone. I'm sure Coach Kerbel wasn't sorry to see it go."

Kerbel, who once told Duane, "I'd love to coach in the NFL someday, but only if I had total control; I don't want some jackass owner telling me what to do," was building a team that was starting to attract scouts from around the NFL.

"The first thing you noticed was Kerbel's personality," says Art Rooney, Jr., who ran the Steelers' scouting operation in those days. "He was a rough guy, gruff, like a DI in the marines."

"The day I was there," says Bobby Beathard, the Redskins' general manager who scouted for the Chiefs and Falcons during the Duane Thomas era, "he got mad at Duane and made him run one hundred laps around the field. And Duane did it, that's the amazing thing.

"Kerbel had a great presence, he was dramatic, but he was rough on assistants, too. I don't know how it would have been to work under him."

"He'd fire assistant coaches right on the sidelines during a game," Duane says. "Then he'd hire 'em back at halftime. An assistant would do something that would get him mad and he'd yell, 'Security! Get that son of a bitch off my sideline!'

"Guys would be snickering on the bench and he'd turn around and yell, 'And that goes for all of you!' The security guy wouldn't know if he was serious—he'd be moving like a snail—and Kerbel would yell, 'And move *your* ass or I'll fire you, too!' Coach Kerbel was into firing people.

"Once he had security escort his wife off the practice field. He said she was disruptive to his practices. She was sitting in the stands and she waved, Hi. He didn't even look at her. He just told security to get her out."

"Remember when we played Memphis State?" Dierking said. He and Thomas had met at a Cowboys' game in the fall of 1987. Dierking was scouting for the Lions, Duane was down for an alumni weekend. They were swapping Kerbel stories, naturally.

"Spook Murphy, the Memphis coach, was as wild as Kerbel was," Dierking said, "and before the game he and Kerbel were screaming at each other in the tunnel. The police had to separate them and escort them out. We won the toss and chose to kick off. They started moving the ball and Kerbel turned to me and said, 'If they make one yard, that's one yard too much.' I was to his right with the defense. The offense was always to his left. I'd do what he wanted me to do, but he'd chew me out and I'd get upset. A year later we got another coach, Lee Harrington, and we stationed him to Kerbel's right, to intercept him. So he'd chew him out. He never would get to me. Lee was the buffer.

"Kerbel's thing was offense. He had no patience with defense. One time he told Sleepy Jack Harris, the offensive line coach, 'Tell those defensive guys to let 'em score so we can get the ball.' "

"He used to run down to the offensive side," Thomas said, "and tell us, 'Men, the defense doesn't want to play today, but we do, don't we, men. *Don't we?*' And we'd all yell, 'Yeah! Right on!' and wave our fists."

"We're playing New Mexico State in Las Cruces," Dierking said. "They hit a pass on our cornerback, Billy Lantow. I was yelling and Kerbel came down the sidelines. 'What happened, Coach? What happened?' I told him, 'Billy screwed it up.'

" 'Well, goddammit, get him out of there!' Kerbel said. I told him I didn't have anybody else and he said he didn't care. We had this kid, Hardy Williams, from LACC. He wasn't ready to play, but I got him up and started telling him what to do.

"Kerbel came over and said, 'What are you doing?' and I told him he said to get somebody else in there. He gave me this real wide-eyed look.

" 'For God's sake, don't give up, Coach,' he said. 'Don't give up.' So Billy stayed in there."

"Hardy Williams," Duane said, shaking his head. "He teaches school now. He'd run down the field under kickoffs like this, looking up. Every kickoff he'd take a terrible hit. He'd look like a windmill, just get wiped out. I used to ask him, 'Hardy, why do you do it? Why do you look up like that?'

"He said, 'I don't know, man. I like to look at the stars.'

"I said, 'Yeah, you'll see stars all right.' Hardy had something going with the stars.

"Once Kerbel got mad at him in practice and he said, 'Son, who recruited you?' Hardy said, 'Coach McCullough, sir.' Kerbel said, 'Dammit, I'm gonna fire both your asses.' "

Thomas saw some action as a freshman in 1966, a 6-4 year. "I played special teams, made all the trips," he said. In his sophomore year he ran in the same backfield with Mercury Morris, who finished second in the country in rushing, behind O. J. Simpson of Southern Cal. The 7-3 season ended with a 35–13 victory over San Fernando in the Junior Rose Bowl.

"I broke my left ankle, running the ball in our sixth game, against New Mexico State," Thomas says, "and I was out for the season. Had I completed that 70-yard run I'd have been leading the country in rushing, ahead of O.J. and Mercury and everybody."

In his junior year Thomas shared the fullback spot with Albie (Double-O) Owens. That was his blocking year. They cleared the way for Morris, whose 1,571 yards broke the NCAA single-season record, but he still finished second to Simpson. The season ended at 8-2, Kerbel's best at West Texas State, and Morris became the all-time major college career rushing leader with 3,388 yards.

"We played Colorado State in Fort Collins," Dierking said. "Mercury was kicked out in the first half for fighting, along with a Colorado State player. In the fourth quarter Kerbel puts Mercury back in and he starts carrying the ball. Mike Lude, the Colorado State coach, was out on the field. What happened was that the officials forgot to write down the players' numbers, so they let Mercury stay in and let the Colorado guy come back. Mercury broke two NCAA records that afternoon—after he'd been thrown out."

"My favorite Mercury story is the time Kerbel punched him on the sidelines," Thomas said. "Right in the stomach. We were playing Utah State. We'd moved the ball down to the 10- or 20-yard line and we were getting ready to go in and Merc fumbled on a sweep.

"Well, everybody had to pass Coach Kerbel on the sidelines on his way back to the bench. He had a rule about it. You couldn't have your head down. He'd say, 'I want to see your eyes.'

"Mercury tried to sneak around the back of the bench, but Kerbel found him. Merc held out his hands like, hey. Kerbel was so mad he was dancing from side to side.

" 'You Pennsylvania son of a bitch!' he yelled. 'You coward! I'm gonna blackball you in every school in the country!' Then he just wound up and gave him this bolo punch in the belly. Merc came back to the bench crying. We were all laughing.

" 'Hey, Merc, your father kicked your ass.'

"That's why I enjoyed playing for Kerbel so much. He was right into it, you always knew where he stood. Like Woody Hayes, when he punched that Clemson guy on the sidelines. I loved it! My old man really liked Kerbel, and he didn't take to many people. I used to complain how hard he was, and my father would say, 'What do you mean, hard? He's a man!' "

For Thomas, Kerbel was the natural extension of what he'd known at Lincoln High, the fire of Iglehart, the wild, sometimes uncontrolled rages, but also the closeness and commitment of both Rabbit Thomas and Iglehart himself. Because Kerbel was not an unfeeling coach. "A black kid from Texas or Oklahoma who gets screamed at by a white coach, well, if the white players get the same kind of treatment, which they did, then he realizes that at least the guy cares. He cares about all of us."

Kerbel had no eye to color. He treated blacks and whites the same, roomed them together on the road, made sure they spent time together. Even his locker room tirades, chuckled at sometimes by the hipper members of the team, served to bring everyone together.

"Typical Kerbel locker room speech," Thomas says. " 'Men, do you know why we're here?'

" 'No, why?' No, no, none of us would really say that.

" 'This team'—and he'd mention the name of the team—'they think that we're gonna go out and lay down. But we know'—that's when we all had to look at him, at the buzzword 'we,' we'd give him our attention—'We know what we're here for, don't we, men?'

"We played San Diego State and Kerbel fell down, coming down the ramp for the warm-ups. He was so fat he couldn't get up. Don Coryell, the San Diego coach, was walking past. 'You fat son of a bitch,' he said, 'that's what we're gonna do to you in the game.'

"When Kerbel brought us into the locker room for the pregame he was practically in tears. 'I was coming down the ramp,' he said, 'and Coryell saw me fall down and called me a big fat son of a bitch. Men, I want to kill those guys!'

"Then he turned around and hit the blackboard—Wham! It cracked. Guys were screaming and pounding on the lockers. 'Yeah! Yeah!' When we ran out, Kerbel would stand at the door and watch every one of us go through. He'd have something to say to each guy.

"Now the brothers, you understand, would be sitting in the back of the room. They didn't go for all that hoorah stuff, but they knew they had to go out and kick ass. That was okay with Kerbel. He accepted everyone as he was. He knew I wasn't an excitable-type guy, but inside I was ready. He'd say to me very softly, 'You ready, Duane-O?' I'd say, 'Ready, Coach.' 'Then let's go, Duane-O.'

"He had this way of sticking an 'O' on people's names, Duane-O, Gino for Gene, like that. It had a certain jingle to it. Phil Pozderac, the tackle for the Cowboys who just retired, once called me that, 'Duane-O.' I thought, 'How interesting.'

"The Cowboys never were like that. They could never adjust to an individual, like Kerbel could. They'd bring a player in and try to reshape him in their own image."

Thomas mentions the lack of envy or jealousy on the West Texas team. They suffered together, partied together. Some of the players, such as Thomas, did promotional work for Levi Strauss. When a case of jeans would arrive, they'd be handed out to everyone.

"We were a close group," Thomas says. "Hotfoot Henderson and A. Z. Drones and Curley Waters and Dave Szymakowski, our Polish brother from Pennsylvania, and Jeff Maillard, a wild and crazy linebacker, a locker-beater, who went to Hartnell JC in Salinas with Rocky Thompson. Once, in my senior year, we were driving out to Salinas on a semester break, and we were going through these lettuce fields and Jeff says to Rocky, 'I'll bet I can beat you running—without clothes on. You black guys think you can run through these fields because of all that jungle blood in you.'

"So there they are, running naked through the lettuce, crazy stuff, all that energy flowing, and Rocky comes out first and hops in the car and I keep driving, and Jeff's chasing us, screaming, cursing, 'I'm gonna kill you guys when I catch you!' and Rocky yells, 'Yeah, but you gotta catch us first.' And every fifty yards or so we'd throw an article of clothing out the car, a shoe, a sock, and Jeff's racing after us, his white body all green from the lettuce, and every time another car comes by he has to take a dive back into the fields. Then we finally let him back in and we're all wrestling and yelling in the car.

"Sometimes, the night before a home game, we'd go over to the hotel where the visiting team is staying and check 'em out. I remember this big, 245-pound linebacker we had, Byron Jones, in the Utah State hotel the night before we played 'em, selling wolf cookies with Altie Taylor and MacArthur Lane, who became so great in the NFL . . . 'We're gonna kick you ass' . . . 'Better pack a lunch, because it's gonna be a hell of a fight' . . . that kind of stuff.

"We had this middle linebacker, George Mohammed Kebe—that was his real name, his father was a doctor from Africa. He was built like Lawrence Taylor and he had this deep, heavy baritone voice. A brilliant player, you couldn't fool him. He operated that defense. He went crazy. He went back home to Fort Worth and decided he wanted this motorbike, so he drove it off the showroom floor, through a plate-glass window. He came back to school all cut up. He just kept drifting, drifted out of school, and I never saw him after his junior year."

They could play, though. They all could play.

The passing offense was ranked eighth in the country in Thomas's freshman year; in the next two seasons the running attack was ranked second and eighth.

"There were times when our offense was just unstoppable," Thomas says. "Our goal was 200 yards by halftime. Most of the time we got it. Against Wyoming we got almost 300 at the half. We'd play these big schools on the road. They'd wonder, 'What is this school? Never heard of it.' When we'd leave they'd say, 'Who were those guys? Goddamm!' "

Sometimes games were hard to come by. They made long trips to strange places, Montana State one week, Memphis State the next, anyplace they could get a game.

"We played Arizona State one year when Travis Williams was their star, a 4.3 sprinter," Dierking said. "He couldn't get into West Texas State because of grades, but he got into Arizona State. We beat 'em 21–20 at their place, and next year they dropped us from the schedule.

Frank Kush figured if he was gonna get beat, let it be by someone else, not West Texas."

"Travis Williams, Jerry Smith, Ben Hawkins, Curly Culp, all guys off that Arizona State team that went into the pros," Thomas says. "Curly ripped our center's earlobe loose in that game. Our star that year was our quarterback, a big, black quarterback called Hank Washington. Kerbel loved him. Called him Hankus Pankus.

"They were leading by 7 with fifty-four seconds to go in the first half. The ASU fans had been yelling at our bench all afternoon, 'Sit down, West Texas!' They were having trouble seeing. Kerbel would say, 'Goddammit, I can't coach and chaperon at the same time.' Anyway with fifty-four seconds left we call time out, and Hank comes over to the sidelines and Kerbel tells him to throw the deep post to Charles Ray Henderson, my old teammate at Lincoln. He was a wide receiver in college as a freshman. Kerbel never minded using freshmen if he thought they could win.

"So Hank threw deep over the middle to Hotfoot Henderson and an ASU man tipped it and Charles Ray caught it lying on his back in the end zone, a miracle play, and we tie the game at halftime. The fans yelled, 'Sit down, West Texas!'

"Kerbel turns around and gives 'em a double finger and yells, 'Fuck all you sons of bitches!' Tell me we didn't love it!

"I'll tell you, we put on a show, on the field, on the sidelines, whatever. Fans would come to our games just to watch Kerbel. We played New Mexico State and their big star was Ron Po James. We had heard about him, but we didn't know how explosive he was. When they introduced him he ran out and jumped up in the air. We're saying, 'Damn, this boy's fired up.' He did it the whole game.

"One time we ran him out of bounds by our bench, and he kind of slid on the ground, and Kerbel had to back up to avoid him.

" 'Did you see that son of a bitch?' Kerbel said. 'He tried to run me over.'

" 'I'll run a mile on your fat ass,' James said.

"One of our quarterbacks, Clarence Pookie Redic, said, 'He just might do it, Coach.' "

For all his theatrics Kerbel was the kind of coach who would have been well suited to the NFL. His football philosophy was very sophisticated, very sound.

"I told Gil Brandt and Tom Landry that if there was ever a coach to prepare a player for pro ball, Kerbel was it," Thomas says. "He knew what everyone was doing on the field. You could come and make suggestions, but you'd better be right. There was a theory behind every offensive and defensive formation, the strengths and weaknesses of it, the flexibility of it. We used a pro set with very little college-style quarterback option plays. Oh, we'd use it sometimes, but as a mixer, to create artificial movement in the defense and to make sure they played it honest. He had a theory for every position on the field. His halfbacks could fumble, even if he did go crazy with Merc that time. But the fullbacks never could. He'd tell the fullbacks, 'You and the guards are the pulse of the running game.' "

There were no free handouts at West Texas. Players got fifteen dollars a month laundry money, "and sometimes he held that back, if your grades were in trouble," Thomas says. "He'd set up a study hall in his office, where he enjoyed looking at you."

Players took part in promoting the program. They'd go to the towns in the area and put on exhibition games. They were encouraged to express themselves in public.

"Kerbel didn't like guys afraid to open their mouths," Thomas says. "And if a guy liked to talk, he'd have him right up there in front of the Boosters Club."

Morris was gone by Thomas's senior year. Thomas's new running mate in the backfield was Rocky Thompson, a Bermuda native who'd come from Southern Illinois and Hartnell JC. A year later Thompson would win the British Empire 100-meter championship and lead West Texas State in rushing, which convinced the Giants to draft him in the first round, but 1969 belonged to Thomas. The offense was fullback oriented.

"Rocky was kind of an oddity at West Texas State," Thomas says. "He liked to dress well, he drove a white T-bird, he had that funny accent, and the guys would crack up when he'd put his British on 'em. After he met with Kerbel the first time, Kerbel said, 'Duane-O, get with this guy and make sure he knows his plays.' "

It was Thomas who first got Thompson into track. "The first day out," he says, "Rocky ran a 9.5 with no shoes on. He did it twice."

Thomas himself had continued to run, the sprints and sprint relays, the high and low hurdles. He was a strength runner—his weight was up in the 230–235 range by then—and track was basically a conditioner. He knew his future lay in football.

In the off-season he ran a conditioning program for volunteers. He pushed them harder than Kerbel ever did. "My trainer," Kerbel used to call Thomas, and when his buddy Hank Stram, the Kansas City

Chiefs' coach, would drop by, he would bring Thomas over and introduce him. "Meet the hardest-working guy on my team," he'd say.

"I knew we had to eliminate fatigue," Thomas says. "We didn't have the depth some of these teams did, so we had to outlast 'em. I'd take a guy out on the road and burn him out, so I could talk to him. Sometimes we'd go in a group. We'd get some students to drive us out, eight miles from nowhere, then we'd run back. I'd hang with them for two miles or so, then I'd go into a different pattern of running, sprint out, maybe a 52- or 53-second quarter, then slow down to a jog, sprint for 100 yards, and slow down. I wanted to show them there was more than one way to run distances.

"That's when they'd start cursing me, when I'd take off. They'd curse everything around them. I'd hear them behind me, 'You son of a bitch.' They hated my guts, but I kept pushing them all the time."

Thomas gained 1072 yards his senior year, tenth in the country, and he averaged 5.4 yards a carry. NFL scouts became a familiar sight on the campus at Canyon. Kerbel was always accommodating.

"He'd highlight a player once he knew what the scout was looking for," Dierking says. "If Duane was running a sweep, he'd make sure he did it perfectly. And he always told people about Duane's strength and blocking. They could see his speed for themselves."

"The day I was there," Art Rooney, Jr., says, "Kerbel let Duane do his calisthenics by himself. He had his own set of stretching exercises. When they started running plays, Kerbel said to me, 'Who are you here to watch?' and I said, 'Thomas.'

"He said, 'What do you want to know?' I said, 'Can he catch?' So Kerbel ran over to the huddle and had them throw to Duane. Then I said, 'Can he run outside?' so Kerbel had 'em run sweeps. It was amazing, a tough old coach like that, showcasing a player for me."

Beathard, who'd seen Thomas in games, called him a "do it all back. One of the greatest ever. A Jim Brown."

Ron Wolf, scouting for the Oakland Raiders, said, "When I got back, they asked me how he compared with Norm Bulaich and Bobby Anderson and Steve Owens, all the guys who figured to go in the first round. I told them, 'He's the best. Better than any of them.' "

The Raiders had the 24th pick in the first round. Dallas beat them by one. On the 23rd choice they selected Thomas. He was the fifth back chosen, behind Bulaich, Anderson, Owens, and Larry Stegent of Texas A & M. He had wanted to go to Kansas City because of Stram.

Detroit supposedly had been interested, "but they backed off," Thomas said, "because they were worried about my brother being a militant, or so I'd heard." Kerbel had wanted him to play for Vince Lombardi, who had just taken the Washington job.

"He said he'd be my kind of coach," Thomas says. "He didn't like the Cowboys, though. He said they played sissy football."

6

EARLY COWBOYS

JOURNAL: To win a championship goes beyond the physical realm because it's dealing with your very soul.

For years Dallas was the team that couldn't win the big one. It's a favorite phrase of sportswriters and fans. Become successful, reach championship level, lose twice or three times (the number depends on the mood of the individual writer or desk editor that day), and you're branded with the stigma: Can't Win the Big One. Of course the weak sisters of the NFL, the perennial washouts such as Tampa Bay, never hear that because, except for an occasional flare-up, they're never near the big one in the first place. It's a phrase reserved for the "Yes, but . . ." teams, the ones that "have it all, except . . ." Don Shula with the Colts and then the Dolphins had teams that Couldn't Win the Big One. Until they did in 1972. The Raiders were a team that Couldn't Win the Big One. Until 1976. The Vikings never have won the big one, but nobody even mentions them anymore.

In 1970 the Cowboys were the original Couldn't Win the Big One team. Tom Landry was the coach, as he has been for all twenty-eight years of the club's existence. They took their lumps as an expansion franchise for half a decade. Then in 1966 they got good. Then came the heartbreaks. Vince Lombardi's Packers held them off from the two-yard line at the end of the NFL championship game after the '66 season. Next year the Packers wedged the ball over in the final seconds of the famous Ice Bowl game for the title, the Instant Replay game.The Cowboys went into semishock after that. Cleveland had their number, beating them badly in two straight opening playoffs.

Psychoanalysts went to work. For all their efficiency and technical precision and sophisticated equipment, the Cowboys were lacking a basic ingredient—heart. Landry maintained an outward calm, as he's always done. Inside he was agonizing.

"I once saw a glimpse of Tom Landry that I think few people have seen," said Dr. Steve Taylor, who worked for NFL Properties in those days and is now a New Orleans psychiatrist.

"I was working in the office a few weeks after Dallas's second loss to Green Bay, and Landry came in for something or other, and all of a sudden he just started talking about those two losses. He wasn't really talking to me—anyone would have done—it was just something he had to say.

"He said, 'It's a lack of character, in the team and in myself. We just don't have what it takes. Maybe we never will. Maybe I never will.'

"He talked like that for a while, and I didn't say anything. It was like a window had been opened. Then it shut. I never saw those kind of quotes from Landry again."

No sports organization except perhaps the Chicago Bears under George Halas has had the operational consistency of the Cowboys. The triumvirate that controls today's football operations was formed in the Cowboys' first season, 1960. Tex Schramm, whose background was PR, marketing and promotions, became the president and general manager. He soon hired Gil Brandt, who had worked for him on the L.A. Rams, as his chief scout, later to be the player personnel director; Brandt's original job was a baby photographer in Milwaukee. The thirty-six-year-old Landry was the coach.

He took a good chunk of football history with him to Dallas. He had played on the Bobby Layne teams at Texas. He had been a cornerback—they called them defensive halfbacks then—for the New York Yankees in the old All-America Conference, and he soon became a favorite of the Bronx kids who would sit in the Yankee Stadium bleachers. They appreciated the flashy guys, tailback Spec Sanders or the speedy little wingback Buddy Young, but Landry gave the defense its fiber of toughness. He was tall, 6-1, and he played a roughneck, strangling type of cornerback that was permissible in those days. New York always has loved the tough guys, and Landry heard his share of cheers on those Sunday afternoons. Fans who remembered him from that era were surprised when his coaching style with the Cowboys became cerebral and unemotional because emotion was his big thing as a player.

Nobody realized then that one of football history's great analytical minds dwelled inside that rugged body, but Coach Steve Owen soon came to appreciate it when Landry joined his Giants, along with other members of the Yankees, in 1950. The twenty-six-year-old Landry became his blackboard guy, his chalk man. When one of Owen's concepts had to be explained and drawn up at the board, Landry was the one to do it.

He drew up the original 4-3 defense on Wednesday, September 20, 1950. It was devised for Cleveland, which ran up 66 points in its first two games and had crushed defending champion Philadelphia, and Greasy Neale's 5-2-4 Eagle defense, 35–10. The idea was to cut off the short sideline passes. The Giants lined up in a 6-1-4, dropped, or "flexed" their ends into coverage, and presto, the 4-3 was born. The Giants won 6–0, the first shutout Paul Brown had ever suffered.

Landry became a player-coach a few years later, and then in 1956 took over the defense himself. The Giants' offensive coach was Vince Lombardi, whose primary concept was Run to Daylight—look to the hole first but be prepared to bounce to the open area. Landry countered it with a gap defense, assigning each player a gap, to shut off the daylight. He coordinated each linebacker with two linemen, forming what his middle linebacker, Sam Huff, called "our own three-man platoon." When Lombardi went to Green Bay, he attacked the Landry defense with traps and counters, so Landry devised the Flex, which dropped the weakside tackle and strongside end off the line. It was basically to cut off the traps.

The Flex became his defensive staple at Dallas, a concept that was hard to grasp at first but gradually took hold when the talent improved. But in an unusual coaching decision, he took over the offense, too. Head coaches traditionally give their major attention to one side of the ball; it's rare for them to do both, but that's what Landry undertook. He realized that his offense, stocked with meager expansion talent, would have to do it through trickery rather than material. Landry's attack became a spectrum of changing sets and alignments, with backs and receivers in motion, a dazzle-and-confuse offense with the linemen doing a quick, jerky, stand up–get down motion before the snap of the ball —to deprive the defense of that last moment of recognition.

In 1961 the Cowboys' offense of castoffs and youngsters finished near the middle of the league standings and only 17 yards per game behind the champion Packers, a remarkable coaching achievement. Next year it was second in the NFL. Few people recognized at the time that Landry was on his way to superstardom.

It was Schramm's job to market the Cowboys and run the day-to-day operation. The real Cowboy craze, the America's Team phase of the operation, with its snazzy cheerleaders and blizzard of trinkets on the national market, wasn't to hit until the seventies, but the organization showed a steady increase at the gate, from an average of 21,417 fans the first year to 67,625, or just under ninety percent of the Cotton Bowl, in 1966. The fact that it dropped thirteen percent in the next five years, all playoff seasons, wasn't taken too seriously at the time, but it was to be an omen of the later fickleness of Cowboy fans.

Schramm moved the training camp from the primitive to the sublime. The first camp was at St. John's Academy in Wisconsin. The players dressed in a dormitory basement so murky they called it The Dungeon. It was dank and clammy, and when the football shoes were left overnight, Jack Eskridge, the equipment man, would find them covered with mold in the morning. Dorm rooms were grim cubicles with a bare light bulb in the middle. At night when lights went out, the halls would be filled with hooting and groaning, and somewhere a player would invariably yell, "Quiet down there. This is the warden!" The biggest camp hero was defensive tackle Ed Hussman, who killed a bat on the second floor.

They moved to St. Olaf College in Minnesota, where the players dressed in a cow barn, then to Northern Michigan University in Marquette, near the Canadian border, a frozen, wind-swept expanse where the pipes would freeze at night and strained muscles never got loose. Finally they moved to Thousand Oaks and the gentle, 70-degree breezes.

As the Cowboys became successful on the field, Schramm's creation gradually took on an aspect of glitter and Texas-style elegance.

"See this," a PR man said, conducting a visitor on a late-1960s tour of the Cowboy offices on the North Central Expressway. "What other people have in concrete we have in terrazzo, what they have in terrazzo we have in Italian marble."

Everything was designed to reflect the Cowboy image, the silver Lone Star on the helmet, the team colors themselves. At first they were just Blue and White, on the official designation. Then they became

Royal Blue, Metallic Blue, and White, and finally, in 1983, Royal Blue, Metallic Silver Blue, and White. The image was perfect—nobility, wealth, purity.

Schramm, who was NFL Commissioner Pete Rozelle's employer on the L.A. Rams in the late 1950s, became a power in league politics. He became the president and spokesman for the Executive Committee of the NFL Management Council, the agency that negotiates contracts with the Players Association. He headed the NFL's Competition Committee; he was the only member it has ever had with no playing or coaching background. Opponents who had trouble in Cowboy games would mutter, "What do you expect; they're wired to the league office."

Gruff and blunt-speaking, Schramm is a strange combination of business promoter and fan. One year he backed a proposal in the Competition Committee that would have moved all postseason games to neutral sites, such as Albuquerque and Phoenix, thus depriving the season ticket holders of a chance to see their team in the playoffs. The motion was soundly defeated.

He sits in the press box during the games, grumbling, cursing the officials, openly cheering for the Cowboys. A fan. In 1970, when New Orleans's kicker Tom Dempsey, a man born with a deformed right foot, set the record for the longest field goal in NFL history, a 63-yarder, Schramm immediately called for an investigation of his shoe. It met with a storm of abuse.

"Wow, what a no-class thing to do," the Jets' kicker, Jim Turner, said. "I sent Dempsey a telegram congratulating him. Lots of kickers around the league did. I don't care if he used a cannon, you've got to admire the guy, not whine about his shoes."

"I'm the one who took the heat on it," Schramm says. "I'd been campaigning in the preseason to standardize the kicking shoe. Then after Dempsey's kick I got all those nasty letters . . . 'How can you destroy this story?' The greatest fairy tale of our times. I learned, 'Don't say it, say it at the right time.' "

Landry and Schramm coexisted through the years, but the coach, as a football man, occasionally resented the intrusion of Schramm and the promoters into the actual playing of the game. In 1978, when Schramm and the Competition Committee pushed through the new rules liberalizing passing offenses, Landry was outspoken in his opposition. He thought the basic problem of controlling defenses that were monopolizing the game should be handled through coaching ingenuity, not by lawmakers.

Every so often Landry, a strong supporter of the Fellowship of

Christian Athletes, got annoyed by some of the flashier aspects of the Cowboys' promotion, such as the famous Cheerleaders.

"We had an argument about that one time," Schramm says. "He didn't like what the Cheerleaders had become, all the flesh they were showing. He didn't approve, because of his religious background.

"I said, 'Tom, just go to the beach and look around.'

"He said, 'Well, they're not wholesome.' That's one of the legal definitions of pornography, 'not wholesome.'

"So I went and got a videotape of the porno flick *Debbie Does Dallas.* That's when we were having the legal battle with them over copyright infringement. They were using our emblem illegally. I put the tape on the machine. It was a scene in the shower, with all these guys and girls going at it, an orgy in the shower. He stood there looking at it in disbelief.

" 'Tom,' I said, 'this is what is meant by "not wholesome." ' He nodded and left and never said anything about it again."

Brandt originally was hired as a chief scout, but he soon became much more. He coordinated the whole operation, he set up the color-coded system that had a tracer on keynote players, such as Duane Thomas, as far back as high school. He used the Cowboys' vast influence in the state and Texas politics to swing deals, getting a ballplayer assigned to the National Guard after he'd been drafted into the military service, for instance. And he signed players to contracts. He was a good haggler. Players always felt that the hand of Tex Schramm was somehow behind the numbers, which generally followed a team scale and were very low, compared to the league average (in an emergency they could always see Clint Murchison, the oilman who owned the team). But when they thought they had gotten the dirty end of a contract or had been lied to or somehow cheated, there was the feeling they'd been worked over by a Schramm-Brandt combination.

"In my next book," said former free agent wideout Pete Gent, who wrote the novel *North Dallas Forty,* a bitter indictment of the Cowboys, "I'm gonna create the most evil person I can think of and call him Schrandt!"

Brandt set up a network of college and high school coaches around the country to grade films for him and help in the scouting. Stanford coach Jack Elway, the father of Denver quarterback John Elway, once did some freelance work for Dallas, grading prospects in the state of Washington. Just for fun, he filled out a form on John, who was twelve at the time.

"I wrote down, 'great arm, good speed, 6-2, 185, outstanding student, knows the game,' " Elway said. "But then I had to indicate he had an 'attitude problem' because he hadn't taken the trash out like he was supposed to."

Brandt used to throw an annual party in his suite in Chicago's Continental Hotel the night before the College All-Star game. I went one year. The room was filled with college coaches and administrators. The liquor flowed freely. The purpose, as Brandt explained it, was to keep in good graces with the collegiate people, to make sure his scouts got decent treatment when they visited the campuses, that at the games they could get a seat in the press box instead of the stands.

In the mid-1960s the Cowboys hired Salaam Karishi, a mathematical genius from India, away from IBM. The purpose was to fully computerize the scouting operation. Other teams had fooled around with computers, but no one had a complete system.

"We knew we needed an edge of some sort," Landry said.

So Dallas became known as a computerized organization. The tone at first was of respect, almost awe . . . look how far ahead of the rest of the world they are . . . but when the fall finally came, the computer became a symbol of everything that was wrong with the Cowboys.

Karishi, incidentally, was later fired by Murchison ("He was not a good businessman"), and the irony is that Karishi ended up in Saudi Arabia, helping to teach the royal family how to computerize its operation and eventually amassing a fortune worth $40 million, while Murchison went broke and had to sell the team. In 1985 Karishi was invited back to Dallas.

> **JOURNAL:** In this computerized world of technology we are able to receive data from almost any place on earth instantaneously. Football has been affected by the revolution as well. The Dallas Cowboys were the first team to computerize its system. Football became less an inherited belief and more of a forced indoctrination. After leaving college I was to become one of those computerized players.

The Dallas drafts were solid enough during the 1960s, at times exceptional in the lower rounds. Fullback Don Perkins, a ninth rounder, became their all-time rushing leader until Tony Dorsett moved ahead of him thirteen years later. Few people had heard of Jethro Pugh or his college, Elizabeth City State, when the Cowboys took him on the eleventh round in 1965, but he became an exceptional defensive tackle for more than a decade. Rayfield Wright, the finest offensive tackle in their history, was a seventh-round choice. So was Olympic champion Bob

Hayes, their best deep threat. The Cowboys were willing to gamble on a player's potential if he had speed and athletic ability, and in those days the gambles were paying off. Everything paid off. They gambled on Roger Staubach's still being functional after a four-year hitch in the navy, and it paid off. They brought in mobs of free agents every year, more than anyone else in the league, and from those hordes came a regular influx of all-pros. They had the good trading instincts. Linebacker Chuck Howley and offensive tackle Ralph Neely both came on trades and both were all-pros.

But the topper, the selection that set the tone for the Cowboys' operation and convinced the world that they truly had the golden touch when it came to finding talent, was Calvin Hill, their first-round draft choice in 1969. First of all, he came from Yale. No one ever drafts Ivy Leaguers in the first round. Secondly, he hadn't even been the focal point of the Elis' attack. Carmen Cozza preferred to build his offense around quarterback Brian Dowling—who later became the model for Doonesbury in the comic strip—and fullback Bob Levin.

The Cowboys' computer told a different story. It digested all the raw materials on Hill—height 6-4, weight 227 pounds, speed 4.55 in the forty, athletic ability exceptional (he had long-jumped 25' 1½" and triple-jumped 51' 5¼")—and the verdict was: Unlimited Potential. When Hill gained almost a thousand yards and made rookie of the year and the Pro Bowl, everyone was surprised except Brandt and his computer-heads.

A year later, when the computer spat out the name of Duane Thomas as the first-round choice, no one scratched his head and said, "What do they need another runner for?" NFL people were not about to second-guess the Dallas computer, not with that track record.

7

THE ROOKIE

JOURNAL: I realized my first year in pro football, now was my opportunity. I saw that many great players didn't make it to the point I had. I just thanked God that I had this chance; out of all the players I'd played with and against, that I'd been chosen to carry the baton. It was a revelation. All the things I had passed up in my life, all the parties I'd missed, didn't mean that much. The only thing that mattered was my career in front of me. In every young athlete there must be a commitment. I made my commitment to pro football. It was my love. There was pro football and whatever was second, which was gradually losing ground.

The newspaper stories were all upbeat. The *Dallas Morning News* quoted chief scout Red Hickey: "He reminds me of Deacon Dan Towler, one of the greatest runners there was." The *Fort Worth Star-Telegram* quoted Tom Landry: "We have unlimited feeling for Thomas. He's the type of running back that doesn't come along every year. . . . He's the one guy I wanted. He was the guy I was sweating out." The *News* again, this time quoting Rams' scout Hampton Pool: "As a college and pro prospect, the best I've ever seen."

Thomas was friendly and talkative to the media. Why shouldn't he be? "I can't express in words how I feel," he told the *Morning News.* "Dallas is my team . . ." (Well, maybe geographically.) "It doesn't matter what position I run out of" was his quote in the *Times Herald.* (Good quote, that. Shows the kid is unselfish.) "There's no place like home, and it's good to be back," wrote the AP, lifting the quote from the Cowboys' official release. (No place except Kansas City or Washington under Lombardi.)

There was only one slightly jarring note. *Sport Magazine* of June 1970 quoted "a scout from another NFL team"—bearers of bad tidings are always anonymous—as having questions about his attitude. "Lackadaisical," he called it. He also mentioned "financial problems," in the form of unpaid bills . . . "I'm not ready to write them off by saying, 'Boys will be boys.' This kid should be one helluva pro back, but I'm not sure he will be."

Those observations were repeated by the Dallas papers, always followed by Gil Brandt's disclaimers. Scouts always say that when they're jealous over a guy you got that they wanted, he said. Kerbel and the Dallas scouts never noticed any kind of lackadaisical attitude. The kid's a terrific worker—and blocker. As for the financial problems? "He had about $1,200 on a credit card that he hadn't paid," Brandt said. "He had some clothing bills. We know about it . . . But the bills are paid now . . . A lot of guys have these kinds of problems . . . We had one guy here who owed twenty times as much as Thomas. . . ."

Duane himself was progressing on a direct line toward stardom. He suited up for the alumni in the annual West Texas State spring game and it was a joke, a man against boys. He gained 210 yards on only 8 carries. Five of them were touchdowns—on runs of 80, 62, 22, 8, and 6 yards.

With 45 credits needed for graduation he dropped out of college and enrolled at UC Irvine, south of Los Angeles, taking courses two days a week and intensifying his training program. The schedule he drew up for himself and maintained was rougher than any coach would have devised.

"My day would start off at five-thirty A.M.," he says. "I'd do thirty minutes of stretching, then eight hundred push-ups and sit-ups in flights, then fifteen miles of roadwork. I'd run from North Hollywood to L.A. International Airport and back. I got to know the city that way. Then

I'd do fifteen minutes of stretching and warm-down exercises. By that time people were just starting their day.

"In the evening I'd work on speed trials—twenty-six to thirty reps of 11-yard striders at half and three-quarter speed, followed by four to six 220-yarders for speed-endurance. Then I'd do four to five miles of roadwork. In the evening I'd go to a health spa for light weights, steam, sauna, and massage."

He turned in his rental car. Who needs a car when you've got two legs? In between workouts, on nonclass days, he'd spend time at the beach, "reading, writing notes on self-improvement."

In the summer he moved into an apartment with linebacker Don Parish and defensive end Cecil Pryor, draft choices of the Cardinals and Bears, respectively. The Cowboys' Les Shy and Claxton Welch lived in the same complex. So did the Bears' Dicky Daniels. Now Thomas had someone to work out with, to talk football with. Sometimes he'd visit his Los Angeles cousin, Dr. Wenefrett Conner.

"His mother used to write to me and say, 'Can you imagine? They want this boy to play professional football and make money with his legs,'" Dr. Conner says.

In July, Thomas reported to the College All-Star camp in Evanston, Illinois. Dallas had already begun its training camp. He knew he was in the wrong place. He never hit it off with Otto Graham, who had been the All-Stars' coach for years. He played one series in the game against the defending champion Chiefs. Someday the Hall of Fame will be filled with players who rode the bench for Otto. John Riggins was termed an "attitude problem" and hardly played. Bob Lilly and Gale Sayers saw little or no action. The list is endless.

"I wanted to be in camp, learning the system, not at some damn All-Star game," Thomas says. "Otto and I didn't get along from day one. We ran a Nutcracker Drill, primarily designed for the defensive linemen. The lineman blocking in front of me slipped. I broke the run outside.

"Otto yelled, 'Run the hole! Run the hole!' I just looked at him. I wasn't going to change my instinct just for a drill. After practice Otto told me, 'You'll never make it in the NFL.' After the season I saw him in Miami at the Super Bowl. I said, 'Coach, I made it. They even voted me rookie of the year.' He just ducked his head."

For the first time Thomas had met famous players from the big-name schools, the guys he'd been reading about. On the coaching staff was Willie Davis, who'd just retired as a defensive end for the Packers.

Eleven years later Davis would be inducted into the Pro Football Hall of Fame.

"I had a lot of respect for him as a player," Thomas says. "He'd been a brilliant player, but in terms of being genuine? Well, I just didn't like him. He had this deep, singy voice . . . he'd say, 'Doo-aayne.' It was all surface. I thought, 'How the hell is he going to know me? He's too busy being Willie Davis of the Packers.'

"I've known some of those old Packers: Willie Wood, Herb Adderley, Forrest Gregg, Dave Robinson. They're all different. Dave Robinson's corporate, but he's still Dave Robinson. Davis reminded me of a pseudo-bourgeois colored man—not a black or a Nee-gro, a colored man. There were black players, the older players, who would tell us to watch out for him.

"In the 1980s I met Reggie McKenzie at a Youth Foundation dinner. He's another NFL showpiece guy, but Reggie's down to earth. He's more real, genuine. He said something spiritual to me, about always keeping my faith strong, no matter what happened. I was thrilled to meet him.

"Davis thought I was strange. We'd get on the elevator on our way to practice, and I wouldn't talk to anybody. I was going to work. The players kidded me. They called me Flex, because I was seriously built. The other day I saw Doug Wilkerson, who'd been on that team and played guard so many years in the NFL, and he started yelling, 'Flex! Flex!' "

Thomas came to the Cowboys' camp with a slight muscle pull. He did not explode in the exhibition season as Hill had done the previous year. The Cowboys' starting backfield of Hill and fullback Walt Garrison was coming off a year in which they'd been the most productive one-two combination in the NFL with 1,760 yards. Behind them was Les Shy. Player-coach Dan Reeves was scheduled to be the first backfield reserve, when he'd recovered from his knee operation. Thomas was the fifth running back, a special teams player and kick returner.

He had shown rookie nervousness, a case of the yips, they call it. He wandered out of bounds on a kickoff return. Against the Cardinals he was running back a kick and he fumbled as he was changing hands.

"I was just paralyzed," he says. "I made the most beautiful move. There was nothing but clear field ahead. I tried to change the ball and I wound up chasing it along the ground.

"This is Tom Landry on the sidelines—teeth clenched—'Ggggeeet, damn rookie!' "

After four games he had carried the ball 12 times for 48 yards. He was running tight, trying not to make mistakes. Then a door opened up. Garrison went down with a knee injury. Thomas would start at fullback against defending NFC champion Minnesota. He decided to let his instincts take over.

JOURNAL: I used to visualize myself a gazelle or one of the big cats. I'd watch *Wild Kingdom* every Sunday. I still watch it. The cats, the way they ran, stroking the ground, then holding it, then again, like slow motion, only fast. I concentrated on that. If you notice, in my running I ran that way . . . hit the ground, really riding off the burst, and in that way conserving my energy. Some defender comes up to challenge me, he's churning whereas I was making one motion to his three or four. I was actually controlling the entire movement, they were overreacting to the movement, wasting energy.

I studied Bob Hayes every chance I could get. On punts or kickoffs I'd go to make a block, I'd look up and he was on the other side of the field, like he'd run through a hole. Okay, see if you can touch me. There was a mystery behind his running. I don't think anyone knew how fast he really was. Running after practice, his cleats would take a clump of turf out of the ground, the drive power of his cleats. That's when I knew I was on the right track. I would combine my style with his, not a lot of movement, more the idea of acceleration based on the flexibility I had. If I could do that, I could increase the drive power.

Watch a cat. It's actually leaping. Watch a gazelle. It's stroking the ground. I started to stroke the ground in my running. They'd time me. I'd run just fast enough to beat the guy I was running with, maybe a 4.6 or a 4.55 forty. I never wanted anybody to know how fast I could really run.

He gained 79 yards on 13 carries against the Vikings. So what? The Cowboys were blown out, 54–13. Next week Dallas played the Kansas City Chiefs, who'd won the Super Bowl the previous year. The Cowboys, a 3-2 team at that point, beat KC, 27–16, and Thomas ran for 134 yards on 20 carries, including a 47-yard touchdown. In two games, against teams that were to finish first and fifth in defense in the NFL, he had gained 213 yards and averaged 6.5 a carry.

"Thomas is what we said he was," Landry said, "a tremendous runner."

Reeves talked about his blocking. "Duane explodes into the defensive guys so much that the first thing you see are their feet," he said.

The legend was growing. He hurt his leg and missed a Monday night game against St. Louis in November. Without him in the lineup the Cardinals crushed the Cowboys, 38–0. The Dallas offense didn't cross midfield until the end of the first half. On ABC-TV, Don Meredith, the color man who'd been a Cowboy quarterback, was practically in tears. "Folks, I have to apologize for what you're seeing there," he said.

The Cowboys were 5-4 and sinking fast. Hill had hurt his shoulder and would miss the Redskins game. Last year's rookie of the year was just about a forgotten man in Dallas, anyway. Landry had two options. He could replace Hill with Reeves and keep Thomas at fullback, or he could go with Garrison, a tough blocker and straight-ahead runner, at fullback and switch Thomas to Hill's halfback spot. In an offense as complicated as his he didn't like to mess with position changes, but he went with instinct. He moved Thomas over.

The kid didn't make mistakes on the practice field—none.

"People don't realize what a smart player Duane was," Roger Staubach says. "He was perfect at practice, and when he got in a game, he seemed to know what everyone else was supposed to do. The guy was amazing. A mind."

"He was always curious about things, always inquiring," Hill says. "I have a friend, Byron Jones—he played with Duane at West Texas and he works for Xerox in Washington now—he said that at school Duane would read a dictionary in his room. He was always trying to better himself.

"When he joined the Cowboys, well, most rookies know point of attack and that's about all. Duane knew everything."

Well, why not? Hadn't his whole training been geared for it . . . Kerbel, Iglehart, Rabbit Thomas and his 'Don't write it down, keep it up here' approach, the idea that you had to know what the entire offense was doing?

"When I got to the Cowboys' camp, I modified Rabbit Thomas's system and devised my own," Thomas says. "There were too many plays and formations on the Cowboys to try to memorize everything, but while everyone else was diagraming the plays in the meeting, I'd just write down the names. I kept the diagrams in my head, and when I got back to my room, I'd draw them up. I'd do twenty-five to thirty a day. I'd memorize them by series, trap series, dive series, play action, toss, sweep, roll. It might have been taken as showing off, but when you're in a game situation, all you have to rely on is your memory.

"I used to watch some of those guys in the rookie meeting room in camp and laugh sometimes. The coach would say, 'Now this is the I-Flip,' and a rookie would say, 'Oh, no, man, I ain't flipping. I ain't doing none of that shit.' And someone would tell him, 'No, man, it's a formation.' I'm thinking, 'Where is this boy's mind?'

"Once I almost started laughing out loud. I thought of an incident in high school, in practice, when the quarterback kept calling over and over again, 'Down-set! Down-set! Down-set!' The coach said, 'Hey, wait a minute. Anything wrong with you?'

"The quarterback said, 'No, sir,' and his eyes were glassy. He'd been hit in the head on the previous play. He was having a brainstorm.

"They filmed all our practices in the Cowboys' camp, and I used to see guys actually trying to hide from the camera. They'd make a mistake and cover their heads. It didn't do any good. The camera had an overview of the whole field. We'd see the film and yell, 'Hey, run that back!' And there would be some guy trying to get out of the way."

Landry knew that if the Cowboys were going to finish in the money that year they would have to do it on the ground. His quarterback, Craig Morton, was fighting shoulder and elbow problems. The backup, Staubach, was still learning. No team in the NFL that year would run the ball as many times as the Cowboys. Or gain more yards. Or complete fewer passes.

Maybe it went back to his days with Vince Lombardi, when he saw the Run to Daylight concept being born, but Landry's basic theory was that first you had to be able to run wide, then run the creases when they pursued, then stop the other people from doing it.

"Duane couldn't have had a better coach at that time," says Hill, who played for the Redskins, WFL Hawaiians, and Browns after he left Dallas. "Landry was a running back's dream. He always geared the running game to a particular back's talents. He'd never attack the heart of a defense; he wanted to get you one-on-one with somebody. Shifts, rolls, influences, everything to help you, and always with a very logical reason behind it.

"Anyone coming from that system and going somewhere else was going to have problems. When I went to the Redskins, George Allen was the most illogical coach I ever saw. He was always attacking the heart of the defense. Afraid of making a mistake. Everyplace I went, I felt Dallas's system was superior. Whenever I could, I leaned on the logic I learned with the Cowboys. Of all the coaches I played for, Landry no question was the best in the running game, the most sound."

He started Thomas at halfback in that tenth game of the 1970 season, and the rookie responded with 104 yards on 16 carries. He took a knee to the head on the opening kickoff, got knocked groggy, and came back to score three touchdowns. On his longest he was hit by two tacklers at the line, bounced off, did a complete spin, and ran 35 yards into the end zone.

The Cowboys beat the Skins, 45–21. They won their last five and captured the division. Thomas went over 100 yards three times in that five-game span and averaged 5.5 yards a carry. At the end of the regular season his numbers read: 151 carries, 803 yards, 5.3 average. He led the team in rushing and kickoff returns. It was no surprise that the wire services named him rookie of the year, the second season in a row for a Cowboy runner. The computer had triumphed again.

"I saw films of him in training camp," a later vintage Cowboy, Everson Walls, said seventeen years later. "I can't compare any running back to him, except maybe Gale Sayers. He could hit a hole sideways and people just fell off him. He could see everything on the periphery, like a wide-angle lens on a camera. He made it look easy."

"When he runs," said offensive coach Ermal Allen, "he raises a wind."

"I could break a tackle," Thomas said, "I could make them miss, through knowledge of what I was doing, plus field knowledge. It made no difference where the defense was, I knew the weakest angle of their positioning, and I attacked it. I knew the strengths and weaknesses of our line, and even when they were tired, what plays we could still run effectively.

"People have asked me, how come I didn't run for 1,500 yards that first year? Our offense was not set up for one person. You had to keep a constant balance. You had to keep everyone involved. It's like a race car. You keep it in storage for a month, it's not going to run with all the precision it should have.

"With me, it wasn't how many yards I gained, but how many I gained in meaningful situations, like third and short. Football is a game of situations. You could be in the fourth quarter, completely pooped, and still be able to say, 'Hey, it's mine.' "

JOURNAL: I never fit in with the Cowboys because I didn't like hunting. Cornell Green, Bob Lilly, Walt Garrison, Ralph Neely ... they were hunters. I'd hunt linemen. If you're going to kill something, kill the son of a bitch in front of you, not some helpless animal.

The Cowboys of 1970 were a curious mixture. They were predominantly a good-ol'-boy team, with 19 of the 34 white players from the South and Southwest and 9 of the 15 blacks. The 49-man total represented the 40 active squad members (as in *North Dallas Forty*), plus the significant taxi-squaders.

Whites generally hung out with whites once practice was over, blacks with blacks, although there were a few mixers, such as Steve Kiner, a rookie linebacker from Tennessee who was drafted in the third round. Kiner and Duane Thomas shared an apartment in a racially mixed section of Dallas near Love Field airport. It caused some muttering, the idea of a black and a white living together, and a southern white at that, but after a while people shrugged it off. Kiner always had been a little free-spirited.

"He was a different kind of guy," said Blaine Nye, the right guard. "He used to drive this old, beat-up VW, and one day he parked it in Tom Landry's spot at the practice field. Now that's a no-no for anyone, but for a rookie . . . ? Well, it takes guts.

"It was raining that day, and here comes Tom into the meeting, dripping wet. He told Kiner the rules about parking spaces.

" 'Gee, Coach, I didn't think it counted when it rained,' Kiner said. Even Tom had to laugh at that."

Lee Roy Jordan, the middle linebacker from Alabama, was the defensive leader, Lilly, the right tackle and a future Hall of Famer, its most prestigious player. But Jordan was the one who took charge, who made the adjustments on the field, who took it on himself to make sure no one messed up in a game, or in practice.

Morton, as quarterback, should have been the offensive leader. Everyone admired his courage in playing with pain throughout the season, and at the end of the year the fans voted him their "Favorite Cowboy," which earned him a trip to Acapulco. But there were still players bitter over the fact that he had crossed the picket line in the abortive training camp strike that year. Actually the offense had no leader—until Staubach emerged a year later.

Leadership was very much on Landry's mind when he recalled the postseason losses to Green Bay and Cleveland. So he imported it, or what he thought would be a reasonable facsimile. In '69 he had brought in Mike Ditka, an all-pro tight end with the Bears and Eagles. In '70 Herb Adderley arrived from the Packers. The following year he was to bring in Gloster Richardson of the Chiefs, Lance Alworth of the Chargers, and Forrest Gregg of the Lombardi Packers. All had played on some kind of championship team. Four of them would end up in the Hall of Fame.

The black players on the Cowboys showed an inordinately high ratio of quality performance, based on their numbers. Five of them—Hill, Hayes, Adderley, and defensive backs Cornell Green and Mel Renfro—had been all-pro. A sixth, offensive right tackle Rayfield Wright, was a budding all-pro. Pugh would end up tying a Cowboy record for longevity with fourteen seasons, and Thomas would become rookie of the year. Eight out of fifteen, or fifty-three percent superstardom.

Privately they had their own opinions about this. "On the Cowboys, you'd better be good if you're black and you want to hang around," Wright said years later, but publicly they kept their mouths shut and paid attention. The closest thing to an incident came in the 1960s when Renfro was denied housing in practically all-white North Dallas.

Thomas didn't fit any image. He came from a black neighborhood in Dallas, but he'd lived in L.A. and hung around with white guys—there and at West Texas State. And he lived with a white player. He didn't fit in with the South and Southwest faction on the team, but he respected anyone who could produce on the field—his Joe Kerbel training had taught him that. Later he was to describe Jordan as "the leader of the redneck faction on the Cowboys," but he also said he respected him more than any other player on the team.

There was another strange little clique forming on the Cowboys, the Zero Club—defensive end Larry Cole, Nye and rookie defensive end Pat Toomay—a group of cynics who saw life through a winking eye and dedicated their club to "the pursuit of boredom and inactivity."

Thomas was very fond of Nye, both as a player ("He and Rayfield and Dave Manders, the center, were just devastating at the point of attack . . . I could run behind those guys all day") and as a person ("very decent, very liberal; the most balanced human being on the team"). He liked Cole as an all-around good fellow. And he thought Toomay, who would later become a successful novelist, was "a lazy son of a bitch."

The players found Thomas "a nice enough fella," according to Nye. "A typical rookie . . . no airs. On the field he had a lot of flair, and when you opened a hole for him he might break it 40 yards. We didn't have that kind of elusive speed before."

"You can't believe what a great guy he was in those days, what a great smile he had," Hill says. "A wonderful sense of humor, too. We were playing someone, I can't remember who, and he ran the 36-Toss and they just knocked the hell out of him. He got up and looked at me and said, 'What's wrong with those guys? Don't they know it's just a game?'

"Another time we were both taking a beating. He said, 'I have to do this, but what are you doing here? You went to Yale.'

"He was a very open person. He'd do anything for you. When I got married, I told him, 'I've got to go out to L.A. and bring my wife back. I don't know what to do about the apartment—it's a mess.' He said, 'Go on out, I'll take care of it for you.' When I brought my bride back, I didn't know what we'd find, but the apartment was immaculate. He'd cleaned the whole thing. That's the kind of guy he was."

The Cowboys liked him best, of course, when he had a ball under his arm. They gave it to him 30 times, a club record, in the divisional playoff victory over Detroit, a mean, nasty defensive struggle won by the Cowboys, 5–0. Thomas gained 135 yards, his highest output of the season.

"It's a funny thing," he said, "but every time the defense does well I seem to do well." The Cowboys' defense was playing in a kind of frenzy at this point. They had gone nineteen quarters without giving up a touchdown. They had allowed a total of fifteen points in their last five games, counting the playoff against the Lions, and they had beaten their old nemesis, the Browns, 6–2.

"I'd stand there on the sidelines watching a guy like Chuck Howley, our outside linebacker, and I'd get fired up," Thomas says. "He's the first one I saw with that kind of anticipation. It's like the quarterback had told him to run out for a pass, like he was in their huddle."

It was only the second time in their history that the Cowboys had won a playoff game. The San Francisco 49ers in Kezar Stadium lay between them and a trip to the Super Bowl. The 49ers, formidable in the passing game on both sides of the ball, had the NFL's number one pass offense, all-pros in quarterback John Brodie and wideout Gene Washington, one of the great cornerbacks of all time in Jimmy Johnson, J.J. they called him, an all-pro outside linebacker in Dave Wilcox, and a rookie sack specialist at defensive end, Cedrick Hardman. But they were a little soft against the run.

> **JOURNAL:** Cedrick Hardman was a very nice person and I had visited him at his house in Palo Alto in the off-season, but he would give you the illusion that he was more experienced and had a greater knowledge of the NFL than you did. He was a very aggressive guy as well as player. He was more interested in quarterback sacks than control football. Before the game, outside Kezar Stadium, he walked over to me in a very proud and authoritative fashion and slapped his arm around my shoulders and said, "Duane, you are in trouble today." I couldn't figure out what kind of trouble I was in. "You will not be gaining all those yards against us because I'm going to stop you."
>
> I looked at Cedrick and said, "You'd best touch me now because you won't in the game."
>
> He stared at me and said, "Duane, you are strange."

The Cowboys beat the 49ers, 17–10, to give them the first conference title in their history. Jordan and then Renfro cut off the 49ers with interceptions, and Thomas had a day that he would never again duplicate in his pro career. He carried 27 times for 143 yards and a touchdown. He seemed to be in a rage the whole game; he broke tackles, he punished the 49ers with his slashing, swerving runs, he gained yards outside. The years of sprinting and interval training and stamina work had paid off in one dazzlingly brilliant afternoon.

Michael Calvert Hudson of the San Francisco UPI bureau, who'd been watching the 49ers since 1946, said, "Never have I seen one player make so much of a difference between two teams."

Thomas himself was analytical about the game.

"San Francisco," he said, "depended on two people to stop the outside running game, strong safety Mel Phillips for the strongside force and right end Cedrick Hardman for the force on the weakside. Cedrick was thoroughly confused or misinformed on his reads. He would constantly overpursue the sweeps. I came back to the huddle and told John Niland, our left guard, to let Cedrick go upfield and then hook him, inside-out, and there would be no way he could recover. It worked. Phillips, an aggressive player at the point of attack, was effectively contained."

The Super Bowl against Baltimore in Miami's Orange Bowl matched two teams that Couldn't Win the Big One. That was a one-day angle. Another was Thomas.

Actually the best Thomas interview was an impromptu conversation he had with a writer who spotted Duane one morning sitting by the beach next to the Cowboys' Fort Lauderdale hotel. He was staring at the ocean. The writer asked him what he was thinking.

"I like the water," Thomas said. "I think about where I am. Just now I was thinking about New Zealand."

"About New Zealand?"

"Yes, it's a good place to retire."

"Retire? But this is only your rookie year."

"That," Thomas said, "is the best time to think about it."

In one of the mass interview sessions he was asked if he were an overnight success.

"Wait a minute, gentlemen," he said. "Are you aware of all the miles of pain involved to get here, all the running? And there's still more."

"Is this the ultimate game?" someone asked.

"Well, they're playing it next year, aren't they?" Thomas said.

"That was my favorite quote," NFL Commissioner Pete Rozelle said years later, "my all-time favorite Super Bowl quote. If it's the ultimate game, would they play it again next year? Perfect."

The ultimate game itself, 1971 version, was an anticlimax. Scalpers were eating tickets pregame, trying in vain to sell them below face value, despite the fact that Miami was blacked out for TV. The longest play of the game came on a deflected pass. Twenty of the 29 points scored in the Colts' 16–13 victory were set up by turnovers. There were ten of them during the afternoon, but the one that Landry cited as the "big play" of the game was Thomas's goal line fumble in the third quarter with Dallas leading, 13–6.

"If he had scored, they would have had a lot of catching up to do," Landry said, ignoring the fact that Baltimore's last ten points, including Jim O'Brien's field goal with five seconds left, were set up by Colt interceptions deep in Dallas territory. Thomas had fumbled on second effort.

"Before they unpeeled, Dave Manders was right on top of the ball," Morton said. "I screamed to the line judge on my side, 'Call the first thing! Call it, you son of a bitch!'

"He said, 'You say one more word to me and you're out of the game.'

"So they let 'em wrestle for it and Baltimore won the wrestling match."

On the bench Thomas buried his head in his hands. To this day he gets upset when he talks about that game, about the unfairness of Landry's placing the entire blame on him.

"Tom got on me about losing the game," he said. "How about Dan Reeves? He tipped the damn ball into Mike Curtis's hands for the interception that gave them their touchdown. At least I scored a touchdown in the game. Did Reeves? After that game I knew that the only way I could survive was to make no errors."

It had been a troubled season in many ways. During the year a wire story mentioned widespread use of drugs on the squad. Wide receiver Lance Rentzel was arrested on a charge of exposing himself to a young girl. Niland had been thrown in jail for brawling with the Dallas police. And years later Morton was to tell a strange story about Thomas on the morning of the Super Bowl game itself.

"I took a walk along the beach by our hotel," the quarterback said. "It was about seven-thirty. I saw Duane sitting there on the curb with his head down. He looked zonked. I don't know what he was on, but it scared the hell out of me. I mean, here was a guy who was supposed to be my main man that afternoon. Well, he got back to the hotel, and before the kickoff he gave me this big wink, so I knew he was all right—I guess."

"I've heard that story," Thomas says. "All those people who never could understand the problems I had in Dallas said, 'Well, he was on drugs.' I've heard it for years, and it's a damn lie. What Morton and others fail to understand is that I'd been running that morning. I ran every morning, including the mornings of the game. Running was my life. I used to see people just getting back to the hotel when I was out on those morning runs, lots of them. A lot of those good ol' boys liked to hit it pretty heavy.

"Guys getting drunk and fighting the cops, a guy flashing in front of a little girl, another one arrested for peeing by the side of the road, oh, yes, that all happened and it was accepted as just a bunch of good ol' boys having fun. No big deal.

"People accused me of not being excited for games. Well, compared to them I wasn't excited, because I wasn't using all those damn bennies they were taking. How many times did I see guys hung over for the games . . . in the fourth quarter they're breathing heavy in the huddle, and I was just getting started. There wasn't one year that I didn't feel sorry to see the season end.

"People were concerned about my behavior, about who I was rooming with, and why. All I was concerned about was winning football games and making a decent living for my family."

8

NORMAN YOUNG

JOURNAL: When we were young, my older brother, Franklin (Sonny), and I would always fight, physically at first, then verbally. Bertrand was the youngest of the three boys, and Franklin had trained him well. He agreed with everything he said. Up to the time of my mother's death I never realized the jealousy and envy among my brothers and sisters. When my parents died, the family just fell apart. My Aunt Beck, whom I love and respect dearly, tried her best to pull us together, but during that time everyone was into his own thing. The three of us boys were away in college, my oldest sister was in California, married and raising her family. My youngest sister was the only one living in Dallas. She stayed with Aunt Beck.

I remember when my mother died and we all returned from the funeral home. I walked outside the house and talked with Bertrand about where we were and growing up and things in general. The only thing he could talk about were the fights we had when we were younger. He still had a great deal of hatred in him. I was ready to hit him. I never felt so frustrated. Within ten months we had lost both parents. Our support system was gone, and I knew our lives were changing, even at that very moment. I walked away from Bertrand in complete disillusionment. I felt he was stupid and immature. He was still living his childhood.

The next day we buried my mother and we returned to school. I hadn't yet gotten over the death of my father. I had a child to take care of and I was uncertain about my relationship there. My wife would write these long letters and remind me that money was needed.

I took my problem to Joe Kerbel. He arranged a telephone conversation with a guy named Norman Young, an agent out of White Plains, New York, who had done Mercury Morris's contract. I arranged for him to represent me. It turned out to be the worst decision of my life.

Norman Young's agency was called ProBus Management Inc., "ProBus" short for Professional Business. He had a set of black stringers working for him, runners, they were called. He concentrated mainly on black players from smaller schools, and he'd send his runners down to contact them.

"Some black guy would tell you, 'Hey, go with Norman, man. He treats our people right,' " said Earlie Thomas, a cornerback from Colorado State who'd been drafted in the eleventh round by the New York Jets in 1970. "So you'd sign. What did you know at the time? You were just a kid."

Norman cut him ten percent, that's ten percent of his entire three-year contract package, plus bonus money, all to be paid in front. Earlie Thomas signed at close to the league minimum of $12,000 a year. His payoff to Norman wiped out his bonus, plus part of his first year's salary. He had signed over power of attorney to Young, which meant that the agent would receive Thomas's biweekly paychecks, deduct his own expenses, pay any of the player's outstanding bills, and send him what was left.

By December, Thomas was receiving notices from collection agencies about unpaid bills. Young, an arrogant man with a nasty, nasal, whining voice, was demanding more money for additional expenses. He threatened to bring the rookie to court and prevent him from playing. Thomas's wife was in her last months of pregnancy. A gentle, sensitive person who was working for a graduate degree in entomology, Thomas went to his coach, Weeb Ewbank, and told him what had happened and that he was so upset he didn't think he could play on Sunday.

Ewbank was known as a cheapskate when it came to player contracts, but he was also a tough little Hoosier who had grown up in the rough and tumble semipro leagues around Indiana. He called Young and let him know what would happen to him if he didn't leave the kid alone. He threatened him with prison, which was where Young eventually wound up. He got Thomas out of his deal with Norman, and the cornerback went on to have a productive, six-year career in the NFL. Oh, yes, he also tore up Thomas's contract and rewrote it, based on his value as a starting player, not only for subsequent years but for 1970 as well. He didn't extend it, he redid it.

Young had gained a very unsavory reputation throughout the NFL by that time. Lee Calland, a Pittsburgh cornerback, had pulled a gun on him in his office. Other players had taken him to court. But Duane Thomas, an undergrad at a small Texas college, a young man with more inner problems than anyone realized, didn't know all that at the time.

"Tell me about agents," Nye says. "I got screwed by one and I've got a Ph.D. in finance. I got served with subpoena papers when we played in New York. They catch you off guard, and you don't learn. I've seen guys caught two or three times."

The surprising thing is that when the story first appeared in the June 1970 *Sport Magazine* that Thomas had financial troubles before he was drafted, no Dallas-area writer tried to find out exactly what those troubles were. No one called him or drove down to Canyon to interview him and get his side of it. They just ran the stuff, let Gil Brandt knock it down for them, over and out.

If they had spoken to Thomas and caught him in the right mood, they might have gotten a different story, of a twenty-year-old sophomore who suffered the heartache of watching his father go through a long, agonizing death from pancreatic cancer, followed ten months later by his mother's death from heart attack—she collapsed in front of their house on Baldwin Street—followed by the nervous breakdown of his youngest sister. They might have learned of the promise he once made to himself to someday take care of his parents, or at least his own family, and then being faced with the reality of not being able to support a wife and two children back in Dallas.

A little digging might have led to an exposé of Norman Young and his cutthroat contracts, and maybe, just maybe, Thomas would have been off to a different start with the Cowboys. In all except one story, a later story written out of town and dealing with Thomas's subsequent problems with the club, the name of Norman Young was never mentioned.

"The first time I talked to Duane," Brandt says, "I told him,

'Whatever you do, don't give this guy the power of attorney. It's the worst thing you can do with these people.' He said it was too late, he already had.

"If I ever did anything like these guys did to the players, they'd send for an exterminator and have me rubbed out. In 1970, Young even sent one of his people, a black guy, down on a plane to pick up Duane's playoff check.

"I said, 'You've got to be kidding, spending $150 to fly down and pick up a check.'

"He said, 'Well, we have to have it.' "

Thomas's original contract called for a $25,000 bonus and salaries of $20,000, $20,000, and $22,000 for three years, plus incentive bonuses that could earn him another $20,000—$10,000 for rookie of the year, $5,000 for all-pro, and $5,000 for 600 or more yards rushing. Part of his first paycheck went to paying back George Powell, a business teacher and a personal friend who had gotten him off-season promotional work with Levi Strauss. Powell had loaned him money to cover his credit card debt. Young cut him $8,700 off the top, or ten percent of the entire package, plus an additional $2,500 that he had advanced Thomas in college. He would subsequently take his share of the incentive money, all of which Thomas earned, plus the playoff and Super Bowl money, plus "another $10,000 that he stole from me by not paying the bills, which he was supposed to do," Thomas says.

The salary figure seems shockingly low now for a first-round draft choice, and in those days it was lower than most teams paid, and certainly lower than the successful teams' scale. But that wasn't the era of big salaries. Hill had signed roughly the same-size contract the year before.

"He came in with two Ivy League lawyers from Yale," Brandt said at the time. "It was like taking candy from a baby."

"From first to tenth rounds, I'll bet the base pay wasn't more than $500 out of line on Cowboy contracts," Nye says. "We were in perfect lockstep. The difference came in the bonus money. But the base was always low. Maybe that's why we tried so hard to make the playoffs every year—for the money.

"Of course the classic story is of Lilly going to the Pro Bowl; he's making about $27,000 and the club tells him to keep quiet about his salary because he'll make everyone jealous. And then he asks around and he finds out that Merlin Olsen, playing the same position, is making something like $80,000. A classic."

Contracts around the league always have reacted to competition.

Little else seems to budge them. The scale was abysmal in the 1950s. Then the AFL arrived in the sixties and salaries took a jump. The same thing happened during the WFL era in the mid-1970s and the USFL's run in the 1980s. But Thomas was drafted in 1970, a dormant period.

A year later Thomas would get back together with his wife, but now they were estranged. He was sending her $800 a month for child support.

"I'd get bills on top of that," he says, "bills for the kids' clothing, a $300 bill from R&P Men's Clothing in Dallas. I asked her, 'Why are you buying clothes at a men's specialty store?' She said she bought her brother a birthday present. The bills kept coming in. I told her to keep a record, to write it all down. She never did. Even if the purchases were in her name, I was responsibie. That was Texas law at the time. It's since been changed."

The Cowboys arranged for a lawyer to help set up a divorce.

"Pete Chantillas," Brandt says. "Duane dropped him after two days."

"Longer than that," Thomas says. "The guy kept getting more and more expensive and nothing was resolved.

"An IRS man introduced himself to me after the Super Bowl. I owed them $10,000. I told him, 'I gave this man power of attorney.' He said, 'Well, it doesn't show up on your record.' At this point I'm ready to kill Norman. He'd been sending me statements that he'd paid them.

"I tried reaching him. He stayed unavailable. I could never get through. Finally I talked to him one last time. He said he'd paid. I said, 'Norman, these people want $10,000.' He said he'd take care of it. He never did. I had to borrow the money from George Powell.

"Midway through the season Tom called me in. He said, 'There's a guy from the sheriff's office to see you.' The man said, 'I hate to give you this, but I'm just doing my job.' That was the R&P bill. I started thinking, 'How many other bills are there out there, waiting for the sheriff to deliver?' I called my wife again. I told her, 'Just let me know about these things. I can't take the surprises.' "

After the season Thomas's teammates saw no change in him.

"We'd get together and work out by ourselves," said Staubach, who was getting ready to make a serious run at the starting quarterback position. "We'd throw the ball around. Duane would say, 'Roger, you need to throw, I'll run.' I'd tell him, 'Remember I said I'm gonna be the first quarterback to gain 1,000 yards rushing.' It wasn't until we got into the season that Duane started moving away from us."

Thomas went to Los Angeles in the spring. When he returned to Dallas, he went in to see Brandt about a new contract. He'd heard some of the numbers other people around the league were making. Facing him was a second year at $20,000. By now he had bought out the remainder of Norman Young's agreement with him and he was on his own.

"Gil told me that under no circumstances would they renegotiate my contract," Thomas says. "I said, 'You did it for other people.' I knew Rayfield Wright had had his redone the year before. Gil said, 'What other people?' and I wouldn't tell him. Then he called Tex Schramm in and Tex repeated what Gil had said—no renegotiation.

"Before I left, Gil said, 'Well, we might consider extending it.' "

"Duane wanted something like $75,000 and $80,000 for his last two years," Brandt said. (Thomas puts the figures at $70,000 and $75,000.) "I told him we'd rewrite his contract and tack on an extra year, and we'd pay him $40,000, $45,000, and $50,000. We had a scale to follow. Hell, Lilly was only making around $42,000 at the time."

A positive and a negative. Lilly, one of the finest defensive tackles in the history of the game, was drawing a peon's wages after ten seasons with the Cowboys, eight of them Pro Bowl years. The message was clear: once you get trapped into long-term agreements it's tough to break out. Lilly had been a good soldier. He had grumbled but he hadn't made trouble.

Brandt had showed Thomas his future. Three more spectacular years, which was a distinct possibility, and he'd still only be at the $50,000 level. He'd be pinned.

"One of the first times I'd ever met Gil I'd asked him, 'How does a person make money playing pro football?' " Thomas says. "Gil replied, 'By producing.'

"I told him, 'If that's the case, I'm gonna make a mint.' "

Some mint. Thomas says the first time he'd ever talked contract with Brandt he asked him what the numbers would be on a one-year deal. He says Brandt told him, "Sixteen thousand dollars, and we'll have to lower the bonus."

The Cowboys had him for two more years, and technically they were obeying the letter of the agreement, and if he wanted more money, why then he'd have to give them another year, and if he ever wanted another raise while the contract was still in effect, well, it would be extended again. And pretty soon, at the age of thirty, he would rub his eyes and say, "Where's all the big money I was supposed to make?"

It happened that way to John Hannah, the great all-pro guard for the Patriots. His contract was extended twice, the last time wrapping him up for six years, and he would have been thirty before he'd have had a chance to earn anything commensurate with his performance. So he quit. Walked off the team. Shock therapy, and he forced the club to rewrite the contract and pay him what he was worth.

"If you sign a player to a long-term contract," says Bobby Beathard, the Redskins' general manager, "and then actually hold him to it, all you're doing is creating an unhappy ballplayer. But teams like to be slick like that."

The Raiders' owner Al Davis has a two-year plan. If a player is clearly outperforming his contract, then after two years Davis rewrites it, no matter how many years are left.

The Raiders have won three Super Bowls, Washington two, but Dallas has also won two, although at the time of the Thomas affair they had yet to win their first. They did it their own way, which has kept the team solvent but has created a lot of unhappy alumni.

Lee Roy Jordan, five times a Pro Bowl choice, got a $17,500 salary when he signed as a first-round draft in 1963, plus a $5,000 bonus and a new car, "which I wrecked on my way back to Alabama," he says. "I hit a cow. Wound up costing me $1,200." In his fourteenth and final season he made $100,000.

Rayfield Wright, the finest offensive tackle in the team's history, a six-time Pro Bowl selection, the Cowboys' captain for eight years, was a 1967 seventh-round draft choice out of tiny Fort Valley State. His original contract was for $57,000 for three years ($17,000, $19,000, and $21,000), plus a minimal bonus and a car.

"They love cars," Wright says, "because they have a thing going with the dealers and they get heavy discounts."

Wright's contract was extended twice. His third-year salary was raised from $21,000 to $24,000 and a year was tacked on—for $29,000 —then the contract was extended again and the new three-year package brought him up to $40,000 in its final year. He'd played seven years in the league, he'd made all-pro three times, and he was getting paid $40,000—in an era in which the new World Football League was routinely signing people for six figures.

He was scheduled to make $60,000 in his ninth season, 1975. He was thirty years old. The end was in sight.

"I told them, give me one contract to end my career on," he says. "I said, 'Give me a million dollars for five years.' They damn near fell out the window. They threw me out of the office."

So he jumped to Birmingham of the WFL. The league folded and he was back with Dallas, playing for $60,000. Next year they gave him his five-year contract, for half of what he'd requested. He was released after the 1979 season, his thirteenth on the team. His final salary was a little over $100,000.

The beginning of that kind of arrangement was being offered to Thomas back in 1971 (he says the Cowboys never came up with actual dollar figures), and he said, no thanks.

"That would just put me back in the same boat," he said. "I had performed a damn sight better than the way they'd paid me, and I wanted them to recognize that."

The complexities of club finance and long-term contracts and deferred payments were lost on him. He was twenty-three years old, he had just completed a sensational rookie year, and he was making peanuts. It didn't add up. In the Green Bay game Thomas had gained more yards than both Packer runners, Jim Grabowski and Donny Anderson, combined. The Million Dollar Babies, they were called—in 1966 they had signed for a combined package of $1.1 million.

"When I wanted something around the house when I was a kid, I simply outworked my brothers and sisters," Thomas says. "I came home from school and didn't say I was tired. I cleaned the tub and drew the bath water for my father. If I worked hard enough, I got rewarded for it. That's the way we were brought up.

"The only thing I wanted when I came to Dallas was a playbook. My responsibility was making their football team, then once I made it, to put yards up and down the field and points on the board. I felt I should be fairly compensated for that.

"I never grew up wanting all this money to be important. We just grew up knowing we were somebody. We knew we couldn't buy this or that, but if we wanted those things hard enough, it would be possible to get them."

Thomas called Brandt in March and told him he was **retiring**.

"He said, 'You can't do that,' " Thomas says. "I told him, 'Hey, Gil, the Civil War's over.' That night I called CBS-TV and told them I had retired from professional football. The guy said, 'Duane, are you sure? You have everything in front of you.' I told him, 'That's the appearance of it, but in reality it's very little.'

"The story broke on the air that night and that's when the town fell on my head. I went from hero to zero."

Thomas says his animosity toward newspapermen started in the days that followed. He said they took the club's side of it, and it was a very hard side, dealing with ungrateful rookies and players who wouldn't honor their contract.

"The day that Duane went in to renegotiate, I was waiting in the outer office," Hill says. "I was getting ready to see them about redoing my own contract. I saw Duane walk out and storm to the elevator. I didn't know what Tex and Gil had said to him, but it scared me so much that I turned around and went home without even seeing them. Dan Reeves once told me that he went in to renegotiate one time and Tex made him feel that he was lucky even to be playing for the Cowboys.

"The organization had that way of making you feel insecure. You felt that just when you were on top, that's when you were standing on the banana peel. First they go about trying to build that family aspect, then you see something or you read it in the paper. . . . I remember reading in '70 or '71 that the Cowboys were thinking of trading me to the Giants for Fred Dryer. I was going to build a house in Dallas, but I never did after that."

"I talked to Tex again," Thomas said. "He said, 'What if you don't produce next year?'

"I said, 'Then you only pay me up to how much I do produce. It's like a guy coming to paint your house. If he only paints half of it, pay him for half.'

"He said, 'We can't structure a contract that way.'

"I said, 'Well, pay me so much per yard.'

"He said, 'No, we can't do that.' "

Thomas would talk to his brother Franklin. They'd have long, philosophical discussions about the whole nature of athletics in the financial arena.

"I tried to explain to him that when you go to school, you're introduced into the labor force, but the only thing is, you don't get compensated for it," Franklin Thomas says. "One of the big football factories will say, 'Well, we're giving you an education.' Fine, you give me one percent of the gate and I'll pay for my own education.

"A young professional player rides the illusion of grandeur without the reality of finance. He soon comes out of the dream world and into reality. I told Duane, 'What you're doing, people pay to see, and you don't get your fair share.' "

Duane Thomas stepped back and took a long look at the whole Cowboy organization and their way of operating. He had done all they asked of him. He'd been a young, gung-ho athlete, far ahead of his contemporaries in both physical training and mental preparation for the game. His whole football experience had been "family." Rabbit Thomas and Floyd Iglehart at Lincoln High—we live together and we die together. Joe Kerbel and West Texas State—let's get them sumbitches, it's them or us. But now he was at war with his own team, his family.

Didn't the organization always talk about the "Cowboy family"? Hadn't he read enough about it in the brochures and fliers they'd sent him after he was drafted? Now even Tom Landry stood behind Brandt and Schramm in their "We don't renegotiate contracts" stance . . . Landry, whom he'd respected so much during the season for his command and his football knowledge. Now he was one of them. He was a football man, not a front office guy, but he was one of them.

"Tom never once called me in and said, 'Duane, you had a great year,' " Thomas says. "That was all I ever asked. Instead, what I got from him was this . . . and this . . . and this . . . the face, the chin, the compressed lips. Gil would say on the sidelines, 'All you need is 10 more yards and you'll have 50.' A carrot. Hey, don't put a limit on me; don't put a roof over me. I'll find my own roof, just give me the foundation. If he would have said, 'You've done everything we asked, you've outperformed your contract' . . . ah, hell."

Thomas's problem was that he had never been exposed to the cold-blooded side of the game. His blood ran hot. Football was his love, his life, uncomplicated, pure. It was his escape from the real world, which had been closing in on him; a shyster agent, an estranged wife, two dead parents. And now he was out of football. Or was he? Maybe there was still a support system available—his teammates. Maybe they could be made to understand that his struggle affected all of them.

"We were one of the lowest-paid teams in the league," he says. "We had to keep winning to make any kind of money at all. Practice times had even been readjusted so we couldn't work a second job in the evening and try to make some extra money. It wasn't just the black players who were getting screwed, it was all of them, even great players like Jordan and Lilly. I didn't think offensive linemen should feel inferior because they were blocking guys who were making two to four times what they were, and then hearing Tom and Gil tell them they're not there yet. I thought that by making a stand it would catch on eventually, that I'd have the support of my teammates.

"What did I hear? 'Well, Duane, you're not gonna change the system.'

" 'But you can give it a shot.'

" 'No, man, the organization's too powerful.' "

"A lot of players supported him but were afraid to come out publicly," Wright says. "You know as well as I do, it makes no difference what kind of ability you have. If an organization wants to rid itself of you, it can do it. We knew there were plenty of players out there who could have been playing the game but were just denied the chance. The whole system is based on insecurity."

"When Rocky Thompson was drafted in the first round by the Giants, he called me," Thomas says. "I told him, 'They're going to offer you twenty in front and twenty for your first year. Don't take it.'

"He called me back a few weeks later and said, 'Man, how did you know that?' I said, 'Hey, these guys all talk to each other. It's one big corporation.' He wound up getting forty and forty."

> **JOURNAL:** People would come up to me on the street and say, "Hey, Duane, you used to be a good football player." Like I'd died or something. Well, Jesus rose from the dead.

By now Thomas was retired and living in Los Angeles. Levi Strauss, for whom he'd done promotional work in college, was offering him a job for $20,000 with no bonus but a stock program. He received occasional phone calls from Brandt and Schramm. By now Chuck Dekado of Dallas was representing him, but no progress was being made. Landry called and requested a face-to-face meeting, which was held in Dallas with the same result. Then Thomas took on Jim Brown, the Hall of Fame fullback for the Cleveland Browns, to represent him, "to represent my ego," he says. The deal was that Brown would take a percentage of any endorsements Thomas would be involved in but would take no cut of his Cowboy money, when and if there should be any more of it.

"We had a meeting with Tex in the spring," Thomas says. "It was very interesting. Tex was completely different when he saw Jim Brown with me. He was scared, stuttering. I was thinking, 'That's Jim's impact. Now I'm bringing in knowledge.'"

Late in June, a few weeks before training camp opened, Brown set up a final meeting in the Executive Inn across the street from Love Field in Dallas. Landry, Schramm, and Brandt represented the Cowboys. Brown and Thomas flew in from L.A. and arrived at lunchtime. The meeting lasted a little over an hour.

"It looked like we weren't going to come to any kind of agreement," Thomas says. "Tom was being silent. Tex was doing all the talking. He wanted to see my reaction. Finally Tom turned to Jim Brown and said, 'Look, we want him to play for us.'

"Jim turned to me and said, 'Okay, Duane, you'll play this year under your old contract and then we'll look at it.'

"I really didn't like it too much, but I went along with it because I felt that Jim saw something later, down the road, that I couldn't see. He said to me, 'They'll be forced to renegotiate your contract next year. You showed goodwill.' But I really wasn't too happy about the situation."

"My primary feeling, and what I told Duane," Brown says, "was that he's a football player and football players play football. He'd be better off doing that than anything else at the time."

"We dispersed," Thomas says, "and they relayed it to the press that I was coming back. The only thing I got out of it was that they wanted me back in camp."

A writer called Thomas, and Thomas told him, among other things, the Cowboys would never have made it to the Super Bowl without him. The quote later would come back to haunt him.

"I never should have said it, but he got me when I was angry," Thomas said. "Of course I didn't take Dallas to the Super Bowl—but I was a focal point. Football's a team game, everyone knows that, but it did get people pissed off in Dallas. Of course they were pretty pissed at me anyway. What had settled into my psyche was that from now on people would have to deal with me, Duane, the person other than the fella who played the humble role, the diplomat . . . just do my job."

Thomas reported to camp. He ran the aerobic mile ("Actually two miles," he says) and did well, as usual. When did he ever have any trouble running?

"That shut 'em up real quick," he says. "They were concerned about my condition. The press had been writing this negative stuff about me all along. The implication was that I'd been cocky. In those days it seemed that anytime a black player spoke up for himself he was written up as being cocky and unappreciative, a disruption to the team, a militant. Once you saw the mentality of it, the consistency of it . . . well, I'd given some interviews and the same thing kept flowing out of them, the same observations.

"After I did that two-mile run in camp I made a statement that I wasn't talking to the press anymore. I'd let my actions speak for me."

He had given one final interview before silence descended—actually it was a press conference that he had called himself on July 20. It was the famous one in which he called Schramm, "dishonest, sick, and totally demented"; Brandt, "a liar"; and Landry, "a plastic man, no man at all."

That's the one that swung it, the Landry quote. Players had called Brandt and Schramm names before. No big deal. But in Dallas, Landry was God. The national media came down on Thomas with a vengeance.

"Why did I call Tom a plastic man?" Thomas says. "Because he had shown no flexibility or consideration for me, a player he'd had direct contact with. He knew me, what kind of a player I was, my interest in the game."

Ahead of Thomas lay a season that would become one of the strangest any player would go through, a season dedicated to silence, which would earn him the nickname The Sphinx.

9

THE SILENT SEASON

JOURNAL: So I stopped talking. I could see the look on their faces ... who does he think he is? Simply a football player. How could they understand that football was my love, my high, the intensity of it, the formations and strategy of attacking a defense, the intricate components to learn, the feel of the thrust of a play taking off, the feel of power in flight.

I knew I had to be perfect in my assignments and my execution. Had I missed an assignment or played below par, Tom Landry would not have tolerated my independence and my desire to be treated as a real human being. This does not mean that I was especially hard and tough, it just means that my faith in God was stronger than my faith in Tom Landry and the Dallas Cowboys. For when everyone was against me, God was for me, and through His mercy and loving kindness He guided me through the valley of death.

The Cowboys' 1971 camp was a strange one. Blaine Nye retired to pursue his studies, then unretired. Chuck Howley, age thirty-five, had decided that twelve NFL seasons were enough and he had retired before the season, only to return the day after Thomas's July 20 press conference. Steve Kiner, Thomas's old roommate, didn't want to go through another year as Howley's backup and he requested a trade. The Cowboys obliged, sending him to the New England Patriots for a fourth-round draft choice.

On Thursday, July 29, Thomas showed up at practice "shadowed by a small, dark man with only one name," as one paper reported. That night, wearing a dashiki, Thomas met with Schramm and Landry and asked to be traded. Aha, the Black Muslims have got him, people reasoned. "There was a rumor going around camp," Calvin Hill says, "that Duane and the Muslims were going to kidnap Tex. Next morning Tex had four or five guards around him. It was wild."

Thomas didn't show up for practice the next day, and on the night of Friday, July 30, the Cowboys made a deal with the Patriots. New England would get Thomas, plus backup lineman Halvor Hagen and wide receiver Honor Jackson for a first-round draft and Carl Garrett, a young halfback who'd gained 272 yards for the Patriots in 1970. Kiner had his old roommate back.

"Oh, he was happy about Duane coming to New England," says Will McDonough, the beat man for the *Boston Globe* in those days. "Steve was already a training camp legend. He had these two sisters living in a trailer behind the practice facility. He used to bring them cheese and fruit from the training table. When he'd gotten there, everyone was waiting to see Coach John Mazur's reaction to him.

"Mazur was an old Notre Damer and an ex-marine officer, and he had a rule about long hair not being allowed. Kiner's was real long. The first time Kiner showed up he was wearing one of those black Amish hats, and the sides of his head were clean. Mazur was happy about that. Then he took the hat off and there was all his long hair, tied up on top in a bun. All the players cheered."

Thomas's short stay in New England was equally legendary. He liked Upton Bell, the general manager, distrusted Bucko Kilroy, a former Dallas scout under Brandt. He regarded Kilroy as Brandt's pipeline. And Mazur, whom he said "was into ego . . . intimidation . . . dictation," he liked not at all.

The stories that came out of the Patriots training camp in Amherst were weird, offbeat . . . Thomas lying on his back on the wet grass, staring at the sky, as a crackling thunderstorm hit the practice field. Thomas chasing away photographers, Thomas returning a platter of meat to Art Warren, who ran the cafeteria.

"Anything wrong with it?" a panicked Warren asked.

"Just remembered, I don't eat meat anymore," Thomas said. He had become a vegetarian in 1971. "My body told me it was healthier," he said.

Finally the famous story—Thomas's walking off the practice field after he and Mazur had gotten into it over his stance. Mazur wanted him in a down position, a three-point; Thomas stayed up in a two-point. His quote at the time—"That's the way we do it in Dallas."

"Oh, man, look at the logic of it," he says. "I told him I wanted to stay up because I was having trouble seeing. We were in an I-formation. The fullback in front of me was big Jim Nance, 245 pounds, wide, broad ass. How was I going to see around that?

"It became a clash of wills. 'You'll do it because I say so!' I never liked that phrase. I never liked hearing parents telling their kids that. 'Because I say so!' Now what the hell does that mean?

"My whole football training had been based on logic and players' input when it made sense. With Kerbel at West Texas, if you saw something wrong, you brought it to the coach's attention right away, and he'd evaluate the information based on the kind of player you were, how much into the game you were. If he didn't agree with you, he'd say, 'Okay, run it my way now and we'll look at it later.' That was logical.

"Whatever I felt about Tom Landry, he was never a 'Because I say so!' coach. Never. If you didn't feel right in something, you told him. People don't understand that about Landry. If you're in a position that's not comfortable for you, Tom will go with you and let you do it your way until you screw up. If you're in a pattern, then based on your read of the linebacker drop, you make your own adjustment. Tom would say, 'Good adjustment.'

"When he'd put a play on the blackboard, he'd always tell you why you were doing something. He loved that. I'd say to myself, 'Okay, you've just explained something to me. You've motivated me.' He used to say, 'You can have all the faith in the world, but without knowledge, you're lost.' I commend Tom on that one. It wasn't like Otto Graham . . . 'Hit the hole! Hit the hole!' . . . or John Mazur, 'Because I say so!' "

After five days the Patriots had had it with Thomas. They called Dallas and canceled the trade. The NFL commissioner ruled that the Cowboys had to take him back. It was a bitter blow to Garrett, who had said what a pleasure it would be running behind the Cowboy offensive line, compared to what he was used to at New England. He swapped teams with Thomas again. Hagen and Jackson stayed in New England and the Cowboys owed them two high draft choices.

The word out of New England was that Thomas had refused to take the blood and urine analysis part of his physical exam, the implications being that he was afraid traces of drugs would show up.

"I did everything the doctor asked me to do up there," Thomas says. "He checked my heart, took my blood pressure, and asked me about any injuries. That was the same night I got to camp. He never asked me to take a urine or blood test."

The question is: If Thomas had flunked his physical, how come he was permitted to practice with the team?

"Good question," he says. "I wonder why there weren't any brilliant minds around to ask it."

He went to Los Angeles instead of joining the Cowboys. His new agent, Al Ross, a West Coast lawyer, had him take a complete physical exam, including blood and urine analyses. The physician who administered it was Dr. Milton Birnbaum. Thomas came up clean. Ross spent time on the phone with Schramm. The topic was still Thomas's contract.

He said that Schramm told him Thomas would get a bonus if he went over 1,000 yards.

"Why not make it ten million yards?" Ross said he told him. "Who needs all these incentives? Pay a guy what he's worth. That's incentive enough."

In September, Thomas decided that he would either have to live with his contract or forget the season. He reported to the Cowboys, who put him on the inactive list. He sat out the first three games. In the third one, a 20–16 loss to the Redskins, Dallas was held to 82 yards rushing, their second-lowest regular season total in three years. Thomas was activated for game four, November 11, 1971, a Monday nighter against the Giants in the Cowboys' brand-new arena, Texas Stadium, in the suburb of Irving.

He played the first half on special teams, lining up at the wing, or outside spot, on kickoffs, playing in the wedge when the Cowboys received. Students of special teams play say that Thomas's performance that night was one for the textbooks. As a starting running back he'd often been exempt from the blocking and tackling aspects of the punt and kick game, and nobody really knew how he'd perform when he had to do the dirty work. He played as if he were possessed.

On the opening kickoff he nailed his old West Texas State buddy, Rocky Thompson, and forced a fumble. He was to bring down Thompson twice more on kick returns, each time with a vicious, jarring tackle. In the second quarter Thomas threw the block that sprung Cliff Harris for a 27-yard kickoff return, flipping his man in the air.

"Beautiful," the receivers coach, Ray Renfro, told him on the sideline.

"Every time I tackled Rocky I said, 'Where you goin', man?' " Thomas says. "He'd get frustrated. He'd say, 'They ain't blocking.'

"I'd tell him, 'Hey, Rocky, you ain't getting away tonight.' "

On the fourth play of the second half Calvin Hill swept left and picked up 11 yards. He came up limping on a badly sprained right knee that was to keep him out of the lineup for seven games. Thomas was in at halfback. He carried on a sweep for 11 yards. Next play he picked up 8 on a trap off the left side. He ended up with 60 yards on 9 carries. He was back.

"I wasn't surprised at his running ability, but I was surprised at his stamina," Dan Reeves said after the game. "He just stays in condition, I guess. I was dying out there and he was just a little winded."

"Sure I kept in shape," Thomas says. "I've always kept in condition. Does someone spend all those years getting his body in shape just to lose it?"

Thomas moved in with his wife, briefly, then he moved out.

"There were guys on the team," Hill said, "who didn't even know he was married."

JOURNAL: Out of all the conflict and fear in this world, silence was my way of creating a perfect place within myself.

So he stopped talking. No, he wasn't totally mute; he'd say a word or two on the practice field, if it concerned an assignment. He'd talk to his wife and kids or people from the old neighborhood, or to his brothers and sisters. The press received only silence. His teammates? Well, that's the relationship no one could understand. How could a guy stop talking to his teammates?

Rayfield Wright put his hand on Thomas's shoulder and was fixed with the cold stare, The Look, the players called it. "Get your hand off me," Thomas told him. Even coaches were nervous about The Look.

Jethro Pugh asked him one day how his sore leg was.

"Why, are you a doctor?" Thomas said. Within twenty-four hours the wire services had that quote around the country.

"I was just smarting off," Thomas says now. "I would say that to him anyway."

Nobody thought he was joking at the time. Pugh didn't.

Former players mention occasions when Duane was friendly to them. Yes, he actually exchanged chitchat. They wear the memories like a badge of honor. Calvin Hill, Tody Smith, the number one draft in 1971, Herb Adderley, whose house Thomas would actually visit on his way to practice—on occasion. Always on occasion. They were black players mostly, although Thomas says he included Bob Lilly in that inner circle.

"I'd go through whole days without talking to anybody," he says now.

Why? Why not a teammate?

"I didn't want to involve them with what was going on with me" was one explanation he offered when someone asked him about it recently. "I didn't like to talk anyway" was another. "I was working when I was in the training area" was still another. "I didn't have time for chitchat."

He has thought about it many times.

"Sometimes I wanted to, I really did," he says, "but I was in too deep."

He reflects on it. Maybe hypocrisy was really the answer, maybe he felt that by coming back and rejoining the Cowboys he was being a traitor; he was selling out players who were underpaid, blacks, anyone who ever tried to fight a powerful system. And at least he could show people he hated being where he was—no, not the football part of it, he could never hate that—it was the regime, the way of life he was rebelling against.

"The story of Faust was always in my head," he said. "I felt like I had made a pact with the Devil . . . submitting to a system like that, reinforcing it while I knew what the outcome would be."

He became a locker room phenomenon. Nobody knew what to expect from him. Some players were nervous, some amused.

"Once he talked to me in the locker room about something," Tody Smith said. "Out of the corner of my eye I could see that everything in the place had stopped dead. Everyone was watching us. Afterward they all came around me. 'What did he say? What did he say?'

"It was like being back in the schoolyard in high school, only worse. These were grown men."

"Gloster Richardson once told me at practice, 'I didn't want to come, but I had to, to see what Duane was going to do today,' " Hill says. "Every time I didn't feel like getting out of bed in the morning I would, just to see who Duane would freak out.

"We were playing in Chicago and we were on the bus to the stadium, and Duane turned around to Richardson and said, 'Gloster, I feel like I'm gonna run a mile today.' Gloster told me later that he didn't know that Duane even knew his name.

"On the flights Duane would pull this stocking cap down over his face and he wouldn't move at all. The stewardess was wheeling the service cart down the aisle and she got even with him and he said, without looking up, 'Could I have a tea with Sweet 'N Low, please.' It freaked her out. She was going to check him to see if he was breathing."

"They've always made a big thing about that cap I wore on planes," Thomas says. "What they didn't understand was that I pulled it over my face because my sinuses always bothered me on planes."

"Once in practice we were in special teams drill and Dave Manders got Tody Smith with a forearm," Hill says. "I heard Tody screaming at him. Next kickoff they're on the ground, fighting. Jim Myers, the line coach, used to be brutal on rookies, and he said to Tody, 'You goddamm rookie!' Tody jumped up and called him a faggot and took off after him. Myers started running toward Tom. Cornell Green grabbed Tody.

"When practice broke up, I'm sitting next to Duane and he was laughing. He said, 'That brother really went off, didn't he?'

"I said, 'I'm telling you.' "

One day at roll call in the meeting room, special teams coach Bobby Franklin took over for Reeves, who was to have his own roll call problems with Thomas later on.

"He calls Duane's name," Craig Morton said. "Duane always sat in the same chair, in a far corner in the back. He'd never answer to his name. We're thinking, 'Is this guy gonna be smart enough to see that Duane's here?' But he keeps calling, 'Thomas, Thomas, Thomas.' Finally someone answered for him, 'Yeah, okay, he's here.' "

"With Kerbel the whole thing never would have gotten to that point," Thomas says. "He would have said, 'Duane-O, what is this stuff? Don't be running that silence crap on me. It's not gonna work. You can talk to me . . . never mind the press, we're family here.'

"But Kerbel was also the kind of guy who wouldn't give a player a scholarship and then run him off. Oh, he'd make him work, but he wasn't gonna be doing some kind of diabolical scheming on your ass."

"Duane had the veterans and the city and the NFL mesmerized by his silence," Smith says. "Beneath that, there was a certain amount of empathy you'd want to express, but you didn't want to be in bad with the Cowboys.

"It was a fear-oriented organization. Guys dreaded Tuesday meetings. Duane, on the other hand, made a mockery of that fear. We'd be on the plane and all the writers would monitor his every move. He'd have that yellow cap over his face, with a book in his lap, Benjamin Franklin or something. Then he'd raise the book and read it through the woolen cap.

"The writers would all be elbowing each other. 'Did you see that? Did you see that?' "

Someone asked Blaine Nye if perhaps Thomas would be a perfect candidate for his Zero Club, his trio of cynics.

"He's got his own club," Nye said.

"I was curious about him," Hill says, "but I suppose that in the deepest part of me was admiration. He was like the silent slave. He said nothing, but maybe he took the gear out of the machinery.

"The Cowboys expected predictable reactions to questions. 'Hello, how are you?' 'Fine, how are you?' A lot of what the Cowboys did was to get predictable responses, so they could be in control. If Duane didn't give them those predictable responses, then he was in control. And it was amazing, the control he had over people. Perhaps secretly it was something I wanted to do myself, to get back at the system.

"Once Dr. Marvin Knight, our team doctor, came in the trainer's room, looking for Duane. 'Where's Duane?' he said. 'Oh, there's the son of a bitch. How ya doing?'

"Duane said, 'When you learn how to address me, I'll tell you how I'm doing,' and he got in the whirlpool and turned his back. I felt like pounding on the table. 'Yeah! Yeah!' "

JOURNAL: How could this little nappy-haired nigger from Dallas, Texas, have this type of impact on these tyrants, these giants? I came in like Moses talking to Pharaoh, knowing he was scared at first and telling God he couldn't even talk properly. Yet he shook an entire kingdom. I said, God almighty, I don't believe it is happening to me, but it was.

Schramm says Thomas "had problems before he ever came to us. The contract stuff was a side issue . . . way off here."

Landry, in an HBO special in the fall of 1987 entitled "The Strange, Silent World of Duane Thomas," said that in the off-season Thomas "appeared to be on drugs." It was strange, indeed, to hear such a serious accusation leveled so casually. It was very uncharacteristic of Landry, who has never said that about another player, despite all the stories that broke in 1970 about widespread drug abuse among Cowboy players—unnamed, of course.

"He was just miserable to be around . . . a goldfish became a shark . . . he was a black sheep," Landry said.

Reeves, as a player and running-back coach, was perhaps closest to Thomas in actual game situations. He called 1971 "the most miserable year I ever spent; there was always tension in the air." He said it convinced him to give up coaching as a profession. He returned after a year when he found out that the outside world wasn't much better. In recent years he has had great success as the Denver Broncos' head coach. He thinks Thomas's problem was twofold—California and marijuana.

"After his first year he went out to the coast," Reeves says. "I've got a friend out there, a law enforcement guy, who called me and said Duane might be messing with marijuana."

"I just can't see that at all," Staubach says. "Duane always kept himself in shape. He had too much respect for his body for that. He played in an alumni touch football game recently and he was in fantastic shape. Look, if you can figure out what his problem was, I'd like to know. It was a strange deal with a good guy."

One thing they're agreed on. Once Thomas took the field there was no problem at all—as far as his performance was concerned.

"He'd make you uncomfortable sometimes," Staubach says. "You'd throw a pass a little behind him and he'd give you this look. He got into an argument one time with Reeves, and I tried to step in and he said, 'Hey, it's none of your business.'

"In practice I'd be very careful to lead him just right on every pass, so I wouldn't get The Look."

Reeves says that the night before the Giants game, when Thomas had first been activated, Duane set up a special meeting to work on game situations.

"He called me at two o'clock in the morning to go to his room and go over his plays with him," Reeves says, "like nothing ever happened."

"Anytime we were looking at films," Thomas says, "I knew they wouldn't say anything to me, because I'd done my job. They'd talk around me. They'd talk about the other guys. With me they'd act like that's what I'm supposed to do anyway.

"In the film room the pride was there. I knew I was going to go in and show those people. I actually enjoyed the idea of looking at those films. I didn't walk in with my tail between my legs."

His view of football became rigid. He was into performance and he didn't want anyone messing with the one constant in his life.

On kick coverage he played L1, wing on the left side. Franklin told him he was moving to L4—not asked, told. He said he was getting Pat Toomay, a rookie defensive end, out of there. L4 is an inside position. The job is to take down the wedge.

"Our kick coverage team had been kicking ass," Thomas says. "I'd been grading out high. They wanted to mess up the whole rhythm of the thing just to accommodate one guy who was too lazy to do his job. I told Franklin, 'Why don't you just get Toomay to work harder?'

"He said, 'You're moving inside.' I said, 'Like hell I am.'

"So I was the bad guy again. But here's the funny thing. When we watched films, if Franklin would have stopped the projector just once and pointed me out and said, 'Nice job, Duane,' I'd have taken Toomay's place without a word. That's all it would have taken."

He enjoyed a strange relationship with Landry. He felt that the man had been on the enemy's side, that he hadn't come through when he needed him, but he also had great respect for him as a coach. In New England he had seen the underside, the "Because I said so!" side. Landry had this in common with Kerbel and the coaches at Lincoln High—he knew what he was doing and he knew how to teach it.

"One day Tom was putting a goal line play on the blackboard," Thomas says. "I raised my hand. Tom said, 'Yes, Duane?' It was the first time I'd said anything in a meeting in five or six weeks.

"I said, 'Who's blocking the fourth man?' I meant the fourth man out from the center on the side I was running. I saw that he had an angle. I had to know.

"Tom said, 'That's a good question.' Some of the guys started sniggering. "He said, 'You have to run over him.' Then he explained that based on the tendency of the guy shooting the gap, even if he got there, there would be traffic and he wouldn't be balanced. He wouldn't be in hitting position. The way he explained it made sense to me.

"You know something? I got a touchdown on that play."

With Reeves the situation was different. Thomas didn't like him. He sensed jealousy. He aligned him with the team's redneck faction. Reeves had spent half the night in Duane's room before the Giants game, going over plays with him, but that was business. This was something else.

Reeves's regular assignment was to take the roll call. Thomas's self-given assignment was not to answer. Ever. "Corporate stupidity," he says now. "Anyone could see I was there." On this particular morning

Reeves decided to make an issue of it. He called Thomas's name. No answer. He did it again, with the same result, only this time Thomas turned in his chair and faced the back wall. A few players laughed. Reeves stormed out of the room and went to see Landry.

"Coach, Duane won't answer to the roll call."

"Well, get on with it. You know he's there. We have a game to get ready for."

People who know Reeves say that he's always had a stubborn streak. In his early years with Denver the Bronco players called a meeting and complained to him personally about his inflexible nature. In 1987, Louie Wright, a starting cornerback, retired without explanation. Privately he told friends the reason was the coach.

"Stubborn, maybe, but I've never been unfair," Reeves says. "I still have nightmares about that roll call. Duane made Landry bend to him and do something I thought was unfair, and I've never forgotten it."

Why did Thomas do it? How much trouble would it have been to answer "Here!" or "Yo!" or just grunted? In his private war this was another battlefield. Everything was, in every working moment. He had his own armies, his own sides drawn up, friends, enemies, neutrals.

Jordan was the most difficult for Thomas to type. A great player, yes, and an inspirational leader on the field. But in the locker room, the leader of the redneck faction. Jordan's army? George Andrie, Ralph Neely, Bob Asher, Reeves, and Don Talbert . . . oh, yes, he was one of the worst. Duane's good guys? Staubach, Morton, Nye, Manders, Mike Clark, Cliff Harris, Charlie Waters, John Niland, Larry Cole, Bob Lilly. Lilly was one of the best.

"A great human being," Thomas says. "Bob could relate to black and white guys alike. He'd let you know what was going on. He'd say, 'If I were you, here's what I would do . . .' "

But any warmth or conversation with those guys? Out of the question.

"I always had a good relationship with Duane," Morton says, "but then I lost communication with him completely. He lost communication with himself."

Thomas had ambivalent feelings about the black players on the Cowboys. At times he felt they were his support system. He'd look around the locker room and feel security in their presence—Renfro, Pugh, Wright, Hayes, Green . . . such great athletes, such great competitors . . . Herb Adderley . . . a real man . . . wasn't afraid to stand up to any coach . . . Hill . . . an intellectual, a thinking person who could understand things . . .

But then, in his moments of depression, they were merely Landry's black legion. Support? What support? Did anyone ever come out and support him publicly? Good ol' boys, black variety. Southern and southwestern, conditioned not to make trouble. Where were they in 1970 when Pettis Norman, the tight end, came out and endorsed a black for city councilman and carried a sign, with his little daughter? Norman had been traded to San Diego after that. Did anyone say anything? Hell, no. Did Pettis himself? No, he went quietly. Another Tom. Underneath it all, just another Tom.

"Duane represented what was in the hearts of most players," Wright says, "but we didn't have the courage to stand up like he did. Duane did what he did for a reason, but we didn't give him the support. We just went along with the system.

"A lot of players supported him but were afraid to come out publicly. You know as well as I do that it makes no difference as to your ability. When they want to rid you from an organization, they can do it. There are a lot of players out there who could have played the game, good players who weren't able to. The WFL and USFL proved that."

Thomas still has trouble focusing on his relationship with his former teammates. Reeves? Bitter fights, but what the hell, they bled together. "I saw him recently," Thomas says. "We reminisced about old times." Staubach? "A guy I could relate to, but corporate. Through his relationship with the Cowboy organization he's become a millionaire." Cliff Harris, who came up as a free agent and became one of the great safetymen of all time? "We were rookies together," Thomas says. "We talked a lot that year. But now he's living in Dallas and making his living there. He has to be careful, corporate."

"The Dallas Cowboys reflect the city of Dallas," Franklin Thomas says. "If the Cowboys could become involved in improving the quality of life, rather than just entertaining, then they'd be something special. Dallas is a city that spends less on people and more on material things than any city in the country.

"How did the people of Dallas perceive the Cowboys? Well, a player who got drunk and got arrested was okay. Raising hell and kicking ass was part of the good ol' boy tradition. 'He got arrested last night.' 'Really? What was he doing?' 'Oh, just raising hell and kickin' a little ass. Nothing much.' It wasn't accepted that football players had minds, too.

"Pete Gent could write. Amazing. With the black athletes, hell, reading and writing were out of the question. And counting money? A novelty. Calvin Hill? The mere fact that this man could find his way to Dallas without a guide dog and a written note was a celestial phenomenon."

So Duane went through his private torment. Had he ever considered seeking psychiatric help? Had anyone in the organization ever suggested it?

"No," he says, "and I probably wouldn't have answered anybody who mentioned it to me. But inside, I would have appreciated his concern."

What was it like? What was it really like in those days?

"A very lonely feeling," he says, "and I realized one thing. I was out there on my own. I was the most glorified, the most talked about, the most recognized, and the most miserable. But I got all my happiness when I hit that field. That was my world, my home. All the things written about me during the week . . . well, I could prove it all wrong.

"I wanted a loose and friendly relationship with my teammates, believe me, that's all I wanted. But I was in too deep. It was wills, one will against another. I was like Darth Vader.

"Ray Renfro, the receivers coach, tried to ease it. He'd talk to me about his hardships as a player, some of the things he had to go through. He'd try to break down some of the reserve. I would just listen. Inside I wanted to say, 'Yes, this is the way it is.' But I didn't know how. It seemed that whatever I could say or do, I wouldn't get the satisfaction I wanted.

"He'd say, 'Buddy, I'm not trying to tell you what to do. I'm just trying to share a little with you.' He's in the construction business in Fort Worth now. He should still be in coaching. The receivers loved him. They were the loosest guys on the team. I liked Ermal Allen too. Maybe because he knew Kerbel and he was down-to-earth, like Kerbel was.

"Writers just came over to add fuel to the fire. They were pro–Tom Landry, pro–Tex Schramm, trying to get into the fringe-benefit program. I'd hear them after games, talking to some guy. 'What was the turning point of the game?' I'm thinking, 'You looked at the game. I was the one turning those points.' A writer who would ask me, 'What do you think about the game?' Well, I wouldn't answer. But if someone really cared . . . if he would have punched the right button . . . he'd have had a story.

"The players weren't really afraid of me, they were afraid of what I represented. A guy against the system. I felt there should have been another voice, just one, but it was never there. They never cared.

"After the Super Bowl game Rayfield ran over and picked Tom Landry up on his shoulders. I said, 'Rayfield, pick yourself up, brother. You won it.' He just looked at me.

"There were times when I enjoyed the solitude, because I felt that I was testing myself, testing my faith. But as a human being, no, I didn't enjoy it. I can talk about it now . . . it's something I held in so long.

"I felt like Job, like God is testing my faith. I thought, 'Why me, God? Why me?' I thought about Jesus a lot. I thought about the symbolic meaning of the biblical scriptures. I thought about walking through the valley of the shadow of death. I thought of Jesus, when he walked on this earth and all of Rome was against him. I went back to the religious teachings of my parents.

"It started coming to life, why all this was so important. Martin Luther King, John F. Kennedy, the loneliness of the presidency, how lonely these people really were. I read what they wrote, to learn how you can build up a certain resistance.

"I decided I would be celibate that season. No sex. During Super Bowl week people would actually be pushing women at you. Women would be coming at you constantly. They wanted to screw the image. They didn't care about you.

"I used to read the Book of Daniel. Dreams, visions. I began to feel that I could see things before they happened, in terms of relationships, how people would see me. I'd think, 'They see me on the field and they love what I'm doing, but why can't they accept what I am? Why do they want me to be something I'm not?'

"The people of Dallas didn't know me. Most people don't know themselves; they only know what they're accepted for, and they can't change—through insecurity."

"I sat in restaurants and heard people talking, and what they said reflected pure selfishness," Franklin Thomas says. "They said, 'I want to see him run more.' They were worried about losing their toy. You can take the food off people's table and they'll complain. Take the TV and they'll go to war. I'd call up Duane and tell him, 'Go back to college and get your degree. Go to work. Stop putting yourself through this.'

"The town was divided, as it always is. The Cowboys had done a good job of portraying themselves as the misused and abused party, Duane the aggressor. The white folks in Dallas were upset. The brothers said, 'Right on, man, go on.' But not very loudly, I assure you."

There was no support center in the world outside football. There was no one to turn to. His boyhood friends had grown up, they had jobs and families to worry about. He hadn't stayed very close, anyway. He'd see them every now and then, when he went back to the old neighborhood. It was "Hi, how are you?" As if they didn't know. Nothing else. Sometimes he'd call his old teachers and coaches from Lincoln.

"I wasn't going to tell him what to do," says Otto M. Friday, Jr., who was Lincoln's principal when Thomas was going there and who says he always looked at him as "my boy." He has risen high in educational circles in Dallas. He is now the acting general superintendent of the Dallas Independent School District.

"I felt, let him get it out of his system," Friday says. "I knew he would not beat the system that way. I knew the system would get him. There are so many different ways to work a system, rather than standing tall as the defiant one."

"Every now and then he'd call me," says Rabbit Thomas, his old ninth-grade coach. "He'd say, 'Hey, Coach, they're saying I'm this . . . or that.'

"I'd tell him, 'Well, you shouldn't have said those things about Tom Landry and Tex Schramm.'

"He'd say, 'It's done. There's nothing I can do about it now.'

"I told him to just be Duane Thomas."

"When I saw a news report that he was getting advice from some Muslim guy, I felt he was getting away from his roots and was ill-advised," says Larry Jefferson, the minister who grew up down the street from Duane.

"Looking back on it, maybe it would have been a good idea for me to advise him—about everything. Had the opportunity occurred, maybe I would have."

"I got very upset with the Cowboys," says Clarence Dierking, who'd been Thomas's "favorite assistant coach" at West Texas State. "I'd hear people defending the Cowboys and coming down hard on Duane and I'd say, 'Wait a minute, do you know Duane Thomas? How do you know what's going on?'

"They'd say, 'Well, I read it in the paper.'

"I'd tell them, 'Well, you don't know what you're talking about so you'd better keep your mouth shut.' "

He was asked if he'd ever seen Thomas during that period, ever talked to him. He thought for a moment.

"I had dinner with Duane and Steve Kiner . . . let's see, I guess it was the off-season between '70 and '71," he said. "I felt something was wrong. What had happened, I don't know, but I just felt he was being influenced by the wrong people. But that's just my opinion."

"Kerbel had called me up during the season to find out what was going on," Thomas says. "I told him everything. He said, 'Goddammit, I knew you shouldn't have signed with that team. The team is not aggressive enough for you. But now you've got to make the best of it.' "

In the winter of 1987 I asked Calvin Hill if, sixteen years later, he could put the whole Duane Thomas experience into perspective. I was in Washington covering a playoff game. Hill works there, as a career guidance counselor. My relationship with Calvin goes back twenty-seven years, back to 1961, when he was a fourteen-year-old freshman end at Riverdale Country Day School in the Bronx, and I was the schoolboy writer for the *New York World-Telegram & Sun*. I was there the first day he stepped onto a football field, and they gave him a helmet with no face bar and told him to work against two linemen and learn how to fight the double-team.

I followed his career with Dallas and then the WFL Hawaiians, where he and Duane would spend long hours together, driving around the island. I followed Calvin when he went to the Redskins and the Browns. In Cleveland he was an integral part of Sam Rutigliano's Inner Circle, a group designed to help drug abusers on the team. I've felt for some time that if a club would ever be serious about hiring the NFL's first black general manager, it would find no better man than Calvin Hill.

So we sat in a restaurant in Washington, and Calvin toyed with his coffee cup and tried to capsulize for me the strange, troubled year of Duane Thomas.

"The first thing you have to understand," he said, "is that when you fall from grace in Dallas, no matter what the reason is, it's incredibly sudden—and complete. My popularity there was amazing my first year. KCIF radio had a Back of the Year contest at the Fairmont. Just for fun I went over there. I wound up winning it. Highland Park, the most exclusive enclave in Dallas, had the largest Methodist church in the world, ten thousand members. They wanted to make me a minister. I was a divinity student at the time.

"But then in my second year I was superseded by Duane, and at the practice field suddenly I was no longer a part of the game plan. I was nothing. It was a dramatic shift that I wasn't prepared for.

"It happened differently with Duane; he was still a focal part of the game plan, but he had fallen from grace as a person. The effect was just as devastating.

"Another thing is that Duane is intellectual in a way . . . he has a very curious, inquiring mind . . . but the key to his personality is trust. He was always looking for someone to believe in. That's why it was so easy for him to get with Jim Brown. Duane trusted people very easily, but he was always looking for a father figure—his real father, who died, his high school coaches, his college coach. And I think that when he joined the Cowboys, Tom Landry became that father figure.

"You believe in your coach. He's the guy who's going to take care of you. In that sense you make yourself very vulnerable. Then you get used—it happens in college, then in the pros—and you get suspicious. You don't trust anyone anymore. You go to the other extreme. Even Pete Gent in his book portrayed Landry as tougher than he was. He had been looking for something in Landry at one time and he didn't give it to him.

"I never met a black player as I was coming up who didn't believe in God. Duane is a very spiritual person. Landry is God-fearing. Then a business decision is made. You're part of a team, you sacrifice, then to be traded or cut, or there's a problem in salary negotiations . . . well, there's a certain trust involved, and when you're let down, it's never the same.

"I told Landry, 'A lot of these players look at you as a father.' He projects the image of stability. A lot of what he says will happen in a game does occur. It's a spiritual thing. It appeals to a lot of people. Tom minimized it. I don't know whether I got through to him.

"In terms of a Duane, or a Bob Hayes, who wound up in prison, the sad thing is that I don't think Tom ever understood how much they depended on him. Look at the Super Bowl picture. The guys lifting Landry on their shoulders are Hayes and Rayfield Wright, two black guys. I don't know if it's just a black-white thing, but it's important to believe in someone who cares.

"The thing about Duane is that he'd always been drifting, always looking. He always had his sense of reality obscured by the ideal. When he found out differently, it was a bitter disappointment. He would open up to people and they'd take advantage of it."

JOURNAL: When I saw Bob Lilly and Jethro Pugh, my two favorite defensive linemen, working in such unison with Lee Roy Jordan, I said look at what they have going together. I said look at what we have ... a championship team, even though some people didn't realize it. Cornell Green, the brilliance of his play was thrilling ... Blaine Nye, Dave Manders, Rayfield Wright, John Niland, impeccable at the point of attack.

I was so thankful to be surrounded by such men on the field. The team was like an orchestra. When it was time for the brass to play, the brass came in perfectly, then the strings. It was so beautiful to watch the flow of execution on that team, consistently unstoppable, the scoreboard going like a pinball machine.

Coaching was easier for Tom. How could you teach a Jordan and a Lilly how to play their positions? Just give them their assignments. The communication with the cornerbacks . . . the great safetymen . . . Cornell Green and Mel Renfro had played both offense and defense in their careers . . . just go down the line. If there was an error in communication it was easy to locate right there on the field. Everyone knew his job. You didn't have to go to a replay camera.

We'd win a game in the first or second quarter. From then on it was just how much resistance we were receiving from a particular team, how much fight was in them. Playing and winning were my life, because off the field there was nothing to go to.

The 1971 Cowboys had nineteen all-pros, past, present, and future. They had six future members of the Hall of Fame, four imported and two, Staubach and Lilly, homegrown. Others undoubtedly will follow. They tied the Vikings for the best record in the NFL that year (11-3). They won their last seven games, averaged 41.7 points in the three leading up to the playoffs, and then swept the postseason, winning the three games by an average of two touchdowns apiece.

Staubach took over as the starting quarterback when the Cowboys were 4-3 at midseason. He had spent the first half of the year alternating with Morton. At times they would switch on every play, a strange Landry concept that made neither man happy. Roger solidified the passing attack, but once again it was the running game that was the showpiece. Over a two-year period the Cowboys were the NFL's leading team in rushing yardage, averaging better than 1,000 yards per season more than they gave up.

Statistically, Thomas had a better year than he'd had in 1970, although his yardage was down by 10 (803 to 793), but he'd done it in three fewer games. Also, the defenses were now keying on him. He became the Cowboys' leading goal line threat. No one in the NFL scored more touchdowns than he did. Despite his problems, he'd had a terrific season. The Cowboys got their $20,000 worth.

"The way he ran . . . I always said I wish I could have seen him play longer," Franklin Thomas says. "They had a club in Amarillo that would show the highlight films of Dallas games. I'd spend the last two or three dollars I had just to go there and get a chance to watch those films. They would talk about the fluidity of his motion, but of course at that time it was liquidity, not fluidity, that he was interested in."

He gave no interviews during Super Bowl week in New Orleans. Mors than 81,000 fans showed up on a chilly, 39-degree afternoon to watch the game in Tulane Stadium.

"When we were coming out," Hill says, "I turned to Duane and said, 'Look at all those fans. This is just like the Romans and the Christians, isn't it?'

"He said, 'Sure is.' "

That's the last recorded conversation Thomas had until the famous locker room interview with CBS-TV's Tommy Brookshier.

With ten minutes to go in the 24–3 Cowboy victory over Miami, a man from *Sport Magazine* took a press-box poll for MVP of the game. For some unexplained reason the NFL still lets this magazine select its official award. Thomas, who had gained 95 yards on 19 carries and burst through the openings so quickly that the Dolphin linemen were barely out of their stance, was the writers' overwhelming choice. I voted coawards, to Thomas and right guard Nye, who had done a terrific job cutting off the Dolphins' middle linebacker, Nick Buoniconti.

In the tunnel outside the interview area, *Sport Magazine* editor Larry Klein announced that Roger Staubach, whose statistics had been modest (12 of 19 passes for 119 yards), was the MVP. The writers let up a howl. We hadn't yet learned about the brutality of magazine editors, and Klein had done a savage editing job on our poll. The reason wasn't hard to figure out. The award was, and is, a promotional tool for the magazine, and when the Super Bowl car is given the winner, at a restaurant in New York, he's expected to stand up and say a few words. Thus Thomas was eliminated from consideration. The uncertainty was too great.

Brookshier stood on a wooden platform in the locker room. Next to him was Thomas, with Jim Brown behind and to the left. In essence the interview went like this:

Brookshier: Duane, you don't look that fast the way you run, but then you're able to outrun the defensive players. Are you really that fast?

Thomas: Evidently.

Brookshier: Do you like football, Duane?

Thomas: Yes, that's why I'm a pro football player.
Brookshier: Why do you weigh 215 for some games and
             something else for others?
Thomas: I weigh what I need to.

"I saw Brookshier recently," Thomas says. "I kidded him. I said 'Evidently' a few times. I told him I thought something was wrong with him that day. He'd been shaking. Maybe a sniper had him lined up or something.

"He said he'd been nervous."

"Nervous? I was scared to death," Brookshier says. "It was bedlam in that locker room. I was doing Adderley up on the platform. Pat Summerall was interviewing Staubach in the crowd. A reporter fell and broke his leg.

"I turned to Adderley and said, 'Would Duane Thomas talk to me?' He said, 'He wouldn't talk to Irv Cross.' Next thing I know, my director says, 'You've got him right behind you.'

"First one I saw was Jim Brown. Then Duane. He didn't look mean, he looked blank. The only thing that flashed through my mind was that he made Buoniconti miss him on the goal line, on his touchdown, and that Buoniconti's a good tackler, but he'd misjudged the angle. So I asked that question about his speed. Duane said, 'Evidently.' I could hear people laughing. I asked some nondescript questions after that.

"Jim Brown saw that I was beginning to sweat. He leaned over and tried to help. He said, 'You're pretty nervous, aren't you?' I said, 'You're darn right I am.' At that point Duane just hopped off the platform and he was gone.

"I got crudely written racist stuff after that, supporting me. 'Don't take that off him . . .' That kind of thing. I still have nightmares about that interview. I think of it and break into a cold sweat. I keep a blown-up photo of it next to my desk—so I'll never forget."

Thomas went back to the Cowboys' hotel, talked with Brown for a while, and went upstairs. He wasn't hungry. He didn't eat. He came down to the lobby for a few minutes. A player asked him if he were going to the team party. He said no. He went back to the room and lay down on the bed and stared at the ceiling.

"I was upset that the season was over," he says. "I didn't ever want to stop playing. I didn't want to come off the field and deal with the outside world. I was thinking about my life, whether I should move back in with my old lady, try to make a go of it. I thought about my kids, that they didn't really know me. I thought about how much I really loved them, and they didn't know it. I was worried about the emotional strain they must be under, hearing all those things about their father. People didn't even know I had two kids. Good. The less they knew the less they could pursue."

Two weeks later Thomas was in the news again. He had been arrested, along with his younger brother, Bertrand, in Greenville, Texas, on a charge of marijuana possession. On February 21, after pleading guilty, they received five years' probation. Thomas would have to report to a court-appointed officer on the 21st of every month.

Thomas did not fly out with the team to the Thousand Oaks training camp in July, 1972. Instead he sent a stand-in, Redderick (Bay Bay) Price, his old Lincoln High teammate. They had been together for one semester at West Texas State. Price boarded the flight in Dallas and sat down in the first class section.

"He was not," Hill said, "your typical first class air traveler."

"He said Duane had told him to try out for the team," Staubach says. "No one wanted to argue. They were afraid he would get mad. He got on the bus with us, and next day in practice he's out there with the quarterbacks and receivers, lining up to catch passes in combat boots and sweat pants. Normally he'd have been thrown out, but hey, this is Duane's buddy. Gil Brandt and all those guys never said anything.

"Landry walks up and says, 'Who the heck is that guy?' Someone tells him it's Duane's friend. Tom said, 'Get him out of here.' Anyway, for fifteen minutes he was out there believing he was gonna be an NFL receiver."

"He was wearing combat boots and sweats because that's all he had," Thomas says. "He was a Vietnam vet. If I'd have known that, I'd have given him a pair of shoes. He was a good receiver. He could get open. He had hands. I told Gil I'd take a cut in pay if they gave him a chance."

"Uh, I don't think he would have made it," Staubach says. "I really don't."

Thomas reported late. By now he wouldn't talk to anybody. For the first time he started missing meetings.

"He was in never-never land," Schramm says. "He was out of control."

"I roomed across the hall from him," Morton said. "He never unpacked his bags. I'd go by his room. He'd be lying on the bed, staring at the ceiling, like there was a visitor from another planet in there. He'd never go out the door. He'd jump out that ground-floor window and go to the cafeteria and bring back food and eat it in his room.

"Every night Ray Renfro had to come to get him for the meetings. Duane would leave when he wanted to. It was so pathetic to me. Renfro would be outside his door, saying, 'Duane, Duane, I know you're in there. Coach Landry wants to talk to you.'

"I'd say, 'Ray, why do you do it?'

"He'd say, 'Coach Landry wants me to.' By then Duane was out the window."

"We'd kid Renfro," Staubach says. "We started calling him Duane-Duane. I used to go into Duane's room to try to talk to him. He'd let me in. I'd do all the talking. I'd say, 'Duane, I guess you want me to leave.' He'd say, 'No, man, I don't mind you staying here.' "

"He missed morning practice one day," Hill says. "They sent Roger over to get him to come to practice. He went through this long spiel, and the whole time Roger was tossing an orange up and down. Finally he got tired of talking. He said, 'What do you think, Duane?'

"Duane said, 'Hey, man, I sure would like a piece of that orange.'

"When we played in the college all-star game he took warm-ups with us, but he wouldn't go in. He took his pads out, then dressed by himself, under the goalposts."

On July 30 the Cowboys traded him for the second and last time —to San Diego for wide receiver Billy Parks and running back Mike Montgomery.

"I don't even know who told him he was traded," Staubach said.

Epilogue: The Cowboys forwarded Thomas's mail to San Diego. Oddly enough, many of the letters supporting him contained poems. The one that he liked the best was written by a white student in Dallas.

A Honky's Thoughts on Duane Thomas Leaving Dallas
—for Dwight Warner—

When white boys grow in Dallas Town,
Make all that bread, win great renown,
And when they move to Highland Park
—Where black folk ain't seen after dark—
They strangely find that's not enough,

That they're not men, that they're not tough
Unless they watch the Cowboys play,
Until they know what Lilly weighs.
This team's the god to whom they pray.

They watched them in the Cotton Bowl,
And thought this showed a lot of soul,
Until that day they took a stroll
And saw East Dallas had turned black.
They feared their team would soon shoot smack
And join big D's Black Panther Pack.

Thus in dark hours white boys did dream:
"Let's move to Irving. It's got a sheen,
Not Afro, but of whiter gleam;
It won't corrupt our Christian team."

So to the dome the honkies ran,
Where darkened skins were only tan.

And have you heard of Lincoln High?
Boys grow there too beneath the sky,
Play ball, run streets, and often die.
A Cowboy played on Lincoln's team
Before he entered Landry's Scheme.

"Duane—if silence has that name—
Now do you really weigh the same,
Or do you change from game to game?"

"I weigh what weights I need to weigh.
Conditions change each time I play."

This man who weighed such different weight
Soon weighed too much for Landry's slate.
Those things he learned at Lincoln's High
Were heavy things for white boy's eye.

So now he's gone from Dallas town . . .
Or, Irving (since I see Schramm's frown).
Still, some men bent their heads far down.

They laid their ears against the ground:
They heard a voice of silence speak,
A roar which absence's throat had shrieked,
A sound which made the Cowboys meek.
They saw the blackness which surrounds
Fair Dallas and its bloodstained ground.

10

GREENVILLE

Are you making any headway with Thomas? Not really.
We need to break him a little more under the hammer. Well,
what are his habits? Let's see if we can do something to whip
that boy into line. . . .

I'll say this about Dallas: They play to win. That's why it's
so hard to make it in this city. Whether it's in business or
with the banks, you'd better play to win or they'll eat you
alive.

Franklin Thomas

The Cowboys had won their first Super Bowl. Thomas had spoken
on TV. A few days later Jim Brown called to tell him that ABC was
willing to pay him to appear on the Howard Cosell show. Thomas turned
it down.

"I thought it was just a setup to wipe me out on TV," he said.
"Besides, I was emotionally wiped out."

He had heard reports that his younger brother, Bertrand, was in
trouble, specifically that he was smoking marijuana.

"I knew people would be checking to find some blemish, either on me or my family," Thomas says.

On Sunday, January 30, Duane and Bertrand Thomas took a drive east on Interstate 30, "just to talk things over," Duane says. They got as far as Greenville, forty-eight miles east of Dallas, when they were stopped.

Greenville is not the place in which a black person wants to stop or be stopped. For years Greenville's most famous landmark was a sign that read: The Blackest Earth, The Whitest People. Shortly before two P.M. Thomas and his brother were arrested for possession of marijuana, a felony in Texas, punishable by two years to life imprisonment. The life sentence actually had been handed out—in Houston, to a young black activist charged with possessing two cigarettes. He was freed after serving a small portion of the sentence when attorneys from all over the country rushed to his defense.

The Thomas brothers had been stopped by Norman Gray of the Hunt County Sheriff's Office and Highway Patrolman Wendell Jeter. Gray's complaint, presented to the Hunt County magistrate at the time of the arrest, was as follows:

> On January 30, 1972, at approximately 12:20 P.M., I received a radio dispatch from the Hunt Country Sheriff's Office stating that a white over orange 1972 Grand Prix Pontiac automobile bearing Texas dealer plates P48 947 and occupied by two Negro males was traveling east on Interstate 30 Highway from Rockwall, Texas. I was further advised that this vehicle had been identified by personnel of the R. O. Evans Pontiac Company in Dallas, Texas, as being the same vehicle that had previously been stolen from that automobile company. By radio information it was verified that an automobile answering that description had been stolen on January 11, 1972, from R. O. Evans Pontiac Company.
>
> I was joined on Interstate 30 Highway by Patrolman Wendell Jeter. At 12:35 P.M. on the same date, Patrolman Jeter observed a vehicle answering this description traveling west on Interstate 30 Highway east of Farm Road 36 in Hunt County. Patrolman Jeter turned behind the vehicle and verified the license number. He radioed to me that he had the car in sight. At 12:38 P.M. on the same date, Patrolman Jeter used his emergency equipment to stop said vehicle.
>
> Patrolman Jeter requested the driver, Duane Julius

Thomas, to get out of the car, and I requested the passenger, Bertrand Lynn Thomas, to get out. Both complied. I advised both of the purpose of their being stopped. I then went back to the above-described automobile to determine the VIN number. Upon leaning inside the car, I smelled the strong smell of burning marijuana. I am very familiar with burning marijuana as I have smelled it many times in the past. I also saw some "Zig Zig papers" lying on the console between the two front seats. I personally know these papers to be used by persons in wrapping and smoking marijuana. I then discovered approximately two lids of marijuana, wrapped and lying behind the ashtray in the console.

Wherein, I ask that a warrant to search for and seize the said narcotic drug [two words illegible] the above-described premises be issued in accordance with the law in such cases provided.

The search warrant was issued. The Officer's Return form, filed by the magistrate, Gayle R. Carden, lists the following contents seized and turned over to the court for evidence:

One (1) cigarette wrapped in yellow paper.
Ashes and residue from ashtray.
Bits of scorched paper and two (2) seeds.
One (1) black coat.

There are many holes in this testimony and evidence, which became the basis for the charge to which Bertrand, and then Duane Thomas, pled guilty. The most obvious is that they were illegally stopped and searched. Gray said that radio information had verified the description of the car, but a license plate check would have revealed that the numbers didn't match. The car Thomas was driving had been leased through Van Winkle Pontiac in Dallas, through Gil Brandt. Even the name of the dealer would have shown as different. Either Gray didn't bother to find out the correct license number, or he knew the car wasn't the stolen one, and he just wanted to stop them anyway. And then why did he have to lean in and check the VIN (vehicle identification number)? Why didn't he just ask Thomas to hand out his registration, which would have verified the plate number, make of car, etc.?

He had searched the car without a warrant. He couldn't have found articles behind the ashtray unless he'd conducted a search—before requesting the warrant. And of course, the articles actually turned over to the judge weren't the same ones he'd described in his complaint. The "two (2) seeds," traditionally used when cops want to plant evidence, are especially suspicious. Why would the Thomas brothers have seeds? They weren't farmers.

Duane Thomas's description of what happened is as follows:

"As we were driving, two guys passed us. They were wearing white shirts and ties with no coats. They were driving a GM car. They were pointing their fingers at me. I thought they'd recognized me in the papers. Bertrand said, 'Let's catch up with those guys.' I said, 'No, leave them alone. Just because a man's wearing a tie doesn't make him civilized.'

"We stopped for some orange juice and chips. We turned around and were coming back to Dallas, and I saw this patrol car in the rearview mirror, really gaining ground. He turned his flasher on. I stopped. I knew I wasn't speeding. A door opened and a guy jumped out and pulled a gun. The other guy yelled through a megaphone: 'Get out with your hands up!' Another car pulled up in front and a detective got out and stood blocking me.

"The patrolman said, 'Do you realize you're driving a stolen car?' I said it was impossible. He said, 'Well, someone reported it.'

"I told him where it was from and said he could call Gil Brandt to verify it or to call the dealer the next day. It was Sunday when we were stopped. I had showed him the correct registration and ownership.

"A detective came up and said, 'I know it's in here.'

"I said, 'What's in there?'

"He said, 'Never mind, I know.'

"He started going through the car and came up with a bag of grass. Right then and there I felt, 'There are some sinister, conniving sons of bitches here.' I said, 'Hey, if you don't want me to play so much, just say so.' It was like I was being followed anywhere I went.

"We were arrested and we spent a night in jail. As we were led in, a black prisoner said, 'Hey, Duane, why don't you run a trap play on these fuckers?' "

Brandt said he heard about it the next day and tried to get a lawyer for Thomas and his brother.

"I gave him a list of three names we recommended," he says. "He didn't use any of them. The guy who eventually represented him was a Greenville lawyer. I was wondering why he'd want a guy from Greenville to be his attorney."

"The judge who sentenced us to five years' probation was Hollis

Garmon," Thomas says. "Bertrand confessed, but Judge Garmon said, 'No, we're getting both of you.' I remember his words. We met Judge Garmon in his chambers a few days after we were arrested.

"He asked me if I had an attorney. I said yes, I had one from Boston. Bob Woolf from Boston had called me and said he'd represent us for free. Judge Garmon said I'd better not get anybody from the outside. He said if I did, he'd send us up for life. He told me exactly who to get . . . Larry Green, a local lawyer from Greenville . . . and how to plead and what to say, and then he said he'd give us five years' probation. Then they went back and wrote everything into the record. The whole thing was scripted. It was a setup."

Judge Hollis D. Garmon still lives in Greenville. He is now senior state judge for the state of Texas, "traveling from town to town on special assignment," he said.

"At the arraignment there were perhaps forty or fifty other people in the room whose names were called," Judge Garmon says. "I think Thomas had been originally arrested for speeding. Then they had searched the car and found one marijuana cigarette. Gayle Carden was reading him his rights at the arraignment and he stood up and said, 'I waive arraignment and plead guilty and put myself on the mercy of the court.' "

Did he have a lawyer?

"I don't really remember. Maybe Phil Bertelson from Dallas. I think he had him before he ever came to my chambers."

Where did Larry Green come from?

"The Cowboys' regular Dallas attorney recommended Bill Pemberton of Greenville. Larry Green worked in Pemberton's office."

Thomas says that he was told to get Green as his lawyer. Is that true?

"No, it's very common to hire a local lawyer when Dallas lawyers and Houston lawyers do not know the names and addresses of people who would serve on a jury here. Duane Thomas got Bill Pemberton here. He'd been a city attorney and had worked in the DA's office for years. He got Pemberton because he was afraid the Dallas lawyers wouldn't know our particular laws."

The interesting thing is that Brandt said that none of the three lawyers he had recommended was called by Thomas.

Duane's probation was later reduced to twenty-two months, which he successfully served. In Texas he was a convicted felon. Bertrand Thomas was not so lucky. Before finishing his sentence he was found guilty on another drug possession charge and sent to prison.

Duane Thomas maintains that he was not smoking marijuana that day in the car and he had no knowledge of the stuff that was found. He thinks it was planted, but it wouldn't surprise him if some of it were Bertrand's. Both he and Franklin had continually warned their younger brother to "watch your habits."

Pete Gent, the former Cowboy wide receiver turned writer, believes to this day that the Cowboys had set up the whole Greenville episode.

"Of course they were behind it," he says. "It would be just like them."

Franklin Thomas thinks it's "quite likely." In the days when he feels bitter, Duane says the Cowboys might have done it, "to keep me in Dallas." During the times when he feels more kindly disposed toward them, he says it's highly improbable.

11

CHARLES CAPERTON

The streets of our country are in turmoil. The universities
are filled with students rebelling and rioting. Communists are
seeking our country. Russia is threatening us with her might,
and the republic is in danger. Yes, danger from within and
without. We need law and order. Without it our nation
cannot survive.

> Adolf Hitler, 1932

The quote, neatly framed, hangs on the wall to the right of the
desk of Charles L. Caperton, attorney-at-law, who in 1984 took on the
job of getting Duane Thomas an official pardon for the Greenville drug
conviction.

"A ninety-nine to one shot at this point," he said in the fall of
1987, "even though the State Board of Pardons and Parole approved it.
The governor still has to sign it, and governors don't like to sign such
things if they plan to run on a law and order ticket."

From the hallway in Caperton's office in downtown Dallas you can
see the Texas School Book Depository building and Dealey Plaza, where

John F. Kennedy was shot. The Book Depository has been renamed the Dallas City Administration Building. Caperton's office itself is a storehouse of memorabilia—a pair of boxing gloves on the wall with the inscription: "All-Army, Light Heavyweight Champion, 1956,"; a framed inscription of Shakespeare's famous quote from Henry VI, "The first thing we do, let's kill all the lawyers"; on a coffee table a bronze sculpted hand with a dollar bill jammed between the fingers, a testimony to Caperton's feelings about the greed that infects some areas of his profession. Caperton has yet to charge Thomas a fee for his three-and-a-half-year battle to restore him to good graces in his home state. One-fourth of his practice in criminal law is pro bono, "for the public good."

Fifty years old, slender and athletic-looking with sandy blond hair, Caperton has made a career out of battling the giants. He went after Syntex Labs, claiming their birth control product produced a brain-damaged baby, and got a settlement, after Syntex had won twelve straight cases. He represented Don Vestal and the insurgent Teamsters Union faction in a pension fund investigation, the same Vestal who ran against Frank Fitzsimmons and the machine and who once punched Jimmy Hoffa in the Fontainbleau Hotel.

"They put 140 bullet holes in his house after that one," Caperton said. "When I first started the pension fund investigation . . . well, I had this old white Caddy convertible, and every day, for five days in a row, I found a dead pigeon on the hood of it, a pigeon with its head pulled off. They were sending me a message.

"My wife, Marilyn, said, 'You know, you just don't understand death.' Death threats . . . I've got a standard line when I get them over the phone. 'If you're gonna kill me, you're gonna have to stand in line.' "

He is no stranger to drugs. He and his wife started a first-offender program in their home territory, Highland Park, evaluating, treating, and educating the youngsters he had sentenced from the bench as a municipal judge (unpaid).

"If the kid wants to keep it off the record," Caperton says, "he pays a $65 fine and he and his parents enter the program. I'll do anything to keep their record clean . . . you don't know what's going to happen down the road . . . anything to avoid branding a kid like that. . . ."

Caperton is a strange mixture, a crusader whose whole background was Dallas good ol' boy, a rose that somehow forced itself up between the cracks in the pavement. His father, Dallas-born, was an advertising manager for Dr Pepper for twenty-two years. Charles Caperton grew up in ultra-white, ultra-conservative Highland Park, in the shadow of SMU. He has never moved out of the area. He went the approved Junior

League route, Highland Park High, SMU, short hair, athletics, and when he expressed an interest in law, his friends and neighbors wondered which major oil company he'd represent. But early in life something different clicked in . . . maybe it was what he saw around him, perhaps it was his fascination for everything written about Clarence Darrow . . . at any rate Caperton decided he'd be on the side of the underdog.

Here and there you can find a good-ol'-boy remnant: his love of boxing, his opposition to stringent gun law legislation. On a wall in the hallway to his office is an article about a prominent gun law trial. It's from *Gun Magazine*, November 1987: "The advocacy side was a clash of titans. For the defense stood Charles Caperton, one of America's most brilliant criminal trial lawyers . . ."

He has yet to smoke his first joint . . . "because one of these days the same sons of bitches who nailed Duane are gonna plant me and I want to be able to get through a lie detector."

Duane Thomas couldn't have found a better person to plead his case.

He had met him through Gene Owen, the southwestern regional sales manager for Londontown Corp., a men's outerwear firm. Thomas had traveled with Owen, selling clothing, from 1979 to 1981, and Owen's home office was around the corner from Caperton's. One day he said to Thomas, "Look, there's a criminal attorney who's considered the best in Texas. Why don't you see him?"

"I didn't know what kind of a person would come walking into my office back there in the winter of '83," Caperton said last fall. "I thought maybe he'd come in and start cursing all the white people on earth. I didn't know whether he'd be wild and unruly, sulking, mad and mean, demanding, or what. I was a Cowboy fan, like everyone else, and my perceptions were only what I read in the papers, that he was an emotionally disturbed misfit, that the Cowboys were righteous and he was just a misfit.

"Then the drug bust came, and I thought like everyone else did in Dallas, well, he's screwed up on drugs. You look at the tenor of all the newspaper stories . . . goddamn, the guy's nothing but a social malcontent and a dopehead."

Thomas told him, "Look, I've got a chance to sell insurance around Dallas, but I can't get the job because of that felony conviction. I thought when I served my probation out it would be off my record. They never explained it to me at the time."

So Caperton explained the facts of life to him.

"I told him, 'Hell, you're a convicted felon,' " he said. " 'You can't vote. There are ninety-six occupations in the state of Texas you can't enter into. You can't be a barber. You can't sell insurance. You can't be a licensed plumber or electrician or tow truck driver, anything that requires a state exam. You can't do anything that calls for you to put up a performance bond. You can't run a cash register in a service station without being bonded. You can't even take the place of one of the Iranians working behind the counter in a 7-Eleven store.' "

"I don't know what to do," Thomas told him. "It's crippled me for all this time. No one ever said anything about it when they had me plead guilty. I don't have a dime, but if I ever get work, I'll pay you."

"I don't want to be paid," Caperton said. "I don't want you worrying about it."

"If only I'd have known you back then," Thomas said. "Damn, I wish I would have known you."

Caperton sat down with Thomas for a few sessions, got the story of his arrest and conviction, and the picture started coming into focus.

"Greenville, Texas, 'the blackest earth, the whitest people,' " he says.

"The sign was in the train station, and do you know, it hung there until the 1970s? So you can imagine . . . a white guy from the sheriff's office seeing two black guys driving a new car. The license plate didn't even match that of the stolen vehicle. It was a different dealer. There was no probable cause on the face of this earth for the search, except it was two black guys driving a new car. A motion to suppress evidence in that case would have kept them from convicting, even if Bertrand hadn't originally pleaded guilty. But they got Duane a lawyer who went in and pleaded him guilty even after Bertrand had said the stuff was his. At the time the papers were full of stories about pending legislation that would make possession of anything under four ounces of marijuana a misdemeanor, and in March, one month later, it was passed. If that two-bit lawyer would have filed one motion, any motion at all, by the time it came to trial it would have been a misdemeanor offense and he wouldn't have been a second class citizen all those years.

"But at that time the punishment for one-third of a roach, or a seed that would germinate, was two years to life. They wet a paper towel, put the seed in, take it to the crime lab, and if it germinates, it's a felony. Life imprisonment, can you imagine? A Greenville jury might have given it to him, too. Their chance to bust Big Duane Thomas, to be famous."

Caperton stared out the window, at the traffic on the Stemmons

Freeway. The door opened and a young black woman, maybe twenty-five or so, entered with a plate of broiled chicken and a carrot casserole.

"Lunch," she said, putting the tray down.

"Robbie Johnson, one of our legal secretaries," Caperton said. "She cooks lunch for me. Saves me the trouble of going out. She came here three and a half years ago, from a temporary employment service. My wife interviewed her, and then came bursting into my office, all excited. 'Do you have any idea what this girl can do?' she said. 'Honey, we're lucky as hell.'

"An IQ of 140, types 120 words a minute. I tell her, 'You know that case about the operation that ended with a dropped foot . . . ?' and she'll say, 'Dr. Lazlow,' and thirty seconds later she pulled the complete file.

"She worked for Blue Cross before she came here. They fired her, fired her because some office manager tried to get some pussy and failed. Then they promote some white chick, probably a 75 IQ with big tits."

He pointed to the sports page of the *Dallas Times Herald,* to a story about Plano High School shooting for a state championship.

"Plano High School in far north Dallas, the right-wing capital of Texas," he said. "They had this pep rally Friday night before they played a black high school. They dressed up three kids in black garbage bags and painted big red lips on them and had them run into each other. Now this is November 1987 we're talking about, not 1930. The principal was called about it. 'Well, I don't know,' he said.

"So there's Duane Thomas, facing a life sentence unless he pleads guilty to something someone else has already admitted to. I'll tell you, the laws in this state . . . do you realize the SS had more reason to kick in a door than our local constable has. If he's in good faith belief, that's all it takes. That's why I keep the Hitler quote up there. I could cry sometimes about what's happening in this country. We've lost more rights with the U.S. Supreme Court than we gained in all the wars we fought . . . the fourth, fifth, and sixth amendments are gone. Our constitution in Texas was better than the U.S. Constitution at one time, but it's been amended 259 times. They voted in a constitutional amendment allowing them to change the indictment when you go to trial. It was passed with flying colors. Can you imagine, preparing to defend one charge and facing another? I wrote an editorial about it.

"Anyway, right now Duane's still a convicted felon, the same as if he went to the penitentiary."

Early in 1984 Caperton drove down to Greenville himself to investigate the conviction.

"When I showed up in Greenville it scared them," he said. "They said, 'What the hell are you doing here?' It didn't take me long to see how phony the whole thing was. The indictment had named both of them. At that time you could have joint possession of a joint if it was in plain view. That's why the patrolman's testimony said that it was in plain view. Now nobody with a joint is going to leave it in plain view, in the ashtray for Christ's sake.

"Anyway, thirty days after Duane was sentenced, the conviction was final, and the only thing I could do was go for a pardon. I told Duane we probably wouldn't get it, but we'll damn sure give it a try."

In June 1984 the letters started pouring into the office of Governor Mark White. Tom Landry wrote, "In my opinion he has paid his debt to society and has proven his willingness to abide by the law . . . I am very confident that he has rehabilitated himself and has worked back into the community . . . I am confident that he has remorse over the offense and is now in a position to make a contribution to society . . ."

And from Gil Brandt this bit of irony, probably unintentional: "During his employment as a Dallas Cowboys player he was always cooperative and was well-liked by his teammates." The letter ended, "I do not hesitate to recommend Duane Thomas for a pardon because he has clearly manifested an intent to abide by the law and be a contributing citizen to our society."

Snowden Isaiah McKinnon, the pastor of the Hope Presbyterian Church in South Dallas, a man who had known Duane and his family for twenty-six years, wrote a deeply moving letter, detailing the circumstances of the death of Duane's parents—"I remember Duane carrying his emaciated father to their station wagon to take him to Parkland Hospital for medical help . . ." He quoted a church officer at Glendale Presbyterian, who said of Duane, "He is one of us," and the Reverend McKinnon ended, "I would, therefore, without one iota of hesitation, recommend Duane as an excellent candidate for pardon at this time."

Larry Miller, the DA who prosecuted Thomas, added his endorsement of a pardon. So did Hollis Garmon, the judge who sentenced him. The letters sat on Governor White's desk for almost three and a half years. The board voted the pardon, but White dragged his heels, even after he was voted out of office.

"Well, he might run again on a law and order platform," Caperton said.

Finally late in 1987 White approved the pardon.

"Now we go for an expungement of the record, so he doesn't still have the arrest next to his name," Caperton said in February 1988.

"The problem is that it's applicable only if he didn't plead to it, which he did. Even so, how do you give someone sixteen years of his life back?"

I asked Caperton if he believed, as Franklin Thomas and Pete Gent did, that the Cowboys were behind the original bust.

"I don't think so," he said. "I think that at the time they just didn't give a damn."

He paused for a moment. "You know, they're expected to play as a team. Well, being a team should go deeper than on the field. When someone in my family gets in trouble, or someone in this office, I take care of them. If they're going to perform for me, I'm damn sure going to be there when they need me. But if something is just a job and the person doing it is a machine, well, say so and don't try to create the illusion of a family.

"If the general overall management and psychology is to be together as a team, and if that's a reality, then I'd rather coach a team like that than one with more talent."

I asked him if all this made him less of a Dallas Cowboys' fan. This time he didn't pause in his answer.

"Hell, no," he said. "It's my home team."

12

AMERICA'S TEAM

There are three types of people in the civilized world.
There are those who love the Dallas Cowboys, those who
hate the Dallas Cowboys, and those who don't know who or
what the Dallas Cowboys are. I call these people Group A, B,
and C, respectively. I have never met a Group C person, but
reliable sources informed me they do exist—they live mostly
along the west bank of the Amazon.

Group B people are paragons of mankind. They are
superior in every way to Group A and Group C. Group A
(except those living in or near Dallas, who have been
brainwashed since birth and have long ago lost all ability to
make rational decisions) should be shunned at all costs. They
are not to be trusted.

Let me profile the typical Group A man for you. He is a
front-runner. In other sports his allegiance is pledged to the
Boston Celtics, New York Yankees, etc. He will be your
friend as long as you are doing well and don't need him. But
when the chips are down, he'll leave you faster than the city

of New York abandoned the Giants for the Jets in the glory days of Broadway Joe. A Group A man will lie about the past. He will, for example, claim to always have been a supporter of whoever is on top at the moment. A Group A man will never take a chance. He is a coward. He will never tell you on Friday what he thinks will happen on Sunday, but he'll always tell you on Monday that he knew.

Knowing whether a person falls into Group A, B, or C is valuable information. If you are interviewing someone for a job, you are not permitted to ask questions relating to sex, religion, or politics. But there is no law against asking them their favorite football team. If they are Cowboy fans, don't hire them. Who needs a front-running, cowardly liar?

> Terrence Gallagher, *Instrument & Apparatus News*
> February, 1982

The fans, who would finally abandon their team during the players' strike of 1987, had much to cheer about in the decade of the 1970s. The Pittsburgh Steelers truly were the team of the seventies, with their four Super Bowl victories, but no one won as many regular season games as the Cowboys. Or played in as many Super Bowls—five. But when they faced Pittsburgh, in the '76 and '79 Super Bowls, they were beaten. A new national image of the Cowboys was forming. No longer could they be called the team that Couldn't Win the Big One. They'd done that. Now they were the team without emotion. Cold and mechanically precise, perfectly attuned to Tom Landry's system, they could be beaten by those whose blood ran hotter, by the teams that would simply knock the hell out of them. But wait a minute . . . hadn't they beaten Denver in the 1978 Super Bowl, and weren't the Broncos a bunch of fire-eaters? Or at least the defensive players were. They played every game in an emotional frenzy. It gets complicated.

"I never agreed with that lack-of-emotion theory," Dan Reeves says. "I know I always played hard, and so did a lot of other guys. It's just that we worked under a very disciplined system."

The clash of ideologies reached its culmination in the rivalry between George Allen's Redskins and the Cowboys. A lot of teams felt they had a rivalry going with Dallas—St. Louis for a while, the Giants in the eighties, now Philadelphia. The Cowboys merely shrug and say, "Come get us, whoever you are." But the Skins-Cowboys rivalry was the real thing, fueled by Allen's burning hatred of Dallas.

"He was obsessed with the Cowboys," said the Rams' general manager, Don Klosterman, when Allen had a brief, abortive run as their coach in 1978. "If a light bulb was out in the hall, he'd screw in a new one and say, 'Can't beat the Cowboys this way . . . they don't have this kind of sloppiness.' He was just nuts on the subject."

"Allen worked on that hatred," says John Wilbur, four years a Cowboy guard, three years a Redskin under Allen. "He cultivated it. It got to you. I mean he never referred to the Dallas Cowboys any other way than the 'Goddamn Cowboys.' I can't think of them as anything else now. My son, Nathan, was calling them the goddamn Cowboys when he was five."

"I can remember George Allen's first speech to us," says Billy Kilmer, the Redskins' quarterback during that era. "He said, 'Our enemy is the Dallas Cowboys. You've got to have hate in your heart for the Cowboys. If you don't, we can't beat 'em.' "

It worked. It all worked, not only on the players but the fans as well. It became a trademark of Redskin-Cowboy games—bad guys against mad guys, aristocrats against working stiffs. There was an angle for everyone. The game became a perennial ratings-buster for CBS-TV. The notion really took hold in the 1972 NFC Championship game won 26–3 by the viciously hitting Redskins; the lingering memory of the game is a constant stream of Cowboys being helped off or carried off the field.

On the morning of the game a group of early rising Redskins, Kilmer's Coffee Club he called it, sat around the table and read Landry's quote in the paper that he liked his team's chances because Roger Staubach was a better athlete than Kilmer. Kilmer, a former high school all-America basketball player, had been offered a $50,000 baseball contract by the Pittsburgh Pirates. In his first two years with the 49ers he was a highly regarded running back.

"I was incensed," he says. "That got my blood hot. I wanted to play right then, but I had to wait till four o'clock." In the game he completed 14 of 18 passes for two touchdowns, and he ran for another one.

Oh, it was a terrific rivalry, all right. Next year on Thanksgiving Day the Cowboys won by a point on a last-minute touchdown pass by Clint Longley, a rookie, a rattlesnake hunter from Wichita Falls, Texas, who hadn't played a down, going in. It prompted Blaine Nye's great line—"The triumph of the uncluttered mind"—which could be taken on many levels.

In 1974 the Cowboys missed the playoffs for the first time in nine seasons. Next year was the big housecleaning. Gone were veterans such as Bob Lilly, Walt Garrison, Cornell Green, John Niland, Craig Morton,

Bob Hayes, and Dave Manders—cut, traded, or retired. Calvin Hill jumped to the new World Football League. In came The Dirty Dozen, twelve rookies who made the squad including the first eight draft choices. It was a rebuilding year but the Cowboys won five of their last six games, made it to the playoffs as the wild card team, upset the Vikings on Staubach's Hail Mary pass to Drew Pearson at the end, crushed the Rams, and reached the Super Bowl, where they lost to Pittsburgh. Some people regard it as Landry's finest coaching year. Two seasons later they would beat the Broncos in the Super Bowl, and the year after that they would lose to Pittsburgh again.

Landry had refused to let his team get old. He had gotten rid of some of the most famous names in the game, and not a ripple was felt. The team kept winning, Gil Brandt and his computer-heads provided a steady influx of talent. A man needs replacing? Well, look to the squad. Everything was done from within. Hill's "standing on the banana peel" was a way of life on the Cowboys.

"Tom Landry knows the system, and when the end is nigh, he can be a cold-blooded son of a gun," Cliff Harris said. "The system worked on insecurity. I never knew whether or not I was gonna be back next year, even in my all-pro years. I'll tell you, that competition kept those performances peaked."

Young legs became a Cowboy trademark. They were known for their strong finishes. "Feel 'em out in the first quarter, establish yourself in the second, take command in the third, and put 'em away in the fourth," became Landry's slogan among the players. It translated to the season as well. December became their month. In their three–Super Bowl period of 1975–78, they were 11-3 in December games, 8-0 in the twin Super Bowl years of '77 and '78.

Occasionally they'd get lucky on a veteran cut by another team, such as Preston Pearson, a great third-down receiver out of the backfield, but they never traded for a vet during this era. They didn't have to. They had enough young people on their own squad. Landry developed a three-year plan—if a player wasn't starting or seriously challenging for a starting position within three years, he was gone.

The trades they did make were for blue chip draft choices, the bluest of the blue, the top players or two on the board, and they gave up reserves from their deep talent well or extra draft choices they'd accumulated. Three of those trades kept them in business for the next decade.

Tody Smith, the defensive end out of Southern Cal, was their next first-round draft choice, after Duane Thomas in '70. He was hurt, he showed some potential, and then two years later he became a key man in the trade for the draft rights to Ed (Too Tall) Jones, the top collegiate prospect in the country. The Cowboys got their money's worth out of Tody.

In 1972, the year after Tody had been drafted number one, Dallas chose Billy Thomas, a big back from Boston College, relying on a formula that had paid off so many times before—size, speed, and potential. He was a "yes, but?" pick, a 6-2, 225-pound nonproducer who could run a 4.6, a guy, in the words of Pittsburgh's chief scout, Art Rooney, Jr., who "looked good in his underwear."

The Dallas press book capsuled it accurately: "His statistics were not overwhelming, but the Cowboys felt his potential was worth a No. 1 pick . . ." Years later this philosophy would burn them badly. Thomas was cut after one year.

"The year after he was cut, I saw him up in Boston," Hill says. "He said, 'What happened to me?'

"I said, 'You did everything wrong. You held out, you got hurt, you married a white girl, and then you had the team host the wedding at the Cowboy Club. You're lucky you lived through the year.'

"Of course, he wasn't a very good player. And of course, I wasn't exactly unbiased. The first day I met him he said, 'Oh, yeah, you're the guy whose job I'm gonna take.' "

The 1973 draft was right on the money—first round—tight end Billy Joe DuPree. Pro Bowl. Second round—wideout Golden Richards. Became a starter. Third round—defensive end Harvey Banks Martin. Pro Bowl and co-MVP of the 1978 Super Bowl. Then, in 1974 began the Rape of the Innocents.

What happened should have become a textbook lesson for weak teams—if there is a super blue chip prospect out there in the draft, and you have a shot at getting him, do not, repeat, do not, trade away the pick. Not for extra choices—"numbers," they like to call them— not for serviceable starters, not even for an old pro quarterback who could fill an immediate need. Hold on to that blue chipper. Future Hall of Famers are not that easy to come by.

It's a lesson that should have been learned, but hasn't. Teams still make the same mistake. "We have so many problems, what difference can one guy make?" they say. Plenty, if you're sure he's the right guy. He can lift the performance level of everyone around him. He can, by his dominance, make other people play better. He can make you a winner.

In May 1974 the Cowboys found a 1-13 pigeon to trade with, the

Houston Oilers, the worst team in the NFL. Dallas gave them Tody Smith and Billy Parks and received the number one draft choice, which would be the top pick on the entire board, plus a number three. The number one turned out to be defensive end Too Tall Jones, who is still going strong after thirteen seasons, two of which ended in the Pro Bowl.

On their third-round choice they took quarterback Danny White, who had set seven NCAA passing records at Arizona State. He received offers from four major league baseball teams, but ended up with Memphis of the World Football League, joining the Cowboys two years later and becoming their starting quarterback for eight years.

Smith lasted less than four years with Houston, playing fairly well, and then he was cut. Parks lasted three years, catching 64 passes for two touchdowns. Oy, what a trade!

Like a drunken sailor the Giants were the next ones to come reeling into the Cowboys' clutches. They were 1-5 in 1974 and badly in need of a quarterback. Dallas offered them thirty-one-year-old Craig Morton, who had lost the starting job to Staubach and was supposedly heading for the WFL next season. In return? Oh, we'll take your number one draft (which could have been the top pick overall, since the Giants had a serious shot at being the worst team in pro football). And you might as well throw in a second-round for '76, just to keep it honest.

The 1976 second-round pick, fullback Jim Jensen, didn't make it. The top pick in '75? Well, it turned out to be the second man selected in the NFL. That was the great Year of the Defensive Lineman—eight of them went in the first round—but the best was Randy White of Maryland, and the Cowboys got him. He's still their right tackle, eight times a Pro Bowler, and a certainty as a future Hall of Famer.

Morton? He finished the '74 season—the Giants went 1-7 under his quarterbacking—and lasted through '75 and '76, which were 5-9 and 3-11 years.

"The most miserable years of my life," he said. "I still have nightmares about them."

In 1977 he was mercifully traded to Denver for Steve Ramsey, a quarterback who never played. The Broncos reached the Super Bowl under Morton's steady hand, only to be overrun by Dallas. White became a co-MVP in the game.

You'd think people would learn. Do not give up your number one choice to the Cowboys. But along came a fresh pigeon, the Seattle Seahawks, apple-cheeked and starry-eyed, a new team on the block, an expansion baby with a 2-12 record in 1976, their first year in the league. They would have the second choice in the draft.

Now you see, son, this here's a pea and here are three shells, and the idea . . . Oh, yes, the Cowboys found another one. Give us your number one pick . . . I mean you're desperate, right? One choice can't help you that much . . . and we'll give you our number one pick and throw in three, count 'em, three, number twos that we've, uh, collected here and there. Waddya say?

Done. Seattle picked a tackle, Steve August, in the first round; a guard, Tom Lynch, and a linebacker, Terry Beeson, on the second; and traded the other second-round choice back to Dallas for Duke Fergerson, a wide receiver who never played. The other three guys were decent, serviceable pros, nothing more.

Dallas's pick, which turned out to be the second man selected in the draft, was Tony Dorsett, the leading collegiate ground gainer of all time. He is now number four on the all-time professional list, and still counting.

The rest of the football world shook their heads. The Cowboys were sharks who patrolled the inland water, looking for victims. But skill? You don't need a computer to find the best or second-best player in the whole draft.

But here's the thing—Dallas put itself in position to make those trades. They had built up the extra choices by having enough depth on their squad to trade it away. And that first-round pick they dealt Seattle wasn't their own. It was a better one, ten spots higher. They'd gotten it from San Diego for Clint Longley. Danny White was on the squad now. What did they need Longley for? The whole thing feeds on itself.

During the late 1970s Dallas was a smug and superior organization—and arrogant. That was the word people used to describe the Cowboys—arrogant.

"When you're winning, you're very confident in what you do," Schramm said. "Maybe that's arrogance."

It crystallized one day at the end of the 1978 season, when Schramm and the boys were trying to find a title for the Cowboys' highlight film. In a few years they would capture the sweep and grandeur of the operation with their movie entitled *Like a Mighty River,* but now they needed something even bigger, more grand. So in a bit of promotional extravagance they came up with the name "America's Team." The response was spectacular. Everyone howled.

"If they're America's team, what are we, Guatemalans?" Raider safetyman Mike Davis said.

The nickname caught on with everyone. It became a headline writer's delight, particularly when things went wrong.

"South America's Team" was one headline when some Cowboy players were busted for cocaine. "America's Scream"—after a loss in which Schramm complained about the officiating. Everyone took a shot at the pretentious nickname, but to Schramm's promotional mind, it had accomplished the purpose. It got people talking about them.

"I'll tell you exactly why we chose that title," he says. "At the time we were selling over twenty-five percent of NFL-licensed products. At every road game there were as many banners and pins sold as the home team's. We held every record for TV ratings. Our own in-house newspaper, the *Dallas Cowboys Official Weekly*, printed in two languages, had a circulation of 100,000-plus, 75,000 outside the Dallas–Fort Worth area, fifty percent outside Texas. It was being sold in every state.

"The phenomenon of our cheerleaders was at its highest. The movie they made, *Dallas Cheerleaders*, was the highest rated made-for-TV film of the year. We made them into entertainers. They traveled around the world . . . right now they're going on a twenty-two-day tour of the Indian Ocean and the Persian Gulf. That's why we called ourselves America's Team."

"In Dallas," said former Cowboy wide receiver Pete Gent, "you saw the future. Corporate America. That's bad enough in the real world, but in sports, well, it's downright depressing."

Beano Cook, working for CBS publicity, met Schramm at a party.

"You're one of the two most efficient organizations of the twentieth century," he said.

"What's the other?" asked Schramm.

"The Third Reich," Beano said.

"Talk to anyone around the league," Pittsburgh middle linebacker Jack Lambert said, "and they'll tell you, 'We don't care who wins, as long as it isn't the Dallas Cowboys.' "

"They want people to hate them," Pittsburgh defensive coach George Perles said. "That's their thing. They love it."

Like a mighty river, America's Team rolled on. Three years later they entitled their highlight film *Star Spangled Cowboys*. Their fans came out to Texas Stadium in Irving—they'd had to buy a $10,000 bond to get a shot at season tickets—and enjoyed the show.

"Texas Stadium," said former Raider defensive tackle Tom Keating, "is the only place that's got a dome with a hole in it that's only over the field. When it rains, the players get wet, everyone else stays dry. The first time I ever played there, it was raining. I turned to Ben Davidson and said, 'Do you know what's happening here?'

"He said, 'Yeah, it's raining.'

" 'But only on the players, Ben. Only on us.' "

Around the league they were known as the team that was wired to the commissioner's office, because of the Schramm-Rozelle connection going back to their L.A. Rams days.

"If there's one team that's going to get a break," Raiders' owner Al Davis said, "it's Dallas. On the officials' calls, on the scheduling, on the Competition Committee, on everything else relating to league matters."

The NFL had a rule against diversified ownership. One person had to own fifty percent or more of a club. Then the eleven-man H. R. Bum Bright group bought the Cowboys and not a word was said.

Detroit had the traditional Thanksgiving Day game. Then in 1970, when the AFL and NFL were realigned, a second one was added. Dallas got it for five years, skipped a couple, then got it permanently in 1978.

"Do you know what a tremendous advantage that is, having ten days off going into December?" Davis said. "How many times have the Cowboys lost the game after Thanksgiving?"

The answer is that they won thirteen straight.

At home or on the road, the Cowboys were a phenomenon, a happening.

"The thing I hate about doing one of their games," CBS announcer John Madden said, "is that they lead the league in lobbies. Normally there'll be thirty or forty fans milling around the hotel lobby where a team's staying. When the Cowboys are in town it'll be more like five hundred. You can't even get in the damn dining room. You have to call room service."

It rubbed off on the players. On the few occasions when they did lose, it was always, "Well, we didn't play our game" or "We were flat." You heard the same thing from the coaches.

"Nobody ever beats the Cowboys," former 49er quarterback John Brodie said. "They always do something to beat themselves. They never give anyone credit. Whenever someone beats them, all you hear is, 'Well, those weren't the real Dallas Cowboys they beat.' How many guys do they carry on their roster, anyway?

"They invalidate the thing they promote the most and have the least of, and that's class."

"They've changed," said Mike Manuche, whose New York restaurant was a Giants' hangout. "In the old days they had stand-up guys, Lilly, Renfro, Garrison. Now it seems like they're all a bunch of whiners."

Not only players and coaches but Cowboy fans came under fire.

Rob Bayley, a former Cowboy season ticket holder, moved to Orlando. Someone asked him what it was like watching a game at Texas Stadium.

"The fans were the biggest whiners of all," he said. "The folks in my section used to complain if the Cowboys didn't score at least two touchdowns at our end of the field every game. They'd all whine, go home, and then let someone else use their tickets at the next game."

"Dallas fans never feel the Cowboys have lost a game," said CBS's Tommy Brookshier.

"It's always that the referees screwed 'em or the Good Lord looked the other way or something. It's the toughest place to broadcast a game. Their fans don't know football, they just know something's wrong if the Cowboys aren't winning by two TDs.

" 'Like a mighty river' . . . boy that's Texas, all right. And John Wayne's the quarterback. You do a game in a place like Detroit, well, the people there have seen a little football. You can't bullshit 'em. But try to tell the truth in Dallas and they'll poison you."

A curious phenomenon rose around the country. Cowboy hatred actually boosted their ratings. In an October 11, 1981, game, in which the Cowboys got crushed by the 49ers, 45–14—a game seen throughout most of the USA—nobody switched off. The ratings steadily increased after the half. At CBS the schedule makers had a slogan—"When in doubt, give 'em Dallas."

"My favorite moment in sports," says Lump Jones, a Pittsburgh fireman and dedicated Steelers' fan, "is when Rocky Bleier leaped in the air to catch the pass that beat the Cowboys in the '79 Super Bowl.

"I loved it because it was done by an overachiever, and that's one thing the Dallas system doesn't have, overachievers. People there either achieve what's expected of them or they fail."

It was shown dramatically in the NFC Championship game after the 1981 season. The 49ers drove 89 yards in the game's dying moments to beat them, 28–27. They gained significant yardage at the beginning of the drive, sending an old warhorse named Lenvil Elliott on sweeps against a unit that strangely refused to get out of its six-defensive-back alignment.

"They were beating us with guys who we didn't even know who they were" was safetyman Charlie Waters's classic line.

"You're always a day late on the Dallas Show," cornerback Everson Walls said when someone asked him why the Cowboys didn't get out of their nickel defense.

In the abbreviated strike season of 1982, the Cowboys beat Green Bay in the second round of what was known then as the Super Bowl Tournament, and then lost to Washington in the NFC Championship. No one knew it at the time, but the Green Bay game was historic in a way. It would be the last postseason game the Cowboys would win. They would lose in the first playoff game twice more, and then bow out of the postseason action entirely.

People looked for easy answers. They're not emotional enough—that's it, they need to pump the emotion back in—was an easy fix. Against the Rams in the wild card playoff of 1983, they came out for the introductions in a full sprint, fists thrust high. They pounded each other's shoulders. In the TV booth Pat Summerall and Madden were remarking how unusual this was, how unlike the Cowboys.

"They really want it today," Summerall said.

Then the Rams took the opening kickoff and drove 85 yards for a touchdown. And stopped the Cowboys on five straight possessions. And won, 24–17.

"Emotion is something that's got to be genuine," Dorsett said. "It's got to be real. You can't force it or turn it on or off. By game time it was too late. We'd already become the team we were going to be.

"We've never been a rah-rah type of team. It comes from the coaches, from the top down. You see that your coach doesn't get excited, you don't either. I don't know if people are afraid that it might look funny, or something, but I think it hurts us."

The Rams beat the Cowboys 20–0 in the 1985 divisional playoff, then darkness set in. They had their first losing season in twenty-two years in 1986, and for the first time in their history they failed to put a player in the Pro Bowl.

They followed it with another, this time 7-8. America's Team had become America's Cream Puff. What happened?

Going into the 1987 season I tried to piece it together. One thing jumped out at me, something I called my Tired Legs theory, relating to consistent collapses at the end of the season. That part of the year always belonged to Dallas, but no longer. They had lost their final regular season game for six straight years. I made up a four-year chart, a month-by-month record from 1983, when Dallas first showed itself incapable of winning a postseason game, through 1986. The results were dramatic—and consistent. This is my four-year Tired Legs chart, from 1983 to '86:

	September	October	November	December	January
1983	4–0	4–1	3–1	1–3	
1984	4–1	2–2	2–2	1–2	
1985	3–1	3–1	3–2	1–2	0–1
1986	3–1	3–1	1–4	0–3	
TOTAL	14–3	12–5	9–9	3–10	0–1
(percentage)	(.823)	(.706)	(.500)	(.231)	(.000)

Tired legs at the end of the season can mean two things. The players have been worked too hard in practice, going as far back as training camp, and the cumulative effect has been to sap the strength from their legs. Or the team has simply gotten old. Old legs mean tired legs. I think the Cowboys were guilty of both.

"We came out of camp tired," Brian Baldinger, a guard, said. "In practice we'd play three games a week. When Randy White was in his prime, Wednesday and Thursday were a nightmare. You'd just pray to get through them. He'd fire up the rest of the defensive linemen, and we'd be coming out of it with broken fingers and everything."

Walls says that Cowboy players went to Landry four times during the 1987 season to get him to cut down on the length of practice and meeting time.

"We accepted the rough camp," he says, "but we suggested that once we got into the season he lighten up on practice—to save our legs. Practice was cut thirty minutes, meetings twenty minutes. Sometimes on Friday they'd cut out the entire afternoon meeting. The uniform for practice, instead of full pads, became shorts and pads on top. Even so, practices were longer for the offense because the coaches, Paul Hackett and Jim Erkenbeck, wanted to run their stuff.

"The defense got less work than ever before because of all the offense."

The Cowboys became an old team, not old up and down the line, just in selected places. Danny White, the quarterback, thirty-four years old in 1986 and out for the last half of the season. Jim Cooper, the right tackle, thirty-one and injured. Unable to finish the season. Randy White, thirty-three and in need of late-game relief, which wasn't there. Too

Tall Jones, thirty-five, and no apparent slippage. Wide receiver Tony Hill, thirty and fading. Dorsett, thirty-two and taking a continual beating. Defensive left tackle John Dutton, left linebacker Mike Hegman, thirty-five and thirty-two, respectively, and supposedly replaceable, but no one had been found to replace them. Kicker Rafael Septien, thirty-two, which is not so bad, but facing a morals charge, which means curtains for him in Cowboyland. Wideout Mike Renfro, thirty-two, tight end Doug Cosbie, thirty, center Tom Rafferty, thirty-two, all functional but hardly the guys to build the future around.

"Getting old came so fast after 1982 that they couldn't get ready for it," Drew Pearson said.

What made Landry unhappy as he surveyed this roster at the close of '86 was that in almost every area there was a significant drop-off in talent behind the aging vets. No more three-year plan, no more standing on the banana peel. The well of talent simply wasn't there. The computer had slipped its microdiscs. In plain terms, Cowboy drafts had been lousy for seven years. The sixteen-game season and artificial turf have put extra burdens on older legs. Youth, there must be youth ready to step in and provide relief.

Dallas's draft failures in the period of 1978–84 have been documented many times. The story has been a favorite off-day feature for any writer with a mind to ripping the Cowboys, and you sense a certain gleefulness with which the numbers are presented. Even the *Dallas Cowboys Official Weekly,* which is given to self-flagellation on occasion, has presented the woeful tale—sometimes even going a step further to point out the players who could have been drafted in a particular spot but weren't, a form of hindsight that's always struck me as unfair. Say it at the time, not seven or eight years later, and we'll listen.

Between 1978 and 1984 the Cowboys had twelve choices in the first and second rounds, six and six, the other two going to Baltimore for Dutton in 1980. As of training camp 1987, only one of those first-round choices was on the squad, Jim Jeffcoat, the starting right defensive end. After five years the coaches were still waiting for him to reach his potential. The second round was a little better, producing one starter, right linebacker Jeff Rohrer, and three backups. In total: Out of twelve high picks, which traditionally should form the veteran nucleus, with a smattering of Pro Bowl choices thrown in, the Cowboys had five players and only two starters, neither of them close to all-star caliber.

In 1976 the draft was moved from January to April, thus destroying the Cowboys' edge, according to Gil Brandt. With everyone getting an extra three months to scout the prospects in depth, the value of all those stringers Brandt had working around the country was minimized. The world had caught up. No more miracles. I first heard this explanation when Aaron Kyle, the number one draft in '76, flunked out.

Explanation number two is that the old habit of drafting for potential, picking "guys who look good in their underwear," as Art Rooney, Jr., said, backfired. Too many Billy Thomas types. Larry Bethea, Rod Hill, Howard Richards—much potential, minimal performance. Three flunks, all first-rounders. Bad luck hit the team on two of its top choices, Billy Cannon, Jr., and Bob Shaw. Injuries ended their careers almost immediately. That's explanation number three.

The fourth explanation was that Brandt, saddled with the extra job of signing players to contracts and keeping his eye on prospective trade material, had too much to handle. He couldn't devote enough time to scouting. Joe Bailey, the former business manager, became the contract signer in 1986. Bobby Ackles was hired to handle pro personnel. Brandt could now give all his attention to the college draft.

"You learn that even people who are considered very brilliant when it comes to drafting can have their down moments," Schramm said. "I've never heard any team in the league brag about its drafting prowess."

Oh, but they did. The Cowboys did. And other people bragged for them. Until the down moments came.

The '85 draft was better. Kevin Brooks, the top choice, would challenge the aging Dutton for his defensive left tackle spot two years later. Crawford Ker, the third-rounder, would move in as the starting right guard. And the fifth-round pick, Herschel Walker, simply made the draft. Coming out of Georgia as a senior, he would have been the top pick on the board. But he jumped to the USFL, and when the Cowboys drafted him, he was the property of the New Jersey Generals, tied up to their owner, Donald Trump, on a personal services contract. When the USFL folded in '85 and Trump turned him loose after the season, people figured the Cowboys had lucked in again, they'd stolen another one. But anyone could have drafted him.

The '86 draft produced Mike Sherrard, a gifted wideout from UCLA, in the first round. He eventually worked his way in as a starter and disappointed nobody. With Sherrard and Walker in the lineup the Cowboys finally had something they had lacked for years—speed. Now they could stretch the defense, scare people. They hadn't had that kind of speed since Bob Hayes.

New scouts were brought in for the 1987 draft, some old ones were let go. Danny Noonan, a massively built defensive tackle, was the top choice in 1987, and he immediately became a contract holdout. The second-round pick, cornerback Ron Francis, was a bit of a sleeper. The Cowboys took one look at the burly little 5-9, 200-pounder in their April mini-camp and penciled him in as a starter. The rest of the draft was interesting for its size—guard Jeff Zimmerman, 316 pounds, tackle Kevin Gogan, 310. They already had a 1986 free agent guard, Nate Newton, who weighted 315. Monsters. Just right for the new line coach, Jim Erkenbeck, and his knock-'em-off-the-ball theories that he'd perfected at New Orleans.

It was a switch for the Cowboys. They'd always gone for mobile offensive linemen, nifty on their feet, able to pull and trap and get outside for the screens and perform all those little misdirection and influence-block techniques that Dorsett was so good at reading.

"They don't come at you, they use you to take yourself out of the play," Washington defensive tackle Dave Butz once said. "It's just happened so many damn times. All your instincts, everything you've learned about playing the run, says fight the pressure. But Dallas will give you pressure, take it away, and then ride you in the direction you're going, while Dorsett bends behind you. It's frustrating and it takes a while to get used to."

But Landry was going to give the Erkenbeck system a try. Big guys knocking people off the ball, and Walker following behind with his 225 pounds—that was going to be the thrust of the running game. He was going to give Erkenbeck his chance, or so he said.

No one knew for sure. The year before, Dallas had hired a bright young assistant from Bill Walsh's San Francisco system, Paul Hackett, to breathe some life into the passing game. If Landry has had one weakness as a coach, it's been his handling of quarterbacks. He's the one who instituted that weird system of alternating Morton and Staubach on every play back in 1971, remember?

"Actually I'd done it with Jerry Rhome a few years earlier," Morton said. "It was a terrible concept. We were like robots. No thoughts, no opinions. Once I asked Landry why he did it. He said because he had a chance to explain the upcoming play to the quarterback next to him on the sideline. He said he knew in advance what a play would do, and he had them called three or four ahead of time—which was nonsense.

"I always used to argue with Landry about passing concepts. I'd say, 'Why can't a receiver stop in a zone instead of going to the next level, and then I'm trying to throw through a linebacker?' He'd say, 'It's not done.'

"I'd say, 'Why can't a receiver do a spin on a sideline pass, instead of always squaring it off?' He'd say, 'Because it isn't done that way.' "

After the 1985 season, which ended with the 20–0 defeat by the Rams in the first round of the playoffs, Schramm wrote in his column in the *Dallas Cowboys Official Weekly:* "I've had to look at our organization and see if it still functions efficiently and do things to keep pace with the opposition."

Keep pace? At one time the Cowboys were the guiding star by which all professional football achievement was measured. Let the opposition keep pace with them.

Anyway, Paul Hackett was brought in. Just how he was brought in became a controversial question. Some people say he was Schramm's man and Landry just rubber-stamped the choice—the same with the Saints' Erkenbeck a year later.

"Tom always used to call when they were considering a coach," New Orleans general manager Jim Finks says, "but this time it was Tex."

Landry says he interviewed both coaches himself and they were his decisions. So let's say Schramm suggested them.

After the 1985 season Landry admitted that the Cowboys' pass offense had flattened out, had tended to "sink back" into predictable formations. Hackett came from a San Francisco system that was anything but predictable. He was thirty-eight when the Cowboys hired him, and ambitious. He had been first lieutenant to Bill Walsh, whose 49ers were 4-0 over Dallas since 1981, averaging better than 36 points a game.

"If you can't beat 'em," Schramm said, "hire 'em."

Landry was sixty-one. His contract was up after the 1986 season. There were rumors that if Hackett was successful with the offense, he'd be in line for Landry's job.

"Look, I'm not trying to hire Tom's successor," Schramm said. "I'm looking for someone who wants a challenge, who's willing to gamble for an opportunity. As Hackett will tell you, he was promised nothing."

Hackett, a boyish-looking, bubbly type of person who had coached eleven years in West Coast colleges before entering the NFL, said, "It was pointed out to me that Tom's not going to coach forever. I figured, here's an opportunity for me, one of the all-time great opportunities. The road toward preparing myself for a head coaching job has taken another turn."

Danny White defended Hackett's predecessor, Jim Shofner.

"Shofner didn't have the control in the offense that they say will be given to Hackett," he said. "He wasn't really permitted to do what he could. Hackett has great ideas, but the question is, will he be able to do them? It remains to be seen. He'll present them to Coach Landry, and he'll either get the go-ahead or his ideas will be shoved away."

Opinion was divided. It has always been divided.

Drew Pearson, who came to Dallas as a free agent wide receiver and became the most productive pass catcher in the team's history, was on their staff as a special assistant in 1985. He quit after one game in 1986 and joined HBO as a feature reporter. He says he quit because his ideas were not appreciated.

"If I was expected to work twelve to fourteen hours a day," he says, "I needed to do more than be a yes-man. You always had the opportunity to supply your feelings, your input, but that doesn't mean they were going to go with it. The input you brought to the staff meetings had to be substantiated by so much fact and evidence that by the time you got to make your point and state your case, you were being shouted down.

"A coach can't be innovative in that system. Hackett might bring in an innovative system, but Landry does it his way. He has a way of discouraging innovation."

Dan Reeves worked on Landry's staff for ten years, two of them as a player-coach. He says Landry was always a "good listener. He made you prepare, but if you had good ideas, he'd listen. He let me adjust certain pass routes. He let Mike Ditka put in the shotgun in '75."

It seems that Landry might let people tinker with his offense, but the defense was his baby. Hands off! Beware of the dog!

Charlie Waters, the former all-pro strong safety, tells this story:

"I was hurt in 1979. I sat out the year. I had a chance to watch what was going on. Next off-season I came in to have a heart-to-heart talk with Coach Landry. I was firmly convinced we should go to the 3-4 defense. We had to get our linebackers off the trolley tracks, give them more flexibility.

"I'd prepared what I thought was a good presentation. I thought Coach Landry would welcome the idea of an older veteran coming in to offer ideas to help the team. Well, I got all wrapped up in my little speech, and then I took a look at Coach Landry.

"His eyes were cold and steely, his jaw muscles were tight. He was staring off into space, waiting for me to finish. Right then I knew I'd done the wrong thing. I'd tampered with something that was his, that was special to him. Our relationship was never the same after that."

The 1986 Cowboy defense gave up fewer yards than it did in 1985, but more points, the second-most points it had allowed since the league went to sixteen games in 1978. Pass defense was better, defense against the run was worse—close to the bottom of the league standings.

"What people don't realize," said Cliff Harris, the former all-pro free safety, "is that over a given period of time any defense that doesn't change will be overcome and annihilated."

Hackett's ideas—dictate to the defense, don't be predictable, don't let it force you to do certain things—have their roots in Sid Gillman's theories when he was coaching the San Diego Chargers in the old AFL. Al Davis, who'd been Gillman's end coach, took them with him to Oakland, and Walsh had incorporated some of those concepts into his scheme when he was a Raider assistant.

Hackett was allowed to restructure the receivers' routes, but the full weight of his ideas was never really felt. The Cowboys were 6-3 after nine games and positioned nicely in the NFC East, one game behind the leaders, but in the ninth game, a 3-point loss to the Giants in New York, Carl Banks came in clean on a blitz from the Giants' left side and tackled White, who went down heavily on his right wrist, his throwing side. The wrist was broken. He was through for the year.

Steve Pelluer finished the season at quarterback, a tall, polite young man who'd been the fifth-round draft choice in 1984. His NFL career, going into the 1986 season, consisted of eight passes thrown. But he had a certain air about him, a feeling of hidden fire beneath his "yes, sir" and "no, sir." In 1985 both White and his backup, Gary Hogeboom, had been hurt, and Pelluer came in and led the Cowboys on the drive that beat the Giants for the NFC East title. Hogeboom, constantly complaining that he should be the starter, had been traded to Indianapolis before the '86 season.

Whatever magic Pelluer had in him was buried under a mass of sacks in 1986. The offensive line was overrun. San Diego sacked Pelluer eleven times, one short of the NFL record. The Bears registered seven against Pelluer and his backup, Reggie Collier. The Broncos dusted Pelluer five times and had him running for his life most of the afternoon in Mile High Stadium.

"Dee-fense! Dee-fense!" the Bronco fans screamed, crashing their feet against the metal stands.

"What the hell do they need defense for?" Schramm muttered in the press box.

Blitzers wouldn't be picked up, adjustments wouldn't be made at halftime, schemes that worked for the defense in the first half continued to work in the second. The offensive line, coached by sixty-four-year-old Jim Myers ("a because-I-said-so coach," Duane Thomas once called him) was overmatched. At the end of the season the Cowboys had given up sixty sacks, second worst in their history. Myers retired, after twenty-five years with the Cowboys.

At the 6-3 point of the season Dallas was first in the NFL in pass offense and third in total offense. In the last seven games, in which the Cowboys were 1-6, the numbers had turned around—third worst in total offense, fifth worst in the passing game. The Cowboys had scored 30 points or more six times in their first eight games, no times in their last six.

The Cowboys point to their second-half collapse in '86 and remind you that they lost their quarterback, and that Walker and Dorsett had leg and knee injuries. But a lot more went wrong, too. The tired legs theory. The collapse of the defense—third best in the league before White's injury, fifth worst afterward. No, it was a team effort, a total failure.

In the off-season the coaching staff looked at their quarterback situation. The fans hollered for Pelluer. They had grown tired of White and his injuries. Fans always love backup quarterbacks. They had called for Hogeboom in 1984. One paper even took a poll of players and fans to see whom they wanted. Hogeboom won, on both ballots. Hogeboom was the man, until he got his starting shot and was exposed as a quarterback of marginal talent. Backup quarterback always is the safest position on a football team.

"The way to stay popular as a quarterback in the NFL," former Pittsburgh QB Cliff Stoudt once said, "is never to play."

In the early Cowboy years the fans booed Eddie LeBaron and hollered for Don Meredith. Then they booed him and demanded Morton. When Morton became the starter, they booed him and called for Roger Staubach. Toward the end of his career, when Roger was having a bad day, the fans wanted Danny White. Yes, they did; Staubach heard his share of boos in Texas Stadium. Now they were booing White and demanding Pelluer, after the Hogeboom thing didn't work.

"I think that Hogeboom-White thing was very bad for the team," Staubach says. "Tom didn't handle it well. To let that fester, or even occur in the first place, was a mistake. As far as the players' poll in the paper, I would have gone in the locker room and confronted every one of those guys.

"Those kinds of excuses . . . blaming it all on a quarterback . . .

well, I can't stand a team hiding behind excuses. That's not a team. When Craig and I battled back and forth for the starting position, I know people had opinions, but they kept them private. But some of these guys don't seem to care.

"It's a setback this team hasn't recovered from. It hurt both quarterbacks. Both became ineffective. You look back, though. Danny White's been a darn solid quarterback. He played great football for the Cowboys. He did not get a fair shake."

The interesting thing about White is that, going into the 1987 season, he was the fifth-leading passer of all time, according to the NFL's rating system. That's right, number five, ahead of Johnny Unitas and Joe Namath and Sonny Jurgensen, Sammy Baugh, Sid Luckman, Dan Fouts . . . practically the whole Hall of Fame roster. Of course the weakness in this argument is the system itself. It places a premium on pass-completion percentage. Three of the four rating categories are keyed to the percentage. It rewards the dink passers, penalizes the high-risk, down-the-field throwers, such as Terry Bradshaw and Namath. But still, you have to have done something right to climb that high in the ratings.

The biggest knock on White during his career has been that he won't take the big gamble. He's played it safe.

"The guy's got a year's supply of dried food in his basement," Pete Gent once said about White. "He's got phone numbers to call when Armageddon arrives. That's the kind of guy you want quarterbacking your team, down 17 points with time running down? Hell no, man. Too logical. He knows you can't come back."

Another knock has been his lack of leadership ability, which might be unfair because he had the misfortune to follow Staubach, who made a career of pulling out games in impossible situations.

"Do you see the players going up and rallying around White?" Cliff Harris says. "Or did you see, quote, Good performance by Danny White, unquote. Give me Billy Kilmer any day."

It was one of the questions confronting Landry and the coaches as they opened their 1987 training camp. Do they go with White, experienced but still recovering from a broken wrist? Or do they start the season with Pelluer, who was in shock at the end of the '86 season?

There was another incident that sent some minor shock waves through the Cowboys in 1986. During the Rams game on the Coast, someone had called stadium security and told them his brother was in the stands with a rifle and would attempt to kill Landry. Viewers on national TV saw Landry led off the field at the end of the third quarter. He came back a few minutes later, heavily guarded and wearing a bulletproof vest under a light-blue sleeveless sweater.

The game was going on. He had to get caught up. He looked a bit puzzled at first. Things had been progressing without him. Some of his former players who watched the game on TV remarked that for the first time they could remember Landry fully looked his sixty-two years. He seemed vulnerable.

In July 1987, Landry signed a new three-year contract. He reasserted his toughness in the days before camp. He said it would be a rough one. People would be put to the test. There was a lot of work to do. Hackett was eager to get Walker into his passing game. Erkenbeck wanted to try out his Hog Offensive Line theory. It would be a busy camp.

13

OXNARD

A man over 300 pounds, with 40 pounds of fat—to me that's not a football player.

Lee Roy Jordan

Four days into the 1987 rookie camp Tom Landry is raving about the potential of the Cowboys' attack. "This is probably the best offensive team we've ever had in rookie camp," he says. He singles out for special praise Joe Onosai, a sixth-round draft choice, a center out of Hawaii. He's 6-3, 283, a Baby Hog compared to some of the serious heavyweights, but Landry feels he's "really powerful."

One day later Onosai goes down with a neck injury in the afternoon scrimmage. Examinations reveal calcium deposits in the spinal canal, a problem that could lead to blockage. Joe Onosai's career is over.

Two days later the Cowboys travel to Oxnard, twenty miles west of Thousand Oaks, to scrimmage the L.A. Raiders' rookies. Dallas loses, three scores to two, as their final play is stopped on the one-yard line. In two scrimmages against outside teams the Cowboys are down by a combined seven scores to two. They've had trouble moving the ball.

They have not beaten anybody since the November 16, 1986, game against San Diego.

The Raiders' camp overlooks a golf course. Their dormitory is the Radisson Hotel. It isn't the kind of thing you'd expect for Al Davis's warriors of the silver and black—a cave would be more like it—but times have changed.

Some of the vets have come to camp a day early to watch the rookies in action. They stand around the sidelines, loose and relaxed in shorts and sandals. Duane Thomas gets a nod of recognition from Jim Plunkett, the thirty-nine-year-old quarterback. He is five and a half months younger than Thomas.

"How ya doing?" Thomas says.

"That's the most you've ever said to me," Plunkett says. "You don't remember me, do you?"

"I remember you," Thomas says.

For less than a week they had been teammates, when Thomas was traded to New England in 1971, Plunkett's rookie year.

"Nice guy," Thomas says.

"How would you know? You never even talked to him," says Howie Long, the all-pro defensive end. We are joined by Mitch Willis, the 6-8, 275-pound noseguard.

"See this guy," Long says, pointing to Willis. "Two years ago, when he was a rookie, we're scrimmaging in camp. Lyle Alzado's our senior citizen, the leader of our defensive line. On this one play Mitch gets handled by the center. He gets body slammed. When he gets up, Lyle's got him by the shirt.

" 'Don't you ever let that happen to you again,' Lyle says. 'You're a disgrace to my whole program.' "

We watch the rookies go at it for a while. We are near the Cowboys' offensive unit. Long and Willis can't take their eyes off Dallas's parade of jumbos, the 300-plus platoon. Afterward we're in the coffee shop and that's all they can talk about.

"Did you see those guys?" Long, who is 6-5, 270 pounds, said. "I mean, where did they come from? They should be mating with cows."

An hour later Thomas and I are on the freeway south, headed for L.A. We're talking about the Raiders, about what kind of a team they are, how loose and relaxed they seem. I told him what his old teammate, Pat Toomay, said when he was traded to the Raiders in 1977. He had said, "All the time I was playing in the NFL I knew that somewhere there must be an organization like this. I just didn't know where it was."

The evening rush hour traffic is building in both directions. The freeway is getting clogged. Thomas guides his '87 Nissan Maxima in and out of the traffic, smoothly, effortlessly. I'm thinking of some kind of an angle, about running style translating into driving style, and then I give it up. When you carry a football there are collisions.

"Traffic is moving now," I say.

"I know one thing," he says. "We're moving."

A highway patrol car pulls even, gives us a long look, and keeps going. The sight of the state trooper unlocks some memories for Thomas.

"All the highway cops around Dallas knew me," he says. "Sometimes they'd stop me just to talk football. Sometimes they'd stop me for speeding . . . you couldn't help but speed on those open Texas highways . . . and they'd wind up talking about the Cowboys.

"I got stopped outside Nacogdoches one time. The cop says, 'You know, Duane, a friend of yours just passed. You're not doing as well as him. You're doing eighty, he was doing ninety-five.'

"I said, 'He's no friend of mine.'

"He says, 'How do you think the Cowboys are gonna do?'

"I said, 'I'm not worried about the Cowboys. I'm wondering what you're gonna do.'

"Another time I got stopped on Route 77. The cop says, 'What's the hurry, Duane?'

"I said, 'See those clouds? I've got to beat 'em before the storm comes.'

"He said, 'No, Duane, they're moving the other way. But that was pretty good. Slow down, okay?'

"I'll never forget a guy who stopped me in Henderson, North Carolina. We ended up talking for two hours. He was telling me about all the changes taking place in the South, and what his life was like, all the things he did.

"He reminded me of Buford Pusser, the crusading sheriff. I still have his card. He said, 'Duane, if you ever have any trouble around here, just call. Everyone knows me.' "

We pass a car that's a tangle of arms and legs, a white foot hanging out the window, sandal flopping, rock music blaring.

"Rocky Thompson and I used to drive all over the country during the semester breaks at West Texas State," Thomas says. "Rocky would turn people on with his Bermuda-British accent.

"We were driving from Carbondale once, from Southern Illinois, where he used to go to school. We're on the freeway outside Osceola,

Arkansas. The speed limit's seventy, and we're keeping it right at that. Cars are passing us. We'd heard about Osceola, Arkansas.

"Rocky's driving a white T-bird. A cop pulls alongside. What does he see but two beautiful black faces in a nice white car. He motions us over, and when we pull over, he jumps out of the car. License and registration.

"I say, 'Excuse me, sir . . .'

" 'You follow me,' he says. 'You're under arrest for doing excessive speed.'

"The jail and the courthouse are all in one, and they're on the black side of town. We pull up. Rocky's telling me how he's going to handle all of this. I mean, he's from Bermuda and he's going to handle it. I tell him to give me all his money. I wait in the car. He told me about the scene he saw inside.

"This black sister's wearing a rag around her head, sweeping the floor. There's a black brother doing some kind of maintenance work, and she's smacking a stick of gum in her mouth and saying to him, 'I want a Coca-Cola. I want a Coca-Cola.'

"The cop comes in with Rocky, and the brother says to him, 'Hi, Captain, got you another one.'

"The cop says, 'Yeah, I got me one.'

"He takes off his patrolman's hat and puts on his gown. He's judge, jury, and everything else, all in one. He tells Rocky, 'You owe me fifty-two dollars and charges.' Rocky says, 'You mind if I go out to the car and get it?' He says, 'I don't care where you got to get it.'

"When Rocky comes to the car, I tell him, 'Rock, if you weren't gonna come out, I was gonna take the car and drive to West Texas.'

"He said, 'Ah, Duane, you weren't gonna do me like that.'

"When we were in school, he used to like to jump on the hood of the car and yell, 'The Rock is back!' Well, they almost had themselves a Rock in Osceola. It was a part of the world he wasn't exactly familiar with.

"We'd see little black kids walking along the highway with no shoes on. We'd see a lot of friendly people. We'd stop to talk to them by the side of the road. I'd say, 'Rock, now you're seeing America.' "

14

A STUDY IN
BLACK AND WHITE

DAGGOO: Who's afraid of black's afraid of me!
                    I'm quarried out of it!
SPANISH SAILOR: Aye, harpooner, thy race is the
                    undeniable dark side of mankind—
                    devilish dark at that. No offence.
DAGGOO (grimly):   None.
                    Herman Melville, *Moby Dick*

JOURNAL: I'm not all black. Both ways, I'm not all black.

Duane Thomas removes a snapshot from a scrapbook. It's a color photo of a white woman with blue eyes and sandy hair. Next to her is a child with dark, curly hair.

"What do you think of her?" he says.

"What do I think? A picture. A woman. What am I supposed to think?"

"My second cousin, Leilani," he says, smiling, "and her little boy. Does she look black to you?"

"Lemme see that again," I say, taking the picture for further study.

"I enjoy watching people's reactions to that picture," he says. "Cool at first, then, 'Hey, lemme see it again.'

"My father's side is the white side. I've got cousins who are white. My grandfather was very light-colored, and his uncle was white. Ask my cousin Wenefrett about it. She knows the genealogy."

"Our great-grandfather, John, was a white man," says Dr. Wenefrett Conner, Thomas's first cousin on his father's side. "He was a farmer and a fisherman. He came from across the Red River, from Louisiana. He was French-Irish. Our grandfather had light, straight hair.

"My hair was blond when I was a child. Then it turned red. I used to get teased about it, but it didn't bother me. They used to call me Red. We have cousins who were self-conscious about the whole thing, but Duane and I didn't pay it any mind."

"There's a whole white cluster in one part of the family," Duane Thomas says, "a recessive gene that kept popping up. They accept me because I'm Duane Thomas who used to play for the Dallas Cowboys, but they regard my side of the family as too black . . . too much dark pigmentation. My grandparents regarded such feeling as bullshit. But it's there.

"My mother used to tell us about segregation and prejudice when we were kids, about whites against blacks, even light blacks against dark blacks. It didn't make any sense to me, but it's something that goes on every day, the kind of thing that puts people in compartments and tells them, 'This is as far as you can go.' I used to get mad at these kind of people for being such imbeciles."

A few months later I met Dr. Harry Edwards, the Berkeley sociologist who is so active in black movements. I asked him if he saw any sociological significance in the story of Duane Thomas's genealogy. He laughed.

"So what?" he said. "I don't even know what my parents were. Every black man in this country has some white in him, somewhere down the line."

I mentioned that at one time Thomas was thought to have been involved with the Black Muslims.

"A jailhouse Muslim," he said. "A guy on the fringes."

The Cowboys suspected the worst back in those days of 1971 and 1972. There was that mysterious figure in robes. ("My spiritual adviser at the time," Thomas says. "Do you know that guy in robes is a millionaire now?") There was the rumor about the plot to kidnap Schramm. They wondered just what was Thomas's involvement.

"Just because you want to find out about something doesn't mean you want to practice it," Thomas says. "I was into awareness. If you read a menu, it doesn't mean you have to eat what's on it. The Muslims and the Panthers were too militant for me, but at the time I wanted to hear what they had to say."

"Duane always was curious about me; he was interested in talking to me because I'd changed my name," says Ahmad Rashad, who started in the NFL as Bobby Moore.

"I told him the Black Muslims were a whole different story than what I was into. I was into the Moslem faith. Something like the Black Muslims didn't sound right to me. It's like a group calling itself the Black Buddhists."

It was a time when Thomas needed a support system. He had religion, he had football, but nothing had prepared him for coping with the world off the field. He had grown up in Dallas, but he had seen it through the eyes of a black kid in a black ghetto.

"My only contact with white kids was through the church," he says. "We were Presbyterians, and at the time they were more liberal in terms of integration. Plus my mother would take us to different churches to meet all kinds of people, but that wasn't a day-to-day kind of thing."

In Los Angeles he had been around white people, but then he went back to Dallas and all-black Lincoln High, and at West Texas State he was an athlete, and they lived in their own world. When he reached the Cowboys, he was naive. You're a football player. What difference does it make what color you are? He lived with a white teammate in a racially mixed neighborhood. But he was soon to learn about the complexities of the black-white world in Dallas, first through the microcosm of the Cowboys, then on a broader scale.

"When I got to Dallas in 1967," Rayfield Wright says, "I asked the team to help find me an apartment. I was a dumb rookie from Griffin, Georgia. What did I know? I wound up in an apartment halfway between Dallas and Fort Worth. It had been built by the Dallas Housing Authority. The apartment house was all black. Later I found out that Mel Renfro had tried to move into white North Dallas and was turned down. It had been a big story at the time.

"After practice white players went their way, black players went their way. Any money to be made off the field was in the form of speaking engagements. There were no endorsements, or very few. Maybe one or two players got them, certainly not black players. When we'd get a speaking engagement, usually it was for goodwill, a church group or youth group, something like that. Occasionally there was minimal pay involved, but it's like there was a hidden agenda, a different pay scale for the white players for their speaking engagements.

"Rooming with a white player in training camp was unheard of. When the forty-man roster was set, they assigned rooms for the road trips. There were thirteen blacks on the team, twenty-seven whites. Everyone had a roommate except me and one white guy. The club paid for an extra room rather than room us together. We showered together, ate together, played together, but we couldn't live together."

Calvin Hill had come to Dallas with a liberal background. He'd gone to high school in New York's fashionable Riverdale, then spent four years at Yale. His first exposure to Dallas was a slight culture shock.

"I roomed with a white first-year medical student," he says. "He had gone down at the beginning of the summer and gotten an apartment for us. When I went over to put my name on the lease, they canceled it, ostensibly because they didn't rent to Cowboys. At least that's what they said. Too boisterous, I guess.

"I was a divinity student at the time."

"The club didn't want the black players in integrated neighborhoods," Duane Thomas's brother Franklin says. "Your life is football and nothing else."

Duane Thomas says he first started sensing problems when his roommate, Steve Kiner, would tell him what was going on in the locker room.

"He said some of the southern guys used to get on him for living with me," he says. "They'd say, 'What do you want to room with a nigger for?' Steve would say, 'Well, at least I know where I am.'

"We were on the bus in Chicago once, on our way to the game, and we passed through a black ghetto—poverty, raggedy-looking kids on the street. We were seeing what the city really looked like. There was this group of guys on the bus who were laughing at the poor people and the way they looked. I've thought back on that many times.

"There was the liberal faction on the team, the redneck faction, and the guys who just didn't want to make any trouble, black guys mostly. The whole thing surprised me. I thought that when I got into pro football the players wouldn't be conscious of color, as far as accepting someone.

"Some things were done in subtle ways. When I first got to Dallas, I'd wear a suit when I'd come to practice. My feeling was that I was a professional and that's what I was trying to project. Tom Landry told me I was overdressing. Then I got more casual, more mod."

Thomas perceived Jordan as the leader of the redneck faction on the Cowboys, and it puzzled him, because he respected him so much on the field as a true battlefield commander.

"I thought the reason he was the way he was stemmed from his Alabama background, where he came from and his lack of real knowledge of black people," Thomas said. "But he was a powerful force on the team. Bob Hayes used to tell me to watch out for him."

"In the early years a lot of people thought of me as being racially bigoted, coming from Alabama," Jordan says, "but I grew up living with blacks. I ate in their houses, worked with them. I evaluated every individual as an individual. I didn't discriminate, black or white; if a teammate didn't give it one hundred percent, next week I'd be out there trying to take his head off.

"I feel that I had a great relationship with Duane Thomas. His locker was right across from mine. He had his priorities right. Football was number one. So it didn't matter whether he talked to me or not. He was a winner as a player. I respect him so much, to this day. In our Super Bowl year he played unbelievable football.

"Maybe some of his problems started with his relationship with Kiner. There were rumors that when Steve went to the islands on vacation he was involved with a drug dealer."

Dan Reeves, who has coached the Denver Broncos to two Super Bowls, was seen by Thomas as not only an establishment figure—but a fringe bigot. "A recovering redneck," is the way Hill describes him.

"Jesus Christ, that's so ridiculous," Reeves says. "Believe me, it's the first time I've ever heard that. All the times I ever talked to Duane . . . well, it was never said that he had a problem with me, personally.

"It just goes to show that you don't have to have a situation where everybody loves each other to have a championship team. I'll tell you, people didn't care less about Duane because they felt he didn't care about them."

It's a touchy and sensitive area, the relationship between blacks and whites who are thrown into daily contact. Tensions exist in almost every area, but football's supposed to be different. The team aspect is stressed, the family. In reality nothing is different. There is always a substrata of uneasiness.

A nucleus of "good mixers" can help relieve it, particularly if they're high-performance people. When Joe Namath joined the Jets, he had a very keen awareness of the type of society he was entering. He knew that in the early 1960s the Jets were primarily a southern team, and the blacks kept to themselves. He would walk into the dining room in training camp, survey the tables, and join an all-black group. Pretty soon another white player would come over, then another. Before long it was an integrated table. It happened too many times to be accidental.

Thomas describes Craig Morton as a good mixer.

"Anytime he threw a party, he would invite everybody, blacks and whites alike," he says. "The blacks would show up and some of the whites, the good guys, not the rednecks."

Roger Staubach, who was and is one of Dallas's most socially prominent citizens to this day, will not join a nonintegrated country club. Thomas considered him one of the more liberal members of the team, but he says, "I was disappointed in him because he knew what was going on but really didn't try to make things better."

In the sensitive world of the black athlete, a look can have significance, a certain form of address. Why should he be different from any other black person?

"The psychology of the black player is different," Hill says. "He's especially aware of how you treat him publicly. A white player has to be very careful of challenging him with an audience around.

"A black man puts his manhood on the table. Maybe it goes back to slavery days, when he was faced with the inability to protect his family. But through the years he has gone to great extremes to prove that he is a man."

"During the week before the Super Bowl in New Orleans," Tody Smith says, "Margene Adkins and I were walking down Bourbon Street with some other Cowboy players. Margene had his little jumpsuit on. We passed a white girl, all dressed up. Margene said, 'Damn, look at that chick.'

"Walt Garrison threw a drink at Margene. I heard Margene yell 'Tody!' They got into a fight. Walt ripped Margene's jacket with a hook knife. A couple of other players came by and broke it up, defused it. Then they said they'd let Margene screw a white hooker, and that would square it.

"Roger Staubach put a stop to it. He took Margene away. He said, 'You'll be okay.'

"Next day at breakfast Margene asked Walt Garrison for money for the suit. I guess Walt must have said no, because Margene hid in the shower room and coldcocked him. That was three days before the Super Bowl game. It was almost one side against the other side."

"There was a level of talent on that team," Thomas says, "that produced success, even though conditions were socially primitive. But once the talent slips on a team like that, there's no backlog of love and emotion and closeness to fall back on. Certain teams were more advanced. The Washington Redskins, who I played for in '73 and '74, would mix more. Guys were more emotional. You could express your feelings. But on the Cowboys? Well, you wanted to be a team, but there were too many barriers in the way, economic, social, even political. You had to be your own man if you hoped to exist there."

O. J. Simpson was one of the brightest stars coming into the game in the Thomas era. He says he knew what Duane went through. He experienced some of it himself, but he came out whole.

"The Cowboys in those days were going through a *North Dallas Forty* syndrome," he says. "The good ol' boys with their 'peench between cheek and gum.' He was a child of the seventies. What people overlook is that you had black players coming in who had never played with white guys in college. When I went to Buffalo, there were a lot of southern players on the team, good ol' boys, black and white. I couldn't communicate with these guys. I'd find a certain level and that was it. Dallas could not have been an easy situation for Duane. It would have been tough for any liberal-thinking inner-city black kid to break in with that group.

"Black guys in those days were either considered militants, like Jim Brown, or Uncle Toms. There were things going on on the Bills that I didn't like, but the black guys just went along with them.

"I had an argument with Harry Jacobs, our middle linebacker. He'd drive to Fredonia for a speaking engagement, and he wanted me to come along—for no pay. I said, 'Hey, Harry, I don't have an insurance company like you do.' I'd majored in business in college.

"He and Bob Tatarek would go after me on the field, every day. It became a tough time for me. Yes, I could sympathize with Duane. I don't think anybody knows what he went through."

In the off-season Thomas used to spend time with Rashad and O.J. and his teammate, Les Shy, and the Smith brothers, Bubba and Tody, on the West Coast.

"At that time black players around the league seemed to have a very sincere camaraderie that black players don't have today," he says. "The basis of it was respect you had for the man on the field; it didn't matter what team you were on. You gained their respect by performance.

There was motivating power in those relationships, the idea of pulling one another along, the hand reaching back to pull younger players up.

"I don't think the owners in the league particularly liked that. Too much exchange of information on salaries."

"Let's be realistic," Franklin Thomas says. "Duane didn't get any support from his black teammates because implicit in belonging to the Cowboy organization was the understanding that if they did anything to support another black player, they wouldn't be there anymore. The enemy was not only outside but within. Duane was in a position where he couldn't confide in those defined as his teammates."

What about the city? What about black Dallas? Individual blacks had risen to positions of prominence, even as far back as 1971. Was there any possible support here?

"Risen to prominence, but only as high as white Dallas would let us rise," says a member of the black business community who's in marketing and promotions. He said he would allow himself to be quoted only if his name were not used. "I've got to live in this town," he said.

"You've got to understand Dallas," he says. "The tentacles are everywhere, and the Cowboys are at the nerve center of everything. Their power in this town is unbelievable.

"If you're a black businessman and you do something to annoy the people in power here . . . well, they'll be very nice to you, very polite, you'll still sit with them at the table. They'll just shut you down to the point where you can't do business. They'll make a phone call. You make a deposit in the bank and the bank will phone them and let them know how much you've got.

"I'm well respected here. Boy Scouts, Special Olympics, I'm on some civic boards. All that can change overnight. You'll find yourself cut off from everything and you won't know why.

"People like Duane, like Everson Walls, who staged his little protest this fall . . . well, I admire them, but I try to explain to them that there's a way to do things in Dallas, and there's a way not to. I tell them, 'Don't forget, you're dealing with impulsive people.' "

The message from Mr. Anonymous: I like you, but I'm protecting my own skin.

"Do you know," Wright says, "that at one time Dallas was on the verge of one of the major race riots of any city in the USA? It still might be. The reason why it didn't happen, and doesn't, is that the black people look to leaders in the community, and the leaders are playing politics."

The Thomas Family in happier times, when they lived in East Dallas and John Franklin Thomas owned a funeral home and Lauretta Jones Thomas had ambitions to teach. The children, Johnetta, baby Duane and Franklin, nicknamed Sonny.

Duane, age 11, during his L.A. period. "I was what they called a Sugar Dude."

Johnetta, Sonny and Duane Thomas again, circa 1951.

The Buffalos of West Texas State: Head coach Joe Kerbel, back row second from left, and his staff. Robert "Rabbit" Thomas, (inset) Duane's ninth-grade coach at Lincoln High.

Duane in his senior year at West Texas State. His actual playing weight was closer to 230.

Super Bowl Score: Thomas takes the handoff from Roger Staubach (above) and goes in for a TD against Miami in the 1972 Super Bowl. The Dolphin on the ground is Nick Buoniconti, who misjudged the angle, leading to Tommy Brookshier's famous postgame question about Thomas' speed.

The Most Famous Interview: CBS-TV's Tommy Brookshier, with Mike, Duane
and Jim Brown in the Cowboys' locker room after the 1972 Super Bowl.
(John Mazziotta)

San Diego, 1972: Duane takes a stroll while his teammates line up for the National Anthem. He was in the uniform for the Chargers in this game against the Cowboys, but didn't play. It was the only time he dressed for a game all season.

(UP1/Bettmann Newsphotos)

The Lonely Charger: Thomas by himself on the San Diego bench.
(James W. Mildice)

Old-Timers Game in Dallas: Duane, 40 years old and 20 pounds below his pro playing weight.

New Wife, New Life: Duane and his new wife, Shatemar Benson Thomas, in 1987.

"The odd thing," Thomas says, "is that in Dallas the white people know more about what's going on than the black people, and the older black people know more than the young ones."

So in his time of trouble Thomas turned toward the Muslim movement. He'd heard of it but he had to find out for himself. He wasn't by nature a militant for black causes. Any militancy in the family was focused on his brother Franklin, who flatly states: "My position with white folks is that you're guilty until proven otherwise. You come together on one common ground, and that is, let's suppress and misuse one segment of our community. Which is based on what? Only on stupidity."

Duane Thomas was disillusioned with the system, and in an era of rising black consciousness it was inevitable that he'd be drawn to the Black Muslims.

"They tried to recruit me at first," he says. "Everyone was trying to put my program together for me. They considered me a Muslim brother because of my thinking. It would be a tremendous asset to them, to their economic base.

"I'd go to Muslim meetings and listen to their philosophy. I started reading books about black history—about people like Toussaint L'Ouverture and Nat Turner and Booker T. Washington. I wanted to see for myself what the Muslims were all about; I wanted to give them a fair assessment.

"I was learning, and I'm still learning. Why is it all right for CBS to invite Minister Farrakhan on their show and wrong for me to try to learn things my own way. I don't have a system as sophisticated as CBS does, so I have to find out myself.

"I found out that I could relate a lot to their work philosophy because it was the way I was brought up myself. Elijah Muhammad's philosophy was to isolate black people in order to deprogram them out of a slave mentality. . . . I related that to Vince Lombardi isolating his team, not telling anyone where he was practicing, not allowing any distractions and keeping them fully saturated with their subject. But just because I listened to someone's theory didn't mean I practiced it. I was into awareness.

"Hating whites? I wasn't into that. They said one thing, but their subjective consciousness didn't register hate. Keep saying 'hate,' though, and you'll feel it. All this time I was just collecting information . . . I was an outsider."

Larry Jefferson, Thomas's boyhood neighbor who became a minister, had seen Duane's connection with the Muslims as "ill advised."

"People saw me talking to a Muslim, so everybody assumed I was one of them," Thomas says. "Larry's a Baptist minister. He was afraid his paycheck would be cut.

"Tex saw me with someone in robes. Orthodox Jews wear a form of robe. So do religious men in India. I don't know why someone wears something, but what does it matter? If I put a robe on, are you saying I'm a Muslim? If I put on a surgical gown, does that make me a doctor? It's an illusion.

"If it was up to me, I'd have been happiest living the life of my grandfather in peace and quiet, where everyone is valued by his production and racism doesn't ever enter the situation. I can't understand why people can't let each other coexist, why religions can't. My mother switched from the Baptist church to Presbyterian. Does that mean she didn't believe in God?

"When I realized that Dallas wouldn't pay me, that they really didn't give a damn about me, I had to find out what other areas were open. It was a matter of survival. I wanted to know what world I was living in. I wanted to be aware . . . then I was considered a militant because I asked.

"The Cowboys were panicking because they saw me with someone in robes . . . I can't get over that. It's like saying, 'All black people steal.' "

Eventually Thomas drifted away from the Muslim movement.

"Too militant," he says. "Yes, I'd feel the pain of things, but I prided myself on being able to handle it and overcome it without a militant group behind me.

"My level of consciousness did change, though. It became more on a national level. I got in touch with Ali and talked to him. We met in New Orleans in 1975, when the Pope turned school out. I met Marian Gage during a Martin Luther King commemoration in Atlanta. I met with some black heavyweights in the entertainment and political world—Harry Belafonte, Maynard Jackson, Julian Bond. I used this for my own strength.

"For about three years I was active politically. I worked for some youth organizations . . . we're talking about churches of all denominations, basically the kind of thing Martin Luther King started. I was a freelancer. I'd do things in Washington, DC, for Mayor Washington's youth program, for the prison system, for orphanages in Texas. Most of them were mixed groups, blacks, whites, Orientals, Vietnamese. You look at the philosophy of these people, you sit down with them and let them see where you're coming from, then ask, 'What programs do you have that I can participate in?'

"In 1976 I met Lincoln Ragsdale, the Flying Mortician. He said, 'Duane, let me give you a piece of advice. You can turn lemons into lemonade.'

"I started appreciating myself, what I could accomplish. It was a relief that I was starting to meet the people I needed to know. I had a sense of inner peace."

The Cowboys have progressed from the days when they refused to break the color line on their rooming lists, when Steve Kiner was considered an oddity for living with a black player. The city itself has undergone gradual changes.

"When I first came here," Tony Dorsett says, "and visited the Cowboys' office, I wondered, 'Where are all the black people at?' Things have changed in ten years. Oak Cliff is integrated. A few blacks are starting to move into North Dallas."

Dorsett arrived in 1977, a feisty kid from Aliquippa, Pennsylvania, who'd led Pittsburgh to the national title, set an NCAA career rushing record, and won the Heisman Trophy. The hat trick.

"It took me five, six years just to adjust to living here," he says. "Where I was from, in the North, if a guy called you a nigger, he'd better be twenty yards away and running. In Texas they'd call you that right to your face and dare you to do something about it. People resented my big contract. There was much jealousy, black and white.

"There's a lot of old money in Texas. Old money runs the city of Dallas. Here I am coming in, a young black man, boisterous, somewhat different from what they were accustomed to, wouldn't conform. A Duane Thomas type—evidently.

"I was going to be my own individual. I wasn't going to be molded, thank God. If they didn't need me, I might have been out of here. I had a couple of dates with Caucasian women. The players said, 'Man, are you crazy?' I found it pretty interesting, too, that every time I went somewhere management always knew about it—and with whom. They have bird dogs all over this city.

"I always felt that this team should do more things together off the field, like Washington with the Hogs, the offensive line all going out together after practice. Back in college we were always doing things together, black, white, Irish, Italian.

"My first two or three years on the Cowboys we had some things that were successful. We'd have an annual outing at the Royal Oaks Tennis Club before camp. It was real successful. We'll have team parties now and guys won't show up. Maybe it's because we're losing.

"For a few years there was a good interaction between blacks and whites. Black guys like Dennis Thurman and Drew Pearson and Robert Newhouse were good mixers. Who do we have now? Blacks go with blacks, whites go with whites.

"Do I miss those days? Sure I do. Things are different now."

15

THE LOST SEASON, PART ONE

For all his agility, the greatness of Tony Dorsett is his toughness. Sitting back there in that I-formation, eight yards deep, he's great running for the tough yards. I don't know what he weighs, 185 maybe, but he hits like 220 . . . shoulders level . . . God, he's a great player. I like to think that our guy, Eric Dickerson, is going to be like that someday.

Los Angeles Rams Coach John Robinson, 1983

"He's the only reason I'm still here, guys like him and Jim Brown," Dorsett said in the July training camp, pointing to Duane Thomas, who was talking to some rookie running backs. "They paved the way for people like me. Then again, if he hadn't been traded, he probably would have still been here when they drafted me in '77 and the Cowboys wouldn't have needed me.

"I used to love to watch him run. I remember in 1973 when we were practicing for the Big 33 game, the Pennsylvania high school all-star game, and we went over to Carlisle to watch the Redskins work out. That was Duane's first year with them. Everyone was doing one kind of stretching exercise, he was doing something else. I admired the hell out of his running style, but I thought he was crazy."

Dorsett was given to strange, moody periods during the 1987 training camp. He seemed to dwell on the depressing aspects of his career, the way Walker was brought in to replace him, the agony he went through in 1986, finishing the season on damaged knees.

"I had a partial tear of the medial collateral ligament in the left one," he said. "They left it alone. Then I hurt the right one, protecting the left. After the season they went in and cleaned out both of them. I don't know whether it was worth it . . . you get to the point where you can't do anything . . . it's just an awful feeling, standing in the background.

"I read about Jim Otto, Pettis Norman, O. J. Simpson, guys whose careers ended with knee injuries . . . about how they get up in the morning and then wait for their knees to stop hurting. I don't want to be fifty and not able to play with my kids."

There was an uneasy feeling among the older veterans when they looked at Dorsett. If he could be phased out, it could happen to any of them. Thirty-one-year-old Tony Hill, the second-leading receiver in Cowboy history, was cut before camp opened. Landry didn't feel he had gotten himself in proper condition during the off-season. "He didn't fire up" was the coach's quote. It was practically unheard of for Landry to demote a starter in the off-season, let alone cut him.

"There has never been a time in Cowboy history when rookies had a better chance to make the team," Landry said early in camp. The veterans with long memories, remembering the Dirty Dozen, the twelve rookies who made the squad after the Cowboys' 1974 season broke an eight-year playoff streak, were justifiably nervous. The title of the highlight film was *Make Way for Tomorrow.*

Jim Erkenbeck, the new line coach, was already shaking things up, trying to make room for his superheavyweights. Starting left guard Glen Titensor had lost his job to 315-pound Nate Newton, nicknamed The Kitchen. Titensor was playing behind Crawford Ker on the right side. The two of them graded out consistently higher than any other offensive linemen in 1986, but Erkenbeck wasn't that happy with Ker, either.

"He has no idea about leverage points, about striking ability," Erkenbeck said. "He's very stiff around the hips." His man was 316-pound rookie Jeff Zimmerman. He also liked another rookie, 310-pound Kevin Gogan, as the eventual right tackle.

The Cowboys already had failed in three attempts to trade for offensive linemen, Irv Eatman of the Chiefs and Ron Essink of Seattle, both for draft picks, and Ron Heller of Tampa Bay, for backup running back Darryl Clack and a late-round draft. They missed out on a draft-day trade for Stephen Baker, a wide receiver from Fresno State. In camp they did swing a major trade—starting right cornerback Ron Fellows to the Raiders for wideout Rod Barksdale, whose total production was 16 catches in two years, thus handing Fellows's spot to rookie Ron Francis. It was the first player-for-player trade the Cowboys had made since 1984.

The receiving group for Paul Hackett's passing game was now composed of one old pro, Mike Renfro, one marginal pro, Gordon Banks, and a bunch of first- and second-year players, led by the breathtakingly fast Mike Sherrard.

Hackett shared a dormitory room with Erkenbeck. They'd been together on the University of California staff in the early 1970s, but they couldn't be less alike. The forty-year-old Hackett believed in "multiplicity," the Bill Walsh system of keeping a million plays in the book and never repeating anything. It was working pretty well in 1986 until Danny White went down.

Erkenbeck was a fifty-five-year-old ex-marine who liked size and toughness in his linemen, blow 'em off the ball and leave the fancy stuff alone. He served in the Korean War but didn't like to talk about it.

And there was Hackett on the other side of the room, with his Wham and Madonna tapes. He was noticeably upset when the Cowboys' training camp schedule did not permit him to see Madonna either in California or Texas Stadium on Sunday, July 26.

"If it was Saturday night, we'd be off, so I'd fly back," he said. "I think she's a major talent."

Thursday, July 30—the national media descended on Tom Landry and the Cowboys. The reason? AIDS. Other teams had offered early AIDS testing to players, but the fact that America's Team did it became a one-day sensation for the media. In a bit of journalistic hysteria, the *New York Times* ran the story on page one.

Landry sat through the press conference, a rather stoic figure, while a few TV types asked such penetrating questions as: "What would happen if Herschel Walker tested positive for AIDS?" And . . . "Don't you think the Cowboys are fueling the hysteria by making this announcement? Why make it now?" (Obviously they announced it at that time because that's when they gave their physicals.)

Landry was terse and polite in his answers. He had other things on his mind. Jeff Rohrer, his best outside linebacker, was on his way out of camp. He had failed to work out his contract and was on his way back to Manhattan Beach to soak up rays and wait for the Cowboys to offer $300,000. It kept the streak alive. The Cowboys had had a major camp holdout every year since 1982, including such notables as Dorsett, Randy White, and Too Tall Jones.

In the off-season Landry announced that this would be the toughest training camp in years. Now he was making good on his promise. The day's practice time was an hour longer. Players were doing more running at the end of drills, more daily scrimmaging, and they were wearing full pads twice a day instead of shorts and helmets in the morning, as they did in '86. Grass drills were reinstated after a six-year absence.

On Wednesday, August 5, the first major disaster of the 1987 training camp struck. In a scrimmage against the San Diego Chargers, Sherrard was cutting inside on rookie cornerback Carl Brazley when his left heel caught Brazley's foot, causing Sherrard's left leg to come forward and kick the back of his lower right leg. His shin bent forward unnaturally. He fell, grabbing his lower leg with his right hand, his free hand outstretched as he called for a trainer. The lower leg was almost bent in half. Players said they could see the bone sticking out of the skin.

Hackett stared at the ground, then bent his head, his hands clasped behind his neck, elbows forward, pulling his head down. His deep threat was now history. Sherrard was through for the year, maybe forever. Landry took note and then watched the rest of the scrimmage. The writers were surprised by his detachment.

"We've got a lot of players," he said later. "This team is not made up of one player. When you get injuries, you've got to work through it."

"I'm still stunned," Hackett said. "What a difference two days makes." He had lost Canadian import Ray Alexander the day before with a broken wrist.

The next day Walker bruised a tendon in his knee in a goal-line drill, and the team announced that he would miss the first three exhibition games. He didn't figure to see much action in them anyway. By the time of the intrasquad Blue-White scrimmage on August 8, there were twenty-one players out with injuries. The banner above the entrance to the Los Robles Regional Medical Center, the hospital one mile southwest of the Cowboys' camp, said it best: Welcome Dallas Cowboys.

On the final play of the scrimmage third-year receiver Karl Powe was lost for three weeks with a bruised shoulder as he hit the ground hard, trying for a diving catch. There were now five receivers out, including Barksdale and Renfro with pulled hamstrings. Two weeks later the Cowboys would pick up Johnny Lam Jones, once a $2-million rookie for the New York Jets and a world class sprinter. He'd been a football gypsy in 1987, let go by the Jets and 49ers. He lasted two weeks with Dallas. The week before he was signed, Schramm had said, "I think he's finished, we're not interested in him."

White's recovering wrist seemed to be holding up so far, but the Cowboys showed their concern when they signed him to an "either-or" contract in the off-season, $750,000 if he started eight games, $500,000 if he started less.

On Saturday night, August 15, the Chargers overwhelmed the Cowboys, 29–0, in the first exhibition game. White's statistics were meager—3 for 8, for 18 yards, but he was untouched in his four series, and his wrist seemed okay. The thing that concerned Landry, though, was his aging defensive line.

The Chargers rushed for 165 yards and a 4.5 average, thanks mainly to a 74-yard run by free agent halfback Kevin Scott at the end. Kevin Brooks, whom Landry was counting on to unseat the thirty-six-year-old Dutton at left tackle, was out with a sore knee and had yet to mount a serious challenge. And Danny Noonan, the 282-pound first-round draft choice out of Nebraska, was still unsigned.

The Cowboys were offering $1.5 million for four years, roughly the same that the Raiders' number one, John Clay, had signed for, three spots lower down than Noonan, and $200,000 less than what the Bills' Shane Conlan got, four spots higher. But Dallas fouled up the negotiations by sending Gil Brandt to Lincoln to talk directly to Noonan, bypassing his agents, Tom Condon and Tony Agnone. For two seasons Brandt's role had removed him from contract negotiations or player trades. That job was handled by Bobby Ackles. Brandt's responsibility was the college draft.

Incensed, Agnone and Condon canceled a Kansas City meeting with Schramm. Noonan, not exactly outspoken, was critical of the Cowboys.

"I was surprised they would do that," he said. "It wasn't right to ge behind Tom's back like that."

Schramm insisted the Cowboys wouldn't go beyond their salary structure to sign Noonan, but of course that structure went out the window when Walker was signed to his $5-million package in 1986.

For some reason the Cowboys still believed there was some mystique about their organization that would permit them to do things other clubs wouldn't even consider.

The day after the 29–0 loss to San Diego, Joe Bailey, the official contract signer, said, "Noonan has less value to us now than he had twenty-eight days ago." Nobody could quite figure out what this meant.

On Saturday night, August 22, Dallas beat the 49ers, 13–3, in San Francisco. The defensive line was out of the Landry Flex eighty percent of the time, concentrating on a variety of stunts and shifts before the snap of the ball. Joe Montana was 0 for 7 passing, but Walsh traditionally keeps his offense under wraps in the exhibition season. Walls, the Cowboys' left cornerback, called the victory "probably the most important preseason game we've ever had."

He talked about the luxury of playing behind a defensive line that spread such confusion.

"When we were coming off the field in the second quarter," he said, "Mike Hegman [the left linebacker] told me, 'God, I feel great.' I said, 'Mike, we can do anything we want when we put our minds to it.'

"With those defenses we really can do whatever we want to."

The same day they signed Lam Jones the Cowboys completed the Essink trade, penciling him in as the eventual replacement for Mark Tuinei at offensive left tackle. The team that never traded now had four players on the roster acquired by trades—Dutton, Renfro, Barksdale, and Essink. But they showed they still weren't very good at it.

A week after they got him, the Essink deal fell through. He retired five days after passing his physical. There were problems with his ankle that did not show up on the exam and that he did not tell the team about. The Cowboys had given Seattle a fifth-round draft choice, which was not conditional on his making the team. All he had to do was pass the physical. Seattle general manager Mike McCormack said the Cowboys still owed them the draft choice. Schramm said no dice. Outsiders wondered how the Cowboys could deal for a player who had missed the last twenty games through injury without insisting on a "make the team" provision. The league office later ruled in Seattle's favor. The deal stood.

Next week the Cowboys lost to the Raiders, 34–10, in their first home exhibition game. Neither team gained many yards, but now the offense was becoming a concern. Through three games the Cowboys had scored 13 first-half points, when most of the regulars usually play. Against the Raiders, White showed little mobility. He threw three interceptions. Pelluer wasn't much better, completing only 2 of 11 passes. The offensive line had allowed 7 sacks.

The most interesting thing about the game, though, was the attendance—46,063, with no home TV. Ticket prices had been raised four dollars to $23 ($24.67 with tax), second highest only to Miami, which would be playing in a brand-new stadium. This was the smallest home crowd since 43,000 showed up for the Rams-Cowboys wild card playoff in '83, but that game was a sellout and televised at home. And the weather was terrible.

A year ago the Cowboys already had sold out three games. In August 1987 none were sold out. The closest thing was 9,000 left for the Redskins. A Monday night game with the Giants still had 14,200 seats left. Schramm insisted it was the product that was keeping people away, not the new price.

On the day of the Raiders game the Cowboys finally signed Noonan. They had raised their offer $124,000 in the last week of negotiations. They told the press he could have made more money by signing earlier. The reporters laughed.

The last exhibition game, against Houston in an all-Texas battle for the Governor's Cup, ended in an 18–13 Oiler victory. The Cup itself was found in a closet in Houston early in the week—after having been missing for more than ten years.

The offense was dreadful in the exhibition season. It scored 36 points and only three touchdowns. No quarterback on the squad completed fifty percent of his passes. Pelluer was the worst, at thirty-three percent, and neither he nor White was responsible for the one touchdown pass thrown. That honor went to third-stringer Paul McDonald, who survived the final cutdown and made the squad. Schramm said that it was a mistake keeping the twenty-nine-year-old McDonald and cutting rookie Kevin Sweeney, a seventh-round draft out of Fresno State, but Hackett, who had coached McDonald at Southern Cal, had the final say. Pelluer had been the biggest disappointment.

"They've screwed him up," one veteran said.

It was a glum-looking Landry who faced the press after the Oilers' loss.

"I don't think I've ever started the season on a lower note than this one," he said. "This is the first year we really haven't had the team ready to go."

There were ten new players on the 45-man roster, five of them drafted rookies. There were five new starters—Brooks for Dutton, Francis for Fellows, Newton for Titensor, Banks and Renfro for Sherrard and Hill—six, if you counted kicker Roger Ruzek for Rafael Septien. The opponent for the opening game was the Cardinals in St. Louis. They were a team the Cowboys had beaten by 24 and 31 points in 1986. This time the bookies made the game pick-'em.

16

STRIKE '87

The fans were against us, the radio and TV stations, the newspapers. After a while I stopped reading the papers. Everything was so negative, but you get used to it. The Cowboys always had a good PR department.

Everson Walls

The Cowboys split their first two games. St. Louis handed them their second opening-day loss in the past twenty-three years, scoring three touchdowns in the last quarter to win, 24–13. White had been sacked eight times. The Giants game a week later was one of those mean, nasty, defensive struggles, won by the Cowboys, 16–14. At the end Dallas pulled a defensive lineman, went into a three-man rush, a prevent defense, and given the luxury of time to throw, Phil Simms took the Giants on their longest drive of the night. It covered 69 yards, from the Giants' 2 to Dallas's 29, where Raul Allegre's 46-yard field goal attempt hooked six inches to the left. The Cowboys were 1-1, but they'd come six inches from being 0-2. The line didn't hold. White was sacked five times but he did a heroic job, throwing under extreme pressure.

The big news, though, was not on the field.

Contract talks between the players and owners had broken off over the weekend. At halftime of the Monday night game between the Patriots and the Jets, the Players Association's executive director, Gene Upshaw, announced that as of midnight the players were on strike. The picket lines formed on Tuesday, September 22.

Unlike 1982 when the owners shut down the game for fifty-seven days, 1987 would see football of a sort, played by any veterans ·who wished to cross their teammates' picket line, plus a group euphemistically termed "replacement players" by management, "scabs" by the vets. Schramm, the most widely quoted member of management's four-man Executive Committee, said they were forced to play the game because of legal reasons. He said that if the players were locked out, they could claim violation of contract and declare themselves free agents.

"Why wasn't this considered in 1982?" he was asked in an interview.

"We didn't think of it then," he said.

The Cowboys had positioned themselves well for scab ball, as the players called it. On the first day of the strike Schramm announced, "We're ready to go right now." The Cowboys were a regular client of Mike Giddings's Pro Sport, Inc., of Newport Beach, California, a private scouting and evaluating service for a limited number of customers. Bobby Ackles had dipped heavily into Giddings's list of UEs (unemployed) and OTs (out there); Gil Brandt rushed to sign them. They also had rookies who had been cut but advised to stick around for the strike. Daryle Smith, who topped Giddings's list of OT tackles, and Kelvin Edwards, his number one OT wide receiver, even became regular starters after the strike ended. Nate Newton was Giddings's top UE guard in 1986 when the Cowboys picked him up.

They were in good shape. Other teams were struggling with bartenders and truck drivers. Scab ball would be just what they liked, an overmatch.

On Tuesday, September 22, more than forty players gathered at a tennis club in Garland owned by former wide receiver Doug Donley and tight end Doug Cosbie, their player representative. In a poll run by the *Dallas Morning News* six had been noncommittal about whether they'd support the strike, Danny White among them. White showed up at the meeting and walked swiftly past the Minicams and reporters.

"I'm just here to see what they have to say," he said. He wore the pained look of a man sentenced to jail for a crime he had nothing to do with.

The meeting lasted about forty-five minutes. Cosbie asked if anyone was not going to support the strike. Randy White stood up and said he was going to keep playing. In 1984, when he had held out for more money, Dallas players wore his number, 54, taped to their helmets as a show of support.

Rohrer asked him why he was going to play. White said he didn't have to justify it.

"This is the problem with the Cowboys," Dorsett said. "We can't do anything as a team."

White and his fishing buddy, defensive tackle Don Smerek, walked quickly to White's pickup as the meeting broke up. White told a reporter he was going back to work. Most of the newspapermen were gathered around Dorsett.

Danny White, looking more comfortable now than when he went in, said he would support his teammates. Not the strike—he made that clear—it was his teammates he was supporting.

"Right now I'm going out with the team," he said. "It's not an easy decision. It's costing me $45,000 a week. At this point the team is the most important thing. At some point the family or my income may become more important. Who knows when that will be—tomorrow, six weeks or eight weeks from now?

"My teammates have supported me through the years and I can't play by myself. The main thing is to do everything we do as a team. When we start playing again there just can't be any hard feelings."

White stayed out for one week. On September 29 he told his teammates at a meeting at SMU's Ownby Stadium that he was going back because he had financial problems.

"Who doesn't?" Walls said.

Wednesday, September 23, was the first day of picketing, the day that Randy White and Smerek became the first veterans to cross the line. Dorsett wore a Scab-Busters T-shirt. Reporters asked him about White.

"He's in there, isn't he?" said Dorsett, eyes flashing, pointing to the club's Valley Ranch offices. "That shows you what he thinks about Jim Jeffcoat, John Dutton, Ed Jones, Danny White, Tony Dorsett. It shows selfishness. As a team captain he let the team down. But he's gonna make all-pro this year, the scabs' all-pro. He's Captain Scab."

On Friday, September 25, Dorsett's alarm clock rang at six A.M. There weren't many things in his life that he would get up for at that hour, but on this day he staggered into the shower, reached into the bureau drawer for gray shorts and a gray T-shirt, as if he were heading for a workout, and climbed into his Mercedes 500 SEL. He was off to the picket line.

"When the alarm rang, I thought, 'Should I or shouldn't I?' " he said. "Once my feet hit the floor I was okay, but I was still asleep, even after the shower. But as a captain I felt I should be out here on the line. I wanted to.

"One of the big reasons for our decline here is that guys really haven't stuck by each other and done things as a team. That's why I was hoping we'd strike as a complete team. After you get off the picket line guys sit down, eat, talk about the issues, maybe have a couple of beers. You really find out what people are made of. Black and white, we're all out here together now. Hopefully this will bring us all closer together—if and when we do get back to work."

Four days later Dorsett told his teammates he was being forced back to play. He and Too Tall Jones and Walls and Cosbie had received letters from management, accompanied by a legal opinion, informing them that they stood to lose their long-term annuities unless they reported. Randy White said he had been told the same thing previously. In Dorsett's case it would have amounted to just over $3 million of his total $6.4-million package.

Walls and Cosbie defied the Cowboys' threat. Walls told Dorsett to see a labor lawyer before he decided anything. Dorsett listened to his friend, but clearly his mind was made up.

He told his teammates on the picket line. A few of them kidded him about catching Jim Brown in one week of scab ball. After two weeks of the season Dorsett needed 598 yards to pass Brown for second on the all-time rushing list. He asked someone what time the Wednesday meeting was.

"How many meetings you going to tomorrow, anyway?" Hegman said.

Fullback Timmy Newsome said Dorsett really felt bad about what had happened.

"It's a very difficult choice, to say the least," he said.

Next day Tony D. parked his Mercedes outside the Valley Ranch driveway and was surprised to see he was the first picketer to arrive. Rather than walk the line alone, he sat in his car while kids and fans gathered round. He told reporters there was no great mystery about what he was going to do.

"What would you do in my situation?" he said. "I'll see you at the press conference Friday morning."

When some other players arrived, Dorsett got out of his car and signing autographs, walked toward the driveway. A very loud car radio was playing across the street. It was a local FM deejay:

"Well, isn't this interesting? Tony Dorsett, the man who called Randy White Captain Scab, may be forced to cross the picket line because of money."

Then the DJ burst out laughing.

Dorsett returned next day. Dressed in gray workout clothes he held a noon press conference. He was more subdued than normal as he tried to explain the frustration he felt.

"I knew all along something like this might happen," he said. "I knew there was a pro rata clause in my contract concerning my annuity. It was just a matter of getting it defined. If I miss a month, my annuity stops.

"I'm not here to apologize for anything I said. I guess I made myself a spokesperson for the team. I don't feel I need to talk to Randy. Randy as a person is a good guy. If he thinks the statements I made were that strong that they would ruin what little relationship we had, then that's the way it will be."

The first Sunday of scab ball, September 27, was canceled. The following week the Cowboys played the Jets in the New Jersey Meadowlands. Oddly enough newspapers had printed a point spread on the scab-ball games, same as always. Bettors who knew which teams had done a good job rounding up replacement players, and which hadn't, had a field day. It was like stealing. Never had the gamblers enjoyed such an edge.

On Tuesday morning the Jets opened up 2½-point favorites, because of home-field advantage. New York, which was to lose two of its three strike games, had done a poor job of finding players. A New Jersey gambler called his bookmaker as soon as he read the line in the paper.

"What's your number on Jets-Cowboys?" he asked.

"No number."

"It says two and a half in the paper."

"So go bet the paper."

The guy asked him if there would be any price at all.

"Call me the morning of the game," the bookie told him. "Maybe we'll put something up as an accommodation. Limit it to a nickel."

On Sunday, October 4, the Cowboys were installed as a 7-point favorite, real price, betting price. Fans called in to place their $500-limit bets—a nickel is $500 in gambler's talk—and cleaned up.

In front of 12,370 fans in Giants Stadium, and almost as many in the parking lot socializing with striking Jets and Giants players, Dallas won, 38–24. Their lineup was filled with rookies, plus Giddings's UEs and OTs. White and Smerek started on the defensive line. The running backs were a pair of rookies, Gerald White and Alvin Blount, who'd been a ninth-round draft choice. Kevin Sweeney, throwing skyscraping, banana passes in the October sunshine, was the quarterback. There were nine turnovers in the game.

Dorsett did not play. He stood for almost the entire game on the 30-yard line, his legs crossed, wearing a hood. Occasionally the New Jersey fans behind the bench would strike up a chant, "Tony, Tony," and he would turn and smile and wave. The rest of the time he watched.

"This is one of the most uncanny experiences I've ever experienced," he said afterward. "Coming in here on the scab team and seeing so few people in the stands. Mentally I just wasn't in the frame of mind I needed to be in to play football."

On Monday, Landry said he expected Dorsett to be ready to play against Philadelphia in the home opener. Dorsett said he'd never be ready.

"I'll just make a plea," he said. "If they want me to beg, I'll go out on the 50-yard line at Texas Stadium and beg them not to play me. I'll do it on national TV. Anything they want me to do. That's how serious I am about this."

He was told that he needed 597 yards to catch Jim Brown.

"I don't want to gain on him in these tainted games," he said. "No one who takes pride in his work would want to. Anyone who knows me knows the pride I've taken in playing against the best football players in the world for eleven years. They know I've played with broken bones in my back, broken ribs, a broken wrist. I'm close to reaching a milestone so don't make me do it this way."

In the days that followed, Landry said he would use Dorsett if he had to, and Tony said he'd been misrepresented—not misquoted, misrepresented. A proud athlete had been reduced to almost cartoon-figure dimensions. He carried four times against the Eagles and gained 27 yards and scored a 10-yard touchdown. The TD run was booed heavily by the hometown fans. No one could ever remember a Cowboy touchdown being booed in Dallas.

The second Cowboy to fall under the hammer of management's annuity letter was Too Tall Jones. The nickname for the 6-9 defensive end was nationally recognized, the person was not. He was in his thirteenth season, one short of the club record, playing the left side, the power side where sacks are hard to come by. He would have tied the record except that he took the 1979 season off to try to make it as a boxer. One year in that business told him it was time to go back to football. He was successful in the ring (6-0), but he said he'd never met so many sleazy people in his life.

His goal in 1987 was to make up for what he considered a rather disappointing 1986 season and eventually to leave the game with a little dignity. Thirty-three NFL defensive ends made a higher salary than he did at the start of the 1987 season, despite his longevity and the fact that he'd played in two Pro Bowls. His money was tied up in an annuity. Staying on strike could cost him most of it, so the letter said.

A proud and decent person, his agony was apparent as he talked about crossing the picket line.

"I've always been a team player," he said. "I've always tried to look at things from the majority's point of view and gone along with them. Now the team's been put on one side of the fence and I've been put on another, because of my contract.

"I've always had respect around the league. I've always had a clean name. That's something I'm proud of. I can explain this to my teammates because they know about annuities—the Cowboys were one of the first teams to use them. But players around the league don't know anything about them. And when they pick up a newspaper or listen to the news, all they'll hear is that Ed Jones crossed the picket line.

"Hey, if it was just my salary, I'd sit out as long as the next player. I'd sit all year. But this is my retirement thing, this is what I've worked for."

Schramm had imposed a Friday, October 2, nine A.M. deadline on Jones. At three minutes to nine he wheeled his jeep across the picket line and entered the training complex, just under the wire. He stopped by the pressroom and dropped off a dozen copies of a four-line statement:

"Based on circumstances regarding my contract with the Dallas Cowboys football club, I have made the decision to return to practice and will play on Sunday. I hope that all my teammates understand the reasons behind my personal decision to return to camp at this time. I have no further comments."

Kevin Brooks was the next to fall. A letter had informed him that his deferred signing bonus of $50,000 a year for ten years might be lost.

"It might amount to $250,000 in the present value," Walls said. "And he wouldn't start getting it until the 1990s. He came back to protect that? He's how old, twenty-four? And he's going to sign how many more contracts?"

Robert Lavette, a reserve halfback, returned to protect his $135,000 salary—he had no annuity—and his shaky roster spot. A reporter asked him if he felt that these picket line crossings were going to tear the team apart.

"I think team unity was lost at the first meeting," he said, "when Randy White and Tony blasted each other."

Doug Cosbie, the player rep, stood firm, annuity or no annuity. He and defensive right end Jim Jeffcoat, the alternate player rep, had worked long hours collecting union dues from the players. Texas is a right-to-work state; dues cannot automatically be deducted from paychecks. In the fall of 1987 Cosbie and Jeffcoat had come in with one hundred percent fully paid, a notable achievement in the traditionally antiunion Dallas environment.

Everson Walls joined Cosbie in bucking management's assault on his annuity, although he stood to lose as mush as Dorsett—$3 million, which broke down to $100,000 a year for thirty years, beginning in 1996. Nicknamed Cubby, he had parlayed a $32,000 free agent's salary into $350,000, after six seasons and four Pro Bowls. The son of a dump truck driver and an employee in the city's General Education Department, he had grown up two miles from the Cowboys' old practice field. He'd always been feisty in his dealings with management.

"I received a very carefully worded letter from them," he said. "My financial people and I stayed up till midnight going over the annuity. The language was very clear. I stood to lose it, plus my future signing bonus, if I failed to perform.

"What kept me out? Well, my wife was very nervous, I was very nervous, but at the same time I was solid in what I was fighting for. When the players struck in 1982, I was a second-year pro. I remember Brian Sipe standing up against Franco Harris, who was bitching about what would happen to his five-year all-pro status."

"Brian said how important it was to bite the bullet so that the younger guys could have it better than they did. He was so adamant, so pumped up. He sounded so truthful. I was twenty-two and I was impressed. If I ever thought of wavering, that put me back on track. I'd idolized Franco throughout his whole NFL career, but I remember thinking, 'How can he be so selfish?'

"Okay, so I lose an annuity that starts nine years down the road. No matter what's lost, you can still gain it back in time, as long as you're still playing football. I'm twenty-seven. I can always gain those luxuries back."

Walls had gone the same contract route Duane Thomas had, although he delayed renegotiating a year until he'd had his first Pro Bowl season. His original contract called for three years at $32,000, $37,500, and $45,000, plus a $1,500 signing bonus. After two years he told the Cowboys he wanted more money. They offered $80,000 for his third year, if they could tack on a couple more. He turned them down.

"They kept sending people to talk to me," he said.

What he ended up with was a five-year package for $1.25 million. He played three years under that contract, three Pro Bowl years, and signed his current agreement.

"I've been through so much with the Cowboys," he said, "that I think they respect me now. But it's a tough system to buck. No one person's going to come in and change it. A lot of people tried, like Duane Thomas. They'll end up ruining themselves trying. That's the cold part of it."

I asked him if he thought the Cowboys would ever change.

"In their own realm," he said, "within their own system, at their own tempo."

Eventually the Cowboys' assault on their players' annuities would become a key issue in the lawsuit the Players Association filed against the NFL. John Weistart, a professor at Duke's law school and a labor law specialist who coauthored the book *The Law of Sports,* said, "This issue will be an easy one for the players to win.

"You can't impose excessive burdens on a person's right to strike. It's a civil violation, not an unfair labor practice. The right to strike is protected by the law, and it's a very dear law."

Meanwhile Tex Schramm was fighting the kind of battle he was best at. He had lost in training camp when he lobbied hard for a roster spot for Sweeney, a player he'd grown very fond of. He'd gone into the coach's room on the night of September 6 to plead his case, and no one listened to him. But he'd played a strong hand during the strike. He knew that the players whose annuities were being threatened would not have enough time to consult lawyers and get proper legal opinion, and he was right—except for Walls and Cosbie.

He liked the scab games because he felt that competition was equal, although the Cowboys had loaded up their squad well in advance.

"What's unique is that this time we all had the same chance and started from scratch," he said.

Landry disagreed. "As coaches," he said, "we have the responsibility to recruit players, to draft them, and to develop them. Normally we're all on equal footing. No one's on equal footing right now because we have no control over the situation. Teams fortunate enough to get players back have a competitive edge."

Before the strike Landry told his players to "do whatever you do as a team." Schramm wasn't worried about disharmony.

"When the players come back, they'll all have a common goal," he said. "It's amazing to me that there have been all these great coaches in football, and they can never agree on whether togetherness can turn a team into a winner or winning brings a team closer together."

His major concern was the fans. They were already screaming about the four-dollar ticket increase. What would happen at the gate when and if the veterans came back?

The Eagles game was a phenomenon. Conservative, nonunion Dallas had turned its back on the strikers, but they fell in love with the fresh-faced replacement players who said how lucky they were to be getting a chance. The local TV Nielsen rating was a block-busting 34, which was higher than the Giants game had been, played with regulars.

The Philly game drew 40,622. Fans hung banners—SCAB BOYS WE LOVE YOU and SUPER COWBOYS ARE BACK and HONOR THY MOTHER AND THY FATHER AND THY CONTRACT. The picketing players were largely ignored, although one scalper ran over to punter Mike Saxon, shook his hand, and said, "I hope you guys stay out on strike. I just sold one hundred tickets for forty dollars apiece."

"Let go of my hand, asshole," said Saxon.

The Cowboys won, 41–22, against a Philadelphia team about whom their coach, Buddy Ryan, would later say: "The worst group, as a team, that I've ever been around. I'll trade it for any other replacement team, sight unseen." At the end, with Philly threatening to score, Landry put his regulars back and the drive was stopped. The move would have serious repercussions.

Fan support was almost hysterical for the Monday night home game against Washington—support for the replacements, that is. The announcement that Danny White would start drew this banner: WHITE'S A WEENIE, WE WANT SWEENEY. Another one read: FANS ON STRIKE NEXT WEEK. A "replacement party" was held that night, to honor the nonstrikers.

The crowd of 60,612 would be the largest to see a Cowboy home game all season. The game itself was viewed with great interest by sociologists and psychologists around the country, because it would match a team sprinkled with seasoned veterans in key places (White, Brooks, Smerek, and Jones started on the defensive line, Dorsett and White in the backfield) against a Redskin group that had none. Not a one. The Skins had remained solid during the strike. No one had cracked. Only five other teams could make that claim. Professional players around the country turned on the TV, even the ones who swore they would never watch scab football, because this was a happening, a milestone kind of game . . . disillusioned and jaded professionalism against eager youthfulness. Bobby Beathard, the Redskins' general manager and chief scout, was no virgin in the talent recruitment game.

Dorsett and White were booed viciously during the introductions and throughout the game. Dorsett fumbled twice and dropped a screen pass. The offense, under White, was stopped on the Washington 13-yard line at the end of the game. The Redskins won, 13–7. The Cowboy defense let the Skins mount one long touchdown drive and two minidrives for field goals.

"I felt like . . . well, I was playing in a game, but I really wasn't," Randy White said.

The strike had already ended. The back-to-work order was issued the previous Thursday, October 15, one day after the deadline for players' reporting, if they wanted to cash a paycheck for the weekend. Twenty-one assorted Cowboys, including squad members on injured reserve, had crossed the picket line during the strike. It was the third-highest number in the NFL. The Raiders, with the highest payroll in the league, had twenty-six. St. Louis was second with twenty-two.

Cosbie, the leader of the picketers, was emotionally drained.

"He had to go out to the Coast, to get away from everything and be by himself," his wife Sherry said. "The calls got so bad that we had to change our phone number. People around here were just so incredibly antiplayer.

"It's going to be hard for Doug to come in and yell and scream and get it up for a game now. He's just exhausted. He has to get himself together."

"There are definitely a lot of hard feelings around here now," Jeffcoat said. "I don't know where they're going to lead. You never know how long these things take to heal, if they do.

"I won't be out there to win it for the Cowboys. I'll be doing it for my teammates who were out there with me. And it'll be tough to win it for the fans when they let us know they didn't care about us."

Later in the season Walls would mention that opposing players complimented him for the stand he took during the strike. He said that

Reggie White, the all-pro defensive end from the Eagles, told him, "I'm proud of you," and that the Giants' wide receiver Stacey Robinson said, "I really admire you for what you did."

As far as the guys who crossed? Well, they'd get theirs.

"There will definitely be a lot of teams that will be gunning for us because we were weak," said Rohrer, who had become a particular target of the fans because of his blunt denunciation of them. He had called the people of Dallas "stupid for being cowed by management" and said they had been "led by their noses."

"The feeling I've gotten talking to other players around the league is that's why this team had trouble winning," Rohrer said after the strike. "There are too many personalities, egos, likes, dislikes. I hope to prove them wrong, but people will be gunning for us because we caved in."

17

THE LOST SEASON, PART THREE

JOURNAL: Too much attention is placed on vanity, which causes the up-and-coming player to think that this is what makes the professional successful. Personal vanity is a disease, a cancer that can eat up the initial talent and sensitivity and capacity of a player. Love the sport in yourself not yourself in the sport.

Degraded by their fans, distrusting and distrusted by their management, the Dallas Cowboys got ready for the Eagles. The Cowboy scabs had won two games, their regulars one, and at 3-2 they were a game behind the Redskins in the NFC East. The Giants, last year's Super Bowl champs, were 0-5 and disappearing from sight.

During the week of the game I called Cliff Harris, the old safetyman who was a regular at Cowboy games, to get his feelings about the contest.

"The Cowboys are going to have trouble," he said.

"Emotion, right?" I said. Nobody could whip a team into an emotional frenzy like Buddy Ryan. Witness the high level of ferocity the Bears achieved when he was their defensive coach. No Eagles had crossed the picket line. Ryan had endeared himself to his striking vets by publicly announcing how happy he was to get rid of the poor excuses for players he'd had during the scab season and get his real players back. The remarks got him in bad with his owner, Norman Braman, which made his vets love him even more. Us against the world, boys, George Allen style. And now they had a score to settle. I mentioned all this to Cliff Harris.

"Uh, uh," he said. "That's part of it, but that's not it."

It's not? What's "it," then?

"Randall Cunningham," he said. "Scrambling quarterback. Coming out of the strike, there's going to be one player that's going to win games and that's the scrambling quarterback, because the defenses won't be organized. For a few games they'll flash brightly, then fade."

His remarks proved to be on the money. The Eagles won their next three games as Cunningham flashed brightly for 139 yards, then they faded. The Cowboy game was their brightest flash of all. Philly won, 37–20, and Cunningham hurt Dallas with 39 yards of scrambles, but the biggest story was Ryan. With time running out he had Cunningham throw deep to Mike Quick; a pass interference penalty put the ball on the Dallas one-yard line. Keith Byars scored the touchdown with one second left. Take that!

"The last TD was very gratifying," said Ryan in his Oklahoma twang. "What goes around comes around. I've been dreaming about it since two weeks ago."

Veteran Cowboy writers said they'd never seen Tom Landry as mad after a game.

"I wouldn't have any comment on that," he said. "I wouldn't justify it with a comment. Everybody has an opinion of what it was."

"We didn't learn anything about Ryan we didn't already know," Tex Schramm said grumpily.

"It's too bad we don't play Philadelphia again this year," Kevin Brooks said. "Buddy Ryan wouldn't be feeling too good after that game."

And on and on, the sour grapes obscuring the fact that:

1) The Herschel Walker–Tony Dorsett combination had only 86 yards, 40 of it coming on one Walker run. Byars outgained both of them.

2) The last time the Eagles scored more points was in 1981.

3) Dallas fumbled three times and had a field goal blocked.

4) The offensive line gave up five sacks and was generally overrun. Jim Erkenbeck's massive rookies, Jeff Zimmerman and Kevin Gogan, started, respectively for left guard Nate Newton, who was recovering

from arthroscopic knee surgery, and right tackle Phil Pozderac, who mysteriously retired three days before the game to "pursue business interests." He needed one game to get another year on the pension.

5) Danny White was lifted for Steve Pelluer in the fourth quarter. Pelluer lasted one play. He scrambled out of the pocket and to his right, ducked his shoulder, and got blasted by linebacker Seth Joyner, suffering a mild concussion. Next play White was back, and he threw a three-yard out pass to Doug Cosbie. In the press box Schramm clapped his hands loudly and muttered, "Great."

On Monday, White was criticized by both Hackett and Landry for running out of the pocket when he didn't have to.

"We had great protection," Erkenbeck said.

When he had calmed down, Landry said about Ryan, "I wouldn't run the score up on anybody. A lot of people will be upset. I wasn't really happy with it."

Will he forget about it?

"No, I'll probably remember."

Neil Armstrong, the Cowboys' head of research and development and a man who hired Ryan as his defensive assistant at Minnesota and recommended him for the Bears job, was more philosophical.

"I think it was more motivational for his team than anything else," he said.

In the locker room the Cowboy players were indulging in their favorite pastime, self-analysis.

"It was like . . . 'Let's get this game over with,' " linebacker Mike Hegman said. Naturally the fans were calling the radio stations with their usual criticism—lack of emotion.

During the week after the game Walker and Dorsett decided it was time to sound off about their roles in the offense. On Tuesday night Walker went on KRLD radio and said the Cowboys ought to pick a tailback and stick with him. "Let the other one be a fill-in," he said. Next day Dorsett agreed.

"I think he's right," he said. "It's going to have to come to that. This isn't the SMU Mustangs' Pony Express. It's the National Football League."

The coaches weren't overly upset. "We've heard all that before," Landry said. "But it doesn't do the team any good to have comments like that."

"I like the way the guy in Chicago, Mike Ditka, would handle something like that," Erkenbeck said. "He'd tell both of them to get screwed."

In the Monday night game against the Giants, Walker lined up all over the place, first at wide receiver, with Timmy Newsome taking his fullback spot, then at tailback, replacing Dorsett, finally at fullback, in the same backfield as Dorsett. Neither he nor Dorsett gained much yardage. Walker carried 9 times for 28 yards, Dorsett gained 3 in 14 carries, an all-time, eleven-year low for him. The Cowboys' rushing total of 26 yards also was a team record low. Erkenbeck said the Giants' defensive scheme was the reason. He said all the stunts were designed to stop the run, not rush the passer. He didn't mention that the Giants got four sacks.

The Cowboys won, 33–24, though, and the victory belonged to Too Tall Jones. Relying on his one favorite move, the wide, sweeping shoulder slap with his left hand, followed by the arm-over or "swim" with his right, he single-handedly destroyed the Giants' offense, and their right tackle, William Roberts, and their quarterback, Phil Simms. And their season.

He got four sacks. By the fourth quarter he had Roberts groggy, a punch-drunk fighter with no referee to stop the fight. Giants' coach Bill Parcells watched, arms folded, as Jones beat his man time and again. Parcells pouted. On TV the ABC Monday-night crew offered such observations as "Well, it looks like he's still mad at his team . . . no, maybe he likes them now. . . ." And still no relief for Roberts, no double-team help from the tight end or fullback, no one to pull him out for a series or two to let himself get together. The Giants' coaching staff was deep in slumber. It was like watching a guy getting run over by a bus—in slow motion.

Jones forced two interceptions, one of which right end Jim Jeffcoat ran in for the tying touchdown. Jones forced a fumble. With a little under three minutes left, he beat Roberts again and flushed Simms to his left, where Jeffcoat rolled into his left knee, spraining the medial collateral ligament and forcing him out of action for three weeks.

The day after the game Schramm was asked about the magnitude of the victory.

"It was a big, big win," he said, and after a pause, "Almost as big as a win over Washington would have been." He still dreamed about his replacement team.

Tuesday was trade deadline day. The locker room had been filled with rumors that Dorsett would be heading to Denver and ex-Cowboy Dan Reeves. A few days before the Giants' game he was laughing and singing in the clubhouse, despite the fact that Schramm, Landry, and Reeves had issued strong denials.

"Am I going, men?" Dorsett asked a couple of reporters. "Do I need to pack my bags, get a new heavy coat?"

"What's up, T?" said linebacker Steve DeOssie in the next locker. "Are we going to have to throw a party?"

"I'll pay for the party, man," Dorsett said. "Go play on that natural grass . . . that'll add years to my career."

Ten minutes later he said he was just kidding and had no desire to leave Dallas.

"I would have pretty mixed emotions if something did happen," he said. "I'm not looking forward to relocating. If I had to, Denver wouldn't be a bad place. But I like where I'm at. I'm not looking to go anywhere."

It was roughly the midway point of the abbreviated fifteen-game season. The Cowboys were 4-3, with only two games left against teams with winning records. If they were to make their move, it was now. After the opening game loss to St. Louis, Landry had said a realistic goal for the season was 9-7.

"If you're over .500, you're just a little momentum away from the playoffs," he had said.

The playoffs? So what? Just to get blown out by somebody in the first round? What does that prove? What about the long haul?

No superrookies had emerged, no Duane Thomases or Calvin Hills. Francis was starting, Noonan was spelling Randy White. With two of Erkenbeck's gigantos now playing in the offensive line, and the running game now devoted less to stylishness and more to power, it was still nowhere, despite the presence of such exceptional talents as Dorsett and Walker. With the season half gone the coaches still couldn't figure out how to use them. In 1986 the Cowboys finished eleventh in the league in rushing, with a 123-yard per game average. Now, in the four nonstrike games, they were down to 90.2. Ninety yards a game! In Thomas's Super Bowl season of 1971 the Cowboys had gone under 100 only twice, in fifteen games.

"We used to run sweeps and traps and screens better than anyone in the league," said Brian Baldinger, a reserve guard, a five-year veteran. "We ran that Near G-O with both guards pulling, kicking out on the two outside men. . . . Herb Scott made a living out of that play for ten years. Now it's not even in the playbook. Everything's straight ahead blocking.

"Maybe inexperience is part of it, I don't know. In the old days you had guys like Billy Joe Dupree, Pat Donovan, Scott, guys who played six or seven years together. After they'd set the roster at the beginning of the season, you wouldn't ever see a new face in the meeting room."

Even worse, the opponents' sack rate was up from 1986, when Pelluer was turned into a basket case. And Danny White was starting to feel the pressure. The assistant coaches knew it was only a matter of time until Pelluer took over.

"In the Eagles' game," Paul Hackett said, "Zimmerman completely misses his man, Pelluer makes a great escape, runs, and doesn't get down. So he's hurt and back on the bench. That's Steve Pelluer."

The night before the Detroit game Erkenbeck told a writer, off the record, that if he had his way, he would start Pelluer, play Timmy Newsome at fullback, and alternate the tailbacks, with Walker being the number one guy. But the decision wasn't up to him. Landry had to make it. Within two weeks that's exactly what would happen.

Hackett, looking older than his forty years—one writer noted that his hairline seemed to recede on a daily basis—was losing confidence in White, in his ability to stay in the pocket or hold on to the ball. His wrist seemed to weaken toward the end of games. He'd been averaging 37 throws per contest since he came back from the strike.

"He's been fumbling his whole career," Hackett said. "I can talk to him about it, we can look at films, but it all comes down to him going out on the field and performing.

"Danny's great strength through the years has been his consistency. Now he has definitely struggled with throwing on the move, and the zip on the ball is not what it has been. I've said all along that he can have his best year with the Cowboys this season. Then he throws four interceptions in the first Giants game and almost costs us the thing, and I have to adjust. I say, 'Yes, he can, but . . .' "

Is it time to lift him for Pelluer? Hackett shook his head. The responsibility for such a move was not his.

"That's Coach's decision," he said. He always referred to Landry as "Coach."

"I watch the quarterbacks every day, but he has to make decisions everywhere, all the time. He has to look at the team and have the feel. Sometimes change gives you a spark. Sometimes that's wishful thinking. You can make what appears to be a fairly simple move, but there's no predicting what would happen."

White was asked about his season. Things had not been going well for him. The companies he owns had not been doing well. There was talk of lawsuits. Constant therapy was supposed to strengthen his wrist, but it was getting weaker. Then there was his position during the strike.

He saved his job in the second Giants game. He had a high percentage night, 24 for 33 with one interception, but the passes were mostly of the safe variety. He worked the middle, went to crosses and slant-ins, and didn't do much downfield or deep sideline throwing.

As he answered midweek questions in the locker room, his eyes seemed tired. There was a stubble of beard on his face.

"There's no question that more is expected of me now than ever before," he said. "It's important that I execute at as high a level as possible. Every time there's a situation where a veteran might be replaced by a younger player, the burden is on the veteran to make fewer mistakes.

"You handle the ball, you run the risk of making the most mistakes, that's the nature of the position. The first Giants game I felt I had to play more aggressively. That resulted in four interceptions but also in some big plays at the end. It's a tough decision for a quarterback, maybe the toughest part of the job—when do you throw the ball away, when do you take a trap, when do you force it into a tight opening? And you have about a tenth of a second to make that decision. The only way you can get good at it is to have it happen to you over and over again."

White had his worst game of the season in Detroit against the Lions, a 1-6 team that would finish with the second-worst record in the league. The final was 27–17 Lions, who tried to hand the game to the Cowboys—quarterback Chuck Long fumbled away two snaps from center—but the offer was declined. White was intercepted four times. He had trouble getting the ball downfield with any accuracy. The Cowboy defense recorded no sacks.

Tex Schramm, on his regular Monday night KRLD radio show, let fly some remarks that were immediately picked up by the national wires. Bitterness, frustration, maybe just the anger of a superfan whose press box tirades during games were well-known to the Cowboy beat writers . . . whatever it was, the part everyone picked up on was a particularly bitter castigation of Landry as a "teacher." In twenty-eight years no one could remember Schramm's publicly ripping his coach.

"We're having a lot of wins and losses that are very difficult to accept," Schramm said on the air. "Maybe that's the kind of year it's going to be, but it's certainly not the type of year I'm enjoying. We had an outstanding opportunity to get our momentum going, to get our team going. It was a terrible failure.

"I can anticipate some of the questions we're going to get tonight, and I can tell you that I have the same questions. And I don't have the answers. Some of the things we're doing are frankly mystifying. It's very seldom I put myself in a position of giving the players a reason for losing, but I'm not sure it's all on the players.

"When things aren't working and you continue to see the same things, it shakes your confidence. There's an old saying, 'If the teacher doesn't teach, the student doesn't learn.' Maybe we've got to start teaching other things.

"I'll sit down with him [Landry], but these are still his decisions. I'm not a technical football man. Those are decisions the head coach and coaching staff will have to make. You have to do whatever you have to do to make a team successful. If you have to make a change, you make a change. But there's one thing to keep in mind. We're still in position to be a playoff team."

Schramm's radio tour continued the next night when he said on his WOAI San Antonio show that it had become apparent that the team would have to focus on one back and that back was probably Walker.

The day after his blast on Landry, Schramm downplayed the whole thing. He told newsmen who called him that he didn't think his remarks were "that direct." Later in the season, though, when he had time to reflect on the national stir he had caused, he looked at it more philosophically.

"I don't feel I have to sit around answering things that people on the outside are saying about my relationship with Landry," he said. "We've been together for twenty-eight years. It's a very unique, strong relationship.

"This is an emotional game, and those things were said under stressful circumstances. I wish I hadn't said them, because they created a misimpression, obviously. I don't have any criticism of Tom's coaching today any more than I've had in past years."

Landry stood up under the heat. Early in the week he said he felt that no changes had to be made for the New England game the following Sunday. He remembered what happened the last time he bowed to pressure and replaced White with Gary Hogeboom, who failed. He remembered Pelluer's miserable preseason. He said that keeping Dorsett and Walker in the lineup together made sense, even if Walker took a turn at wide receiver every now and then, because when you've got talent, you don't want to waste it on the bench.

Schramm's remarks? Oh, yes, he knew about them. Landry had read the newspapers that were left on his desk every morning. He was not always as unflappable as he liked to project himself.

"Sometimes after a loss you get frustrated and you say things," he said. "But there's nothing you can do about it. You just go on to the next game."

But to be ripped like that? "If the teacher doesn't teach . . ."

"It's been the ideal situation here through the years," Landry said. "I've never had any problems in that area at all. You can look for that if you want to, I suppose. But that's not my nature."

The soap opera continued. On Wednesday, November 11, it was Herschel Walker's turn. This time the vehicle was the conference call to the out-of-town writers, one of the modern conveniences for advancing a game. This was what the New England writers heard over the phone:

"I don't feel like I carried the ball enough last week [13 times for 65 yards]. It's very frustrating. I'm not a wide receiver. I want to help any way I can, but I'm a running back. I must not be the type of runner the Cowboys are looking for. If that's true, I'd rather they let me play somewhere else where I am that type of runner."

He had been calling his agent in Cleveland, Peter Johnson, on a weekly basis to complain about his role with the Cowboys and how unhappy he was. On Thursday, when the Dallas writers talked to him—after he made national headlines—he went into his backstroke. In a strange, disjointed kind of interview that local newspapermen had come to know so well, he said the following:

"I jump around a lot. I don't always say what I believe because that's not what is important. What's important is to answer the questions. They probably left out the questions—which is unfair to me— but I take most of the blame because I gave them the answers."

After they had compared notes and finished scratching their heads, the writers decided that what he meant was that the questions were asked in such a way that his answers came out looking stronger than he intended. Whatever he intended, his remarks had the desired effect, because on Friday Landry announced that Walker would start against the Patriots and Dorsett would be his backup.

Actually the beat writers had sensed that this would happen the day before, when Landry called Dorsett in to talk to him about his future with the Cowboys. This was clearly unusual. Maybe he had taken Dorsett's training camp remarks to heart.

Afterward he told the reporters that his talks with Tony had been "personal," but he mentioned that Dorsett could see what was coming. The coach's eyes grew sad as he discussed the greatest running back in the club's history. He seemed to be putting him in the past tense.

"Our future is in Herschel," he said. "Everybody knows that, even Tony knows that. I have a strong feeling for Tony. He's meant a lot to this team. I'd love to see him get out by getting the records and the goals he has set for himself. Sometimes it doesn't happen that way."

Dorsett was upset only with Schramm's politicking for the change on the radio.

"I've given them almost 12,000 yards," he said. "You'd think he would be more diplomatic than that."

Again the Schramm-Landry divergence, this time over method, had caused unhappiness on the team—or at least a small portion of it.

On Friday, the Cowboys released thirty-six-year-old John Dutton, the oldest member of the team. The dozen players who were thirty or older at the end of the '86 season had been cut to eight. But was this a more talented team? Probably not. Dutton represented the top draft in 1979 since he had come on a trade for the pick, and now the Cowboy squad had only two first-round picks from the past ten years, Jeffcoat and Noonan, and only one was starting.

It's another Saturday night in another Cowboys' hospitality room on the road, this time at Boston's Marriott Copley Place. The Cowboys are one of the few teams that maintain this tradition that once was a necessity when the clubs actively promoted themselves. Some of the younger writers around the league never even heard of it. On a Philadelphia trip one of the Dallas beat writers told a friend of his, a Philly writer, to meet him at the Cowboys' hospitality room at the Franklin Plaza.

"The what?" he said.

Something resembling a party is going on in the Cowboys' hospitality room at the Copley Marriott . . . media people, the airline crew, a few Cowboys' personnel, maybe twenty-five people in all. In an adjoining bedroom Dick Nolan, the defensive backfield coach, Steve Orsini, the ticket manager, and Tim Cowlishaw of the *Dallas Morning News* are watching football highlights on TV. Schramm is on the phone nearby, talking loudly to CBS's Irv Cross:

"No, that's already been strongly denied!" a red-faced Schramm bellows. "No, he never said that! Hey, why don't you tell me who you've talked to so I can tell you whether I'm going to answer the questions?"

It's been a busy week for Schramm, who had been campaigning for change—across the state of Texas on his radio shows. To this point he has not complained to the reporters who reprinted his remarks.

He hangs up and turns to go out the door, then he comes back to Cowlishaw, watching the highlights.

"And next time you write what someone says on the radio," he says, "write the whole thing!" he shouts.

"I wrote what you said," Cowlishaw tells him.

"But you didn't write the whole thing, you wrote what you wanted to write."

"The show's forty-five minutes long . . . how can I run an entire transcript . . . ?"

"Oh, screw you," Schramm says, poking the reporter in the arm and storming out.

Next morning Schramm runs into Cowlishaw in the Sullivan Stadium press box.

"Good morning, Timmy," he says pleasantly. No one as yet has been able to figure out what mood the general manager will be in on any given day.

The Cowboys beat the Patriots, 23–17, on Walker's 60-yard run in overtime. White brought the offense 78 yards down the field to set up Roger Ruzek's 20-yard field goal that tied the game in regulation time. The defense used a five-man line at times, with Noonan lining up at noseguard. He was especially effective driving the Patriots thirty-six-year-old center, Guy Morris, into the backfield, collapsing the pocket around Steve Grogan, who was knocked out of the game in the third quarter.

Walker carried 28 times, four short of the team record, and gained a career high 173 yards. Dorsett's activity was limited to six plays. He carried the ball once for 5 yards and picked up 19 more on two pass receptions.

"That's what I saw Walker do in the USFL," said Erkenbeck, who had been on Jim Mora's staff in Philadelphia and Baltimore. "Just like that. Just like that! He's a scary guy to have around."

With Miami coming to town for a Sunday nighter, bringing the NFL's fourth-worst rushing defense, Walker was the natural focus for the midweek feature stories. On Thursday he treated three writers to another of his rambling, head-scratching type of interviews:

Q: What's your favorite color?

A: Well, if it's a car, I like blue. In a football jersey I kind of like the silver and blue. Cowboys' colors make me look okay. I don't like red.

Q: Then why'd you go to Georgia?

A: I didn't think about colors back in those days. It was too silly. But you know, it's a funny story how I ended up at Georgia. I hated Georgia. I didn't want to go.

Q: Why did you?

A: I was sort of forced. My parents, even though they didn't tell me, they said it would be good to go to Georgia. And when I flipped the coin, it came up that I would go to Georgia. People don't believe that, but that's the way I make all my decisions. It was between Clemson and USC. I flipped for Clemson and Georgia first, and Georgia won. Then USC and Georgia, and Georgia won, so I just said I'd go to Georgia. But if one of those schools had won, I probably would have gone there. 'Cause like I said, people don't realize that you make a mistake in your life, you don't lay down and die or whatever. That's not the way it is. If I make a mistake, I made a mistake. Okay, time to move on.

Q: What did the USC coaches say when you told them you flipped a coin?

A: Well, you know John Jackson was recruiting me, and I think he really thought they had me because that's when SC was always having those tailbacks, and he figured they'd win. When he lost and I told him why, he couldn't believe I'd do something like that. It was just like I flipped a coin to decide whether to come to the Cowboys, even though Mr. Trump told me he thought it would be a good idea if I continued to play. But I flipped a coin to see if I'd play. Heads I go and tails I stay in New Jersey with Donald Trump. It came up heads.

Q: If it had been tails, you would have sat out last year?

A: Yeah, if it had been tails I probably wouldn't have played. To be honest with you, I'd love to go into the FBI or any criminal justice area.

Q: Have you talked to them about it?

A: Well, see, I can do it because my internship was with the FBI training center, but see, my wife has already told me she doesn't want me to go into it. So the only dream I can have is to go on *Miami Vice* or pictures like *Hunter* and play out the dream.

Q: You're not really going to flip another coin in December or January, are you?

A: Not really, but see, I don't think that far ahead. Once you start thinking that far ahead you get lost and stuff. That's why I can't predict what I'm going to do Sunday. That's too far off for me.

Almost overlooked in the come-from-behind victory over New England was the fact that on the last drive in regulation time, the one that tied the score, Patriot linebacker Johnny Rembert dropped a White pass that hit him in the numbers. Had he caught it, the game would have been over and the Cowboys would have been 4-5. Now they were 5-4 with a serious shot at the playoffs. Only four NFC teams had better records. The up-and-down drama continued.

By Wednesday it became obvious that Pelluer would be the starting quarterback against Miami. He was working with the first unit. White was taking treatment for his sore wrist. Landry was asked if the wrist could get any better.

"No," he said.

During the lunch-hour break White was open and candid about the change. He seemed strangely relaxed, a marked contrast to the tearful remarks he was forced to make at a press luncheon in 1984 when Landry surprised him and everyone else by naming Gary Hogeboom as his opening day starter.

"Pelluer needs to not do what I was doing," White said, "trying to create things. He needs to play within the confines of the personnel he's got.

"It's a good opportunity for him because there will be less pressure from the Miami rush. But the throwing part will be critical because Miami will use seven, sometimes eight, defensive backs. Coach Landry has always been an insightful coach. I think he's being insightful right now."

Many people felt it was the urging of Hackett and Erkenbeck that had forced the change. Hackett was excited as he talked about the new quarterback.

"It's an ideal time for it," he said. "It was a great decision by Coach in terms of timing. Who would have thought it, but he just senses things. It's exciting. It's an awful exciting time for the whole football team."

The offense Pelluer would run would be very basic, compared to what the Cowboys used to run. The line had been reshuffled again, and George Lilja, a free agent pickup, a five-year vet who'd been cut by the Rams, Jets, and Browns, would start at center and share time with thirty-three-year-old Tom Rafferty. The 310-pound rookie, Kevin Gogan, would start at right tackle. Nate Newton, 315, was back at left guard, but he was out of shape, still recovering from knee surgery. The massive front wall averaged 6-4½, 294, tackle to tackle. It was the biggest in the NFL but it was slow—and inexperienced.

A visitor to Hackett's office asked him about the '85 Super Bowl, when he was Bill Walsh's offensive assistant and the 49ers had dazzled Miami, 38–16, and quarterback Joe Montana and the offense had set records for yardage.

"Jeez, I haven't even thought about that game," Hackett said, walking up to his filing cabinet and pulling out the 49ers' offensive plan for the Super Bowl.

"All sorts of great plays in here," he said, thumbing through the five drafts of the game plan.

"How many, exactly?" he was asked.

"You want to know? I'll count 'em if you want me to. Let me find the final draft . . . here it is."

He began counting. "Ninety-eight passes, thirty-six runs, not counting goal-line and short yardage, twelve short-yardage plays. How many is that?"

He was told 146.

"Well, we've got about forty now, for our Miami game Sunday night. About twenty-five pass plays and fifteen runs. But you're talking about a very experienced offense in San Francisco. It's two completely different situations.

"You know, Bill scripted the first eighteen plays of the Super Bowl . . . called 'em ahead of time . . . and never changed any. We tried scripting the first few plays here but dropped it early in the season. Coach just wasn't comfortable with it."

Pelluer, who would be getting his first start since December 14, 1986, tried to stay calm as he discussed the game with a few writers. Speaking softly, his voice occasionally cracking, he said, "I've tried to put last year out of my mind. What matters is the next couple of weeks. If I do well, that's what I'll focus on and everyone else will focus on."

Someone asked him if he hoped to outperform Dan Marino, and for the first time he laughed.

"Obviously I don't think I can match him," he said. "Hopefully it won't be my last chance to try."

18

DALLAS REVISITED

JOURNAL: The road is very narrow when you travel at warped speed. Now I go slower, so the road looks wider.

Campisi's Egyptian is the kind of restaurant every serious sports town has, or should have. In San Diego it's Pernicano's Casa di Baffi; in the New Jersey Meadowlands, across the river from New York, it's Manny's of Moonachie; places where the players can come for a beer and a late snack without being bothered by drunks and autograph hounds. The "Egyptian" in the name goes back forty years, when the place was The Egyptian Lounge. When Joe Campisi opened his restaurant in 1939, he removed the word "lounge" ("because I wanted a family establishment") and left Egyptian alone. Either he ran out of money to pay the workers tearing down the neon signs or he sort of liked the sound of "Campisi's Egyptian," he isn't sure which.

The restaurant is on East Mockingbird near Greenville, across the street from the Dr Pepper plant. The food is Neapolitan, heavy on the garlic. You can smell it out in the street. It's a hangout for Cowboy players and management. There's a Randy White Ravioli on the menu.

If the restaurant is full, which it always is, you might find yourself in Joe Campisi's office, eating your lasagna off his desk. There are always people eating in his office, cops, city politicians, businessmen, Cowboys.

Gil Brandt likes to have his meals in Joe Campisi's office. Tom Landry orders his pasta to go. Even in the time of his troubles Duane Thomas was a regular in the office, where he could relax with Joe and his son Corky. On Saturday night, November 21, the night before the Dolphins beat the Cowboys 20–14, we are sitting around the desk in Joe's office—Duane Thomas, myself, and seventy-year-old Joe Campisi.

An ex-FBI man, a ticket broker, and a member of the Stadium Authority are seated in the room, drinking coffees with shots in them.

"You grew up in Dallas, didn't you, Duane?" the ticket guy says, and Thomas nods.

"What part?" he asks, as if he didn't know. Where did he figure Thomas grew up, Highland Park?

"South Dallas," Thomas says, "Baldwin Street," and the ticket guy nods his head gravely, as if he'd been given a piece of vital information.

To get to Baldwin Street, and I assume you're coming from the north—everybody is—you drive down on the North Central Expressway, past the Cowboys' old office building, past Mockingbird Lane and Highland Park, through the downtown area, and you get off at the Cotton Bowl exit, right after the billboard that says: "Jesus Is the Reason for the Xmas Season, Buy Gifts at Jenkins Christian Store."

You skirt the southeastern edge of the Cotton Bowl, past Fair Park.

"I used to climb that tree right there to watch the fireworks," Duane Thomas says. We are taking a drive through South Dallas, visiting his old neighborhood.

Clapboard houses, here and there a hedge or a small, neat cactus garden, weeds, vacant, garbage-strewn lots, a billboard—"Coors Is the One"—a half-court basketball court of pitted asphalt with a shoulder-high hoop, at Foreman and Metropolitan a sign—"Sharpshooter's Sportsman Club"—the paint peeling, revealing whitewashed clapboard underneath. No white faces.

We stop for a light. A thin man in tattered army fatigues comes up to the car.

"How's everything, brother?" he says, smiling and showing a lot of missing teeth.

"Do I know you? I'm Duane Thomas," Duane says, sticking out his hand.

"I'm Scott, man. It's been a long time." Then turning to me—"I was raised up with this young man here."

He gets serious. "Duane, I'd like to talk to you for a moment, if I could. I'm trying to get to Oak Cliff, and I need a dollar and a half so's I can ride the bus . . . I'll pay you back."

Thomas hands him a couple of dollars and watches him leave.

"Do you remember him?" I ask.

"His whole family," Thomas says. "Good people."

We turn on the corner of Foreman and Baldwin.

"Bethlehem Baptist Church," Thomas says. "Our mother used to take us here sometimes. My house was seventeen doors from the church. I'd count the houses. See this vacant lot here, next to the church? Miss Lilton's house used to be here. She had a stand where she'd sell snow cones.

"The neighborhood's changed. Used to be kids playing in the street all the time."

Baldwin Street, neat, poor, quiet except for the crowing of a lone rooster.

"This house here used to be beautiful," Thomas says, pointing to a rundown-looking single-story. "Everyone kept their property up. We used to go up and down the street with lawn mowers, cutting people's yards.

"We didn't have a key to our door. It was never locked. Nobody ever thought of stealing anything.

"Right here's where our house was, number 4527," he says, as we stop in front of a bare, empty lot. "I still own the property. It fell into disrepair. We tore it down. People were coming in from outside the neighborhood, stealing the plumbing fixtures, everything.

"The house looked like that one," he says, pointing to a yellow shingle house across the street. "We'd sleep out on the front porch in summertime, or we'd go in the backyard and build a tent and sleep there. My grandfather gave me two little ducks from his farm. I kept them as pets. They used to stay out in back, in the barn where my father kept his tools."

Harold Chambers, Duane's boyhood friend, lived next door, at 4523. They used to climb the tree in Duane's backyard together, swipe fruit down the street together. A young woman with glasses is sitting on the front steps of 4523.

"Where's everyone?" Duane says.

"Harold's in Oak Cliff, Glenda's in Oak Cliff," she says, "Liz is in New York now, Mary's in Mesquite, Charles is in Hawaii, I'm Helen and I'm still here, and Patsy's here, too, but she's really in Pleasant Grove. I knew you wouldn't remember me. I was too young.

"Everyone was so proud of him," she says to me. "They'd say, 'Lookee here, he lived right next door.' I wanted to be like Duane Thomas. I wanted to do something. People said, 'Go to trade school, stay around,' but I went on to college . . . SMU, graduated from East Texas State. And here I am."

I ask her what she does.

"I had an elementary ed degree, now I work for the government," she says. "Central records and tax liens."

Harold Chambers is inside, visiting his sister. He wears jeans and a sweat shirt that says "Dallas Firebusters." He works as a fireman in Dallas. He tells me about their childhood together, about how close they were at one time. I ask him what he did when Duane was having his troubles with the Cowboys.

"I was overseas in Vietnam," he says. "I heard about it. I wish I could have seen him, found out what was on his mind."

I ask him when did he get back.

"April 6, 1971," he says. "Yeah, I guess he was still here."

"Did you see him?" I ask, and Harold Chambers looks a little guilty.

"I saw him in passing," he says. "I never phoned him. He was living with his wife. I didn't have the number. He'd come by. I'd cut his yard. He seemed distant, different. You could tell he had something on his mind. It was his business. I didn't ask him about it."

He thinks for a moment. There seems to be a need for justification of a sort.

"People I worked with would be misinformed about him," he says. "They acted like they knew his family. One time someone said his mother's living on Warren Street, and I said, 'Oh, yeah? It so happens she's passed away.' I'd set them straight, but no, I wouldn't argue with them."

Larry Jefferson, the Baptist minister who'd grown up with Duane, is standing in front of his house farther down on Baldwin . . . "fourteen Jeffersons in the family living in a house no bigger than mine," Harold Chambers says.

I ask Larry Jefferson about his relationship with Duane during 1971 and '72 and he mentions his uneasiness when he found out Duane was seen with Muslim figures. I ask him if he'd seen him then, tried to talk to him.

"I met him on Hall and Oak Lawn one time," he says. "I was working as a florist and he was coming out of a doctor's office. He mentioned that he didn't think the team was treating him fairly.

"He was dealing with it, but different from the way I feel his parents or friends from childhood would have advised him. I really didn't think I could advise him, primarily because I was just trying to get the straights of it."

A friend joins us. We talk about the neighborhood now.

"You're looking at the drug capital of Dallas," he says. "This never used to be a big drug area. A guy had to know someone who knew someone who knew someone to buy one stick of weed. Now it's heavy. Guys are riding down the street on skateboards selling it.

"The night before last . . . hey, you're not using my name for any of this stuff, are you? I don't want to end up as a body in the river."

I tell him I'm not using his name.

"Well, the night before last they park here in this street and walk over to the next street, to Metropolitan. We call that The Trail, from Jamaica to Baldwin to Metropolitan . . . it runs behind Duane's lot. These two white guys get out. When you see a white guy pull up in his car, he's either a narc or he's buying drugs.

"See that white house over there? That's a drug house. There are twelve in this area, forty or more in South Dallas. I was in that tree there. I climb down, jump the fence. The two guys follow, one with a pistol, one with a shotgun. Boom-boom!"

"Kids in the neighborhood are on stuff now," Larry Jefferson says. "You see these kids just wasting away. It's a lot different from what it used to be."

Trying to cope with a neighborhood that became drug-ridden, trying to make a living for their families . . . the people who knew Duane Thomas from the old days had more on their minds than one guy's problem with a football team, or whatever the problem was . . . they weren't sure.

We drive to the house of Rabbit Thomas, Duane's old ninth-grade coach, past Julia C. Frazier School, which Thomas attended as a youngster, past Hatcher and the railroad tracks and the reservoir ("I'd walk on the wall sometimes on my way home"), past Lincoln High and the practice field.

We turn and head west, and then up the I-35. "P. C. Cobb Stadium, our home field," Thomas says. "All the black schools played there."

An imposing, shiny white latticework building stands there now. A trade center. We head back and get on the Central Expressway.

"Gregg Park for junior high and JV games," Thomas says, pointing. "You can't see it. The freeway blocks it. It's where I scored my first TD . . . an 80-yard pass. The freeway was there in those days, too. It was the only one in Dallas at the time."

We visit with Rabbit Thomas, a tall, heavy, friendly man. He says he had talked to Duane a few times when he had his problems. He says he had told Duane to "be himself." He had defended him.

"Most of the people I knew and hung around with wouldn't say anything derogatory about him around me," he says, "because they knew how I felt about him."

Otto M. Friday, Duane's former principal, whom we visit in his large and lavishly furnished office in the Dallas Independent School District building: "I never could understand Duane's agenda and never talked to him about it when he came to see me."

And so it went, back in 1971 and '72 . . . a word here or there, a hint, a suggestion, nothing in the way of real support.

"People didn't want to jeopardize their own positions," Thomas says, "or the lives they had built up for themselves."

And on July 30, 1972, he was traded to San Diego. In some parts of Dallas, perhaps you could hear a sigh of relief.

19

★

THE GYPSY

JOURNAL: As the wind blows the plants nearby, my dreams and hopes are in the heavens. A day of rest ... peace and God's divine will stretch across the land. Blue sky. Where ... where?

It's a strange, disjointed story, the San Diego odyssey of Duane Thomas. It's filled with "He said" . . . "No, he didn't" . . . "Well, this is what he said he said." It's a bizarre tale of aberrant behavior, of a team gone bad, a secret plane trip in the night . . . and it lasted almost a year, until the Chargers, as Dallas had done, threw up their hands and peddled Thomas to the next buyer. And underlying everything was the hint of drugs. Nobody could act that whacky on his own, people figured. He must have been on drugs, cocaine or mescaline or psychedelic mushrooms—*or something.*

But here's the interesting part. No one ever saw him do anything more serious than smoking a joint. No, not in Greenville that day. He was clean on that one. We're talking about when players got together in the dorm or in the off-season and lit up, which most of the Cowboys did. He had one, too. Guilty. Let's face it, like it or not it's something many young Americans are guilty of, and some not so young. I wouldn't like it if my kids told me they smoked marijuana. You wouldn't either, even if you were doing it yourself. But in the NFL it is, and was, a fact of life. They work hard, their bodies take a beating, at night they smoke one or two to ease the pain or relax or for whatever reason people smoke those things. But they do it.

Thomas says he never fooled around with stronger stuff. Never. People on the Cowboys who knew him, Roger Staubach, Calvin Hill, said he had too much respect for his physical conditioning to do something that would break him down. He was a maniac on keeping his body in condition, they said, and they added that they never saw him out of shape, even years after he had stopped playing football. Hard drugs eventually would have caught up to him. Hill was with him in Hawaii, where drugs were plentiful. He said Thomas was clean the whole time.

People who socialized with him in L.A. in the off-season, even during his erratic period in San Diego, said he never messed with drugs.

"We used to kid him about being strange," said O. J. Simpson, who saw Thomas frequently in L.A. "A bunch of us used to work out a lot together. We used to eat at this soul food smorgasbord at night. Duane took a lot of kidding from us and laughed it off. You know, jock humor type of stuff . . . 'We ain't buying none of your crap, Duane.' That type of thing. We'd get on him hard.

"But when he got up and walked across the street, he was a stranger, a completely different person, hard and defiant.

"As far as drugs? We never saw him fool around. You're looking at 1972 and '73. Cocaine wasn't really fashionable then. LSD was already passé. What could he have been taking, mushrooms, mescaline? Uh, uh, we would have known it, as much as we were around him."

The most logical solution, which seems so hard for people to accept, is that this was a highly disturbed young man, lost in his own world most of the time. And in the 1972 and '73 Chargers he found a team as strange as he was.

In a 1969 game against Miami a hip injury ended the career of Houston Ridge, a San Diego defensive end. He sued the Chargers, claiming the drugs the team had given him for the game, a painkiller, a muscle relaxer, and three amphetamines, had aggravated an already serious injury and turned him into a cripple. The court awarded him $260,000 plus $35,000 for future disability. In May 1973 the California Board of Medical Examiners and the State Board of Pharmacy complained about the Chargers to the district attorney, who declared the case "officially reopened." In a sworn deposition Jimmy Van Deusen, the former trainer, said that in 1969 alone he gave out 2,600 pep pills to the players—along with other drugs.

"Bennies, Quaaludes, they had a gum-ball machine full of them in the locker room," Thomas says. "All a guy had to do was turn the handle and he got as many as he wanted."

Late in the 1973 season, four months after San Diego traded Thomas to the Redskins, the league levied fines totaling $40,000 against the Charger team, general manager, and eight players, placing the Chargers on "probation" for uncontrolled drug use, mainly amphetamines. The whole affair would later become the subject of a book, *Nightmare Season*, by Dr. Arnold Mandell, who had been hired as a special psychiatric consultant by Harland Svare, the coach who later became general manager. Mandell had authorized many of the drugs himself. A story had already broken in the *San Diego Union* that the Chargers were heavy drug users.

"It's bad, really bad," Chuck Dicus, a wide receiver said.

"The Chargers are the cesspool of the league," a man from the NFL office said.

Next year they hired Jack Norris, an FBI agent for twenty-two years, specializing in kidnap cases, as their "health coach."

This was the team to which the Cowboys had sent Thomas.

The coach when he arrived was Svare, nicknamed "Swede," despite his Norwegian descent. Immediately after the 1972 Dallas game, the only game Thomas dressed for, Svare was given a new five-year contract by owner Gene Klein, despite the team's 2-5-1 record. Klein said he decided at halftime. Next year Svare was fired after eight games, with the Chargers' record at 1-6-1 ("I have never seen a team go this sour," said their forty-year-old quarterback, John Unitas, the former Colts' star). Svare was made general manager and fired two years later. He had personally been fined $5,000 by the league for "lack of supervision" in the drug case.

The squad the Chargers had assembled in the two seasons, or pieces of seasons, that Thomas was with them was a foreign legion of aging players who'd been great elsewhere—Unitas, Deacon Jones of the Rams, John Mackey of the Colts, Lionel Aldridge of the Packers, Coy Bacon of the Bengals, Dave Costa of the Broncos, and Thomas's old teammate, Pettis Norman of the Cowboys. Plus a few imported younger whackos such as former Eagle Tim Rossovich, who announced he would sell his hair for $5,000 and his mustache for the same price. Oh, it was a collection, all right.

"When Duane came, the fit was perfect," said Bobby Hood, the administrative assistant.

After the trade was announced Svare tried to reach Thomas by phone . . . "Fifty unanswered calls," he said. Someone asked him if he were ready to give up on him, a silly question, since the trade was unconditional. The Cowboys had seen to that.

"I'll wait a while for him to report," Svare said. "My gut reaction was to take a chance. You have to roll the dice. This is a rare talent, a superior football player.

"If you take a little bird in your hand, you don't squeeze it."

"We'll welcome Thomas with open arms," defensive end Deacon Jones said. "This is a close, friendly team."

Four days after the trade Thomas was in the headlines. He'd been thrown off an American Airlines flight for playing his tape recorder too loud. In Dallas his friend Harold Chambers read the story and shook his head.

"I had no defense for that," he said. "I mean, if it was too loud he should have turned it down."

"I'm sitting there waiting for the plane to take off," Thomas says. "The stewardess says, 'You have to turn it off.' I tell her I'll turn it off when the plane takes off. She says, 'No, right now.' I say, 'I'll turn it off when we start.' She says, 'I said now!'

"I say, 'You'd better learn how to talk to people.' Then security was on the plane escorting me off. They took me into the office and questioned me. I caught the next plane. A communications problem, sure, but I had a lot of stuff on my mind."

He showed up at the Chargers' complex on August 3. Pat Rogers, who'd been a secretary with the club for nine years, remembers him as "very polite."

"He chewed tobacco," she said. "When he was waiting in the office he said, 'Do you mind if I spit?' and I said no. First time anyone ever asked me that."

"I got lucky, I got him for a TV interview," says Jerry Gross, who was with the CBS affiliate in San Diego, KFMB.

"I just bumped into him in the locker room. I started the camera. I asked him three or four questions. He answered them in quick sentences. He looked over me and through me. It was like looking at two empty eyes. He had a classic closing line, though.

"I said, 'Duane, now that you're here, what do you have to say to the fans in San Diego?' He looked at me.

" 'Hello,' he said."

Thomas had one meeting with Svare. He calls it "a numbers bout."

"He said, 'Okay, Duane, I'll give you fifty.' That's the same thing the Dallas owner, Clint Murchison, had agreed to in the off-season. I'd gone in to see him up in his office on the fiftieth floor. He wanted to have a meeting with me. He took me to the window and started telling me about the new civic center he wanted to build and talked about all the business developments down there in Dallas. Then he asked me what I wanted, and I said, 'I'll play for fifty and make no waves,' and he said all right. I thought everything was go, but that was the last I heard about it. When I talked to Tex in training camp, it was the same story all over again—no renegotiation.

"Anyway, Svare offered me fifty, and started telling me that's what Mackey and Deacon and Aldridge and all those guys made, all the black former stars, like they were all on the same agenda. I told him that the buying power of $50,000 in San Diego was a lot lower than in Dallas, plus I needed relocation and moving expenses.

"He said he wanted me to return punts and kickoffs, as well as play running back. I said, 'Okay, that's two more positions I'm playing, so pay me an extra $20,000 for each position.' He said, 'We can't do that.'

"I said, 'Okay, pay me $65,000 and give me 300 tickets to every home game.'

"He said, 'Oh, no, we can't do that.'

"I said, 'What's the difference? You're not selling out anyway,' At that point we broke off the talks and I went back to Dallas."

But only after holding one press conference with San Diego and Los Angeles writers who had gathered outside Svare's office when word reached them that Thomas was in town. Charles Maher of the L.A. *Times* covered the press conference and reported the following conversation:

Writer:	Do you have any animosity toward us?
Thomas:	Let's not get off into animosity.
Writer:	Is your weight up or down? What is it?
Thomas:	I weigh about 250. Sometimes I weigh 500.
Writer:	What causes this fluctuation?
Thomas:	When I get a reaction.
Writer:	What kind?
Thomas:	It's something you feel. Say right now I can be looking at you and I feel like jumping over there on you.

Writer: I might be thinking the same thing.
Thomas: Well, jump.
Writer: I'll give you the first jump.
Thomas: Sometimes the first jump is the last one.

And on and on in the same vein. Looking over the transcript sixteen years later, it doesn't make comfortable reading. It seems as if the West Coast media was goading him, trying to get a reaction, so they could have a neat little off-day feature. Look what that crazy guy said yesterday, folks. It has the sick look of someone poking an animal with a stick.

So Thomas went back home. The exhibition season had started. Would he be fined for missing camp? No one really knew, and the club wasn't saying. Technically he was still under contract. Two other players, Walt Sweeney and Pete Barnes, had been fined $1,000 for reporting late.

Svare told the press he had permitted him to leave, "to clear up personal problems."

Duane was seen at the Chargers' office on August 17. He met with Svare again. He showed up at the practice field, went to the training room, and asked for a pair of sneakers, not football shoes. The equipment man ran to get a pair. When he returned, Thomas was gone.

He was seen in Dallas; he was seen on the West Coast. The *San Diego Tribune*'s Rick Smith reported that he was seen near the University of California at Irvine campus, "wearing a sombrero." On August 28 the club announced that Thomas was suspended and would be fined $150 a day. Writers called Thomas's probation officer, Bill Haddock of Greenville. He wouldn't offer any information other than: "He is not in violation of his probation and is in good standing with this office."

George Powell, the former West Texas State business school instructor who'd been close with Thomas back in college, had bought a house on the beach in Del Mar, north of San Diego.

"One morning, early, Duane showed up at my door," he says. "He was wearing a business suit. He was unshaven . . . he looked so strange. He said he was staying with his cousin in L.A. and he was driving back in a rental car and it broke down near Oceanside. He said he'd spent the night hitchhiking. He wanted me to drive him up to where his car was so he could call Hertz.

"Well, we drove up, and we looked in the ditch he said his car had gone into, and it wasn't there. We went into a restaurant to have lunch. He got up and went to the bathroom. Ten minutes went by and he didn't come back. I looked for him.

"He was out on the road hitchhiking. He'd completely forgotten about me. I picked him up. 'Duane, where do you want to go?' I said. 'Downtown,' he said. So we drove downtown. At a stoplight he got out and walked away."

Powell said Thomas would drop in from time to time. Once he stayed with him for two days.

"We'd take walks on the beach," Powell says. "He'd be totally silent. My little girls adored Duane. He'd given my oldest daughter his Rookie of the Year award when she was eleven or twelve. At West Texas he and Rocky Thompson would come over and take my youngest daughter out horseback riding.

"But at dinner at our house in '72 . . . well, right in the middle of conversation he'd become totally silent. He wouldn't even talk to the girls. You could talk to him and he wouldn't acknowledge it. Then an hour later he'd be normal. The girls were scared that something might be wrong with him, that he was, maybe, sick.

"The idea of drugs never entered my mind. He looked good. He was on a vegetarian diet. His weight was down to about 205. I'd had parties in my house where alcohol was served. He'd never drink it. He wouldn't even have a beer after we'd been out jogging. It was always soda pop. He was so attuned to keeping his body in shape."

The Chargers flew to Miami for a game with the Dolphins on October 15. Thomas showed up for a workout in Fort Lauderdale. Svare announced he'd be activated. Then Thomas walked out.

"I don't think he'll ever play for the Chargers," the coach said.

Abner Haynes, the former Chiefs' star who'd graduated from the same South Dallas high school as Thomas, Lincoln, was Thomas's agent in Dallas. Duane asked Powell to handle his dealings with the Chargers. He did it—on an unpaid basis.

"Locating Duane was a problem," he says. "I talked to Svare a few times. We felt the money could be worked out, but Duane wouldn't sign. He wouldn't show up. I'd go to the airport to meet him and he wouldn't be there. I even called Rocky Thompson. He couldn't get through to him, either."

Finally Gene Klein stepped into the picture. He managed to get Thomas out to his home in Palm Springs for a private meeting.

"I was the official gofer, responsible for getting Duane from point A to point B," Bobby Hood says. "Airport to the office, office to the hotel, whatever. I'd ask him where he wanted to go and he'd just mumble. I had to guess.

"The night that Gene Klein sent for him I picked Duane up in San Diego. There was no flight from San Diego to Palm Springs. I had to charter a plane. I put him in the back. I didn't want him anywhere near the controls. Writers were bird-dogging us, I was trying to lose them. I felt like the CIA.

"On the plane Duane said to me, 'Hood, what do you think about me playing for $50,000?'

"I said, 'Frankly, Duane, you should be happy. If you're not happy, don't take it. Don't make everybody else miserable.'

"He looked at me and said, 'Okay.' That's all he said."

Klein remembers the meeting as "one of the most bizarre things I ever went through. A strange guy—with enormous talent. Svare had called me and said, 'I've had the goddamnedest two-hour meeting with Duane Thomas.'

"I asked him, 'What did he say?'

"He said, 'Nothing. He just stared at me the whole time.'

"Well, I took Duane to my house. I sat and talked. I told him we wanted him, we needed him, he was a great running back, he could help the club. We'd do everything we could to make him comfortable in San Diego.

"He just stared at me. I mean it was eerie. After two hours I said, 'You want to go back?' and he nodded his head. I've had some interesting ballplayers—Rossovich, a certifiable character. Setting his hair on fire, eating light bulbs, but he wasn't like this guy.

"I've negotiated a great deal of my life. I've been in very difficult situations, but never anything like this. Harland told me that's what would happen, but I figured maybe I could do something. At least I'd try to make a deal."

I asked Klein if Thomas had ever gotten money from the Chargers.

"To my memory there was never any contract," he said. "He didn't get paid, except for the few days he was in training camp in '72 and '73."

Thomas remembers his meeting with Klein as completely different. He said a deal of sorts was struck, and although the contract figures were not finalized, Klein agreed to give him $25,000 for moving and relocation expenses.

"He had his secretary write me a personal check," he says.

The story checks out because on December 20, 1973, the Chargers sued Thomas for $12,264, claiming he borrowed it between October 27, 1972, and July 25, 1973, as an advance against his salary. They had traded him to Washington on July 19, 1973. Why they would lend him additional money after he was gone is a mystery. And whether Klein let the rest of the $25,000 slide is also unclear. He said he never gave Thomas anything, but obviously he did. The Chargers had part of Thomas's Redskins' salary garnished in 1973.

Klein's version of the meeting in Palm Springs . . . the icy stare, the lack of communication . . . well, it's a nice story, but that's not the way Thomas tells it.

"A limo picked us up at the Palm Springs airport and drove us to Klein's house," he says. "We talked the first night and he put me up . . . I stayed over . . . then we talked the following day. I met his wife. We talked about African art and the artifacts in their home.

"We went back to Klein's office. Every day he had a catered lunch there, enough food to feed a family of fifty. That's when we got into the serious money part. Klein offered $50,000 on top of the $25,000 moving and relocating expenses. I wanted $85,000. And that's where we left it—after he gave me the check for $25,000.

"Dallas was coming to town. I knew he wanted me in uniform for that game—to help sell tickets. I'd told him I'd suit up, even though I hadn't signed a contract, but I wouldn't play. He said okay."

Thomas reported for practice and was immediately activated for the game, without explanation.

The lasting memory of Thomas's 11½-month odyssey in San Diego is the series of pictures that came out of that November 5 game against the Cowboys. Thomas, bent at the waist, staring at the ground during the team warm-ups, a position he held for perhaps twenty minutes . . . Thomas alone on the bench during the national anthem . . . everything encapsulated; misery, defiance, despair, loneliness, sickness.

"He came out separately," Cowboy quarterback Craig Morton recalls. "I'll never forget the national anthem. It was a weird thing. We're all looking at him out of the corner of our eyes. His team was completely apart from him."

"We go out to warm up," says Calvin Hill, who was in uniform for the Cowboys that night. "Everyone's stretching. Someone says, 'Hey, check out Duane.' He's assumed a yoga position and he held it for twenty minutes or so. Hadl or someone's trying to throw passes, and there's Duane in the middle of it.

"Finally he moves and the crowd goes bananas. Midway during the 'Star-Spangled Banner' he walks away and sits down and assumes a position on the bench. It was distracting to us. It broke our concentration before the game.

"In the second quarter I'm drinking Gatorade. Everyone on our sidelines starts yelling, 'Hey, Duane's leaving!' He got up and walked into the locker room. Then in the third quarter he came back out."

Thomas's memories of that day are surprisingly casual, as if it were no big deal at all.

"I remember it was a nice, clear day, like this one here," he said, pointing to the sunlight streaming in. "I wasn't doing anything. I was just out there on the field. I wasn't part of the team yet.

"Some of the Cowboy players yelled, 'Hey, Duane, c'mon over here! I waved. I didn't feel I was part of them, either. I wasn't, you know, part of the game."

He thought for a moment.

"I won't deny the fact that I was in need of some kind of help," he said. "The club suggested psychiatric counseling. I wasn't going to do anything they were going to put me in, because I didn't trust them. I didn't trust anybody.

"I was being tough and wild, I admit, but it was the system that had created the monster. It was the worst period of my life. I was floating, drained, with nothing to lean on."

On Wednesday, fortified by his new five-year contract, Svare reserved Thomas for the season. He was through for 1972. He went back to Dallas and moved in with his wife, Imani Pamoja, the former Elizabeth Thomas, and their two children. Except for brief visits during their off-again, on-again relationship, it was the first time they'd really lived together—after eight years of marriage.

"Duane would be moody and sullen one day, fine the next," Imani Pamoja says. "Most of the time he seemed okay. He would take the kids places, to the park, to the zoo. Of course at that time the press was trying to make him a villain.

"There would always be reporters coming around. They'd try to interview me, my mother, people in the neighborhood."

"We'd go on camping trips," Thomas says. "We had a schedule of things to do every day. While the kids were in school I'd work on the yard a lot. We had the best-looking yard in South Dallas.

"I heard he was having psychological problems," Rabbit Thomas says, "so I went to see him one day. His wife greeted me. Duane was working out in back. When he came in, we talked about this and that, I can't even remember what. I lit up a cigarette. He said, 'Coach, I'd appreciate it if you didn't smoke in my house.'

"I respected that. I've got rules in my house, too. But I didn't think he was crazy."

"I never watched any football," Duane Thomas says, "never watched the Cowboys on TV. I think I saw one of their playoff games, but my mind wasn't on it.

"I'd work out every day. There was a park across the street. I always tried to live near a place to work out, always a park. In the morning I'd run between ten and fifteen miles, on farm roads mostly.

"At first I used to change my road route every day, plus I'd start at different times. I was security conscious. This was guerrilla warfare. People would drive by and honk their horns. Some would stop, expecting me to stop and talk. Then they'd catch up to me and drive alongside. I'd slow down to half speed. They'd ask me if I was coming back. They'd say, 'We really miss you.'

"Early in the morning was the best time for running, for being alone with my thoughts. I'd have all sorts of thoughts while I was running, sometimes spiritual thoughts . . . let God take care of it . . . sometimes violent ones . . . I'm going to hire a hit man to knock off Gil Brandt . . . I'm going to blow up Dallas. They'd bother me, then I'd think, 'I'm a soldier and soldiers have thoughts like that.' Then I'd think, 'God knows that in my heart I wanted to be a good, loving husband and father, a good citizen,' but it was hard.

"Then I'd bring it into the park and stretch out and sprint, then go home and wash my clothes. In the evening I'd do speed work, 100s, 220s, 330s, stamina-building things, then I'd do some roadwork and warm down. I kept some weights in the house. I'd do high reps with light weights. Then I'd do sit-ups and push-ups.

"Sometimes I'd ask myself why. I figured, I'm running for health. In the back of my mind I thought that maybe a team would call, one of the West Coast teams, but no one ever did. As the '73 season started nearing, I felt I wanted to get back into it, give it another shot."

Early in July Thomas was in the Chargers' office for four straight days, talking contract and working out. The team assigned Dr. Mandell, who would later be implicated in the league's drug action against the Chargers, the job of bringing him around.

"He came over to my hotel after I'd been out there for a while," Thomas says. "I still hadn't agreed on a contract. He tried to come through the door without my letting him in. His brother was with him. I said, 'Both of you get out.'

"Every time I was around there I felt the eyes of Mandell on me. One day he came up to me and said he thought I ought to go into some kind of communal group program for disturbed people. I said, 'Just give me a salary and a house and I'll be fine.'

"I used to run three miles from the hotel to practice. One morning Deacon Jones caught up to me in his car. He said, 'You want a ride?' I said, 'No, I'm staying in shape.' He said, 'You sure you don't want a ride?' I figured it meant something to him, so I got in.

"He started telling me, 'Everything's going to be all right, it's gonna be worked out.' I listened to him. I figured, 'Another club plant.'

"One time when I was negotiating with Svare he brought Rosey Grier into the picture. Rosey said, 'The most I ever made was $14,000.' I hit the ceiling. I said, 'Brother, if that's the most you've ever made, it's all the more reason to get even with these sons of bitches.' "

"I remember we were working out at UC Irvine," says Dan Fouts, who was a rookie in 1973, "and Duane showed up with these two guys . . . they were both in these black leather jackets . . . it must have been ninety degrees that day.

"Duane says to Johnny U, 'Would you throw them a couple of pass patterns?'

"I'm thinking, 'Better throw, John, they might have guns.' I was just trying to stay out of the way. Rookies were losses in those days."

On July 10, Ron Mix, the Chargers' executive counsel, said he and Thomas's agent, Abner Haynes, had reached agreement and Thomas would be in camp with the vets on the official reporting day, Sunday, July 15. Thomas failed to show. He came in at eleven-thirty A.M. on Monday, after the morning workout, and was suspended by Svare.

"Nobody can come wandering into my camp anytime he wants," Svare said, adding that he gave Thomas a plane ticket back to Dallas.

"He seems to think he is bigger than the club," Deacon Jones said.

On Wednesday, July 18, Svare reinstated Thomas. He had practiced with the team and had what the coach called "a good workout." He said Thomas had called him and asked to come back.

On Thursday, Svare termed Thomas's practice "lackluster." That night Thomas was traded to George Allen's Washington Redskins.

"I'd told Harland," Gene Klein says, " 'Tell him you want two first-round draft choices. If he offers you a first and a second, don't hang up.' "

"I have no remorse at all about giving up the NFL's greatest runner since Jim Brown" was Svare's announcement to the press. "Maybe someone else can solve a problem I can't."

"I took him to the airport and got him the ticket," Bobby Hood says. "I said, 'Duane, where do you want to go?'

"He said, 'Duzzz.' I told him I didn't know what he was saying.

"He said, 'Duzzz.' I said, 'Ah, the hell with it.' I asked the girl at the counter, 'Do you have a flight that goes to both Dallas and Dulles in Washington?' She said they did. I said fine.

"I gave Duane the ticket. I told him, 'Duane, here's your ticket. You can get off in Dallas or Dulles or whichever.'

"I think he must have gotten off in Dallas because the Redskins started calling . . . 'Where the hell is he?'

"I said, 'He's either in Dallas or Dulles, but you've got to find him now.' "

Thomas says the first day he met with George Allen he signed his contract—$65,000 in salary, plus a $20,000 signing bonus, plus a $5,000 incentive bonus for playing time, which he hit, and another one for yardage, which he missed. A number one and a number two draft seemed like a lot to give for a player who had missed a whole season, but Allen was obsessed with the idea of beating the Cowboys, and what better weapon to beat them with than a former Cowboy star?

"George seemed happy to get me," Thomas says. "He told the press 'Now we can beat Dallas.' I talked to the writers. I could feel things gradually lifting from my shoulders.

"George was my type of guy. We'd eat in a restaurant in L.A., his cousin owned it. We stayed in a hotel, he had a piece of it. The people in Carlisle, Pennsylvania, where we trained, were complaining about us using the parking lot. George went and bought the lot.

"He said, 'Men, it's okay to park there now.' "

It would be nice to report that Thomas had a great year for George Allen's Redskins, that he was back to his old self and the yardage came in chunks. Such was not the case. The Redskins' backfield was set. Halfback Larry Brown was coming off four straight Pro Bowl years. Charley Harraway, the fullback, was a crushing blocker. The combination had been good enough to get the Skins into the Super Bowl the previous season, and Allen wasn't about to be breaking it up.

But Brown, a ferocious little back who seemed to run in a constant rage, had been taking some terrible hits. "He plays too tough for his body" was the way the scouts put it. It would only be a matter of time for him. Thomas was Allen's insurance policy, although he didn't know it at the time.

He worked hard in the two-a-days at Carlisle. He spent time by himself hitting the linemen's eleven-man blocking sled, twenty reps with the left shoulder, twenty with the right, five sets of each. The Redskin players, sweating under the hot sun, thought he was nuts.

Statistically the Skins had the second-worst running game in the league that season. On the average, 3.1 yards per carry, they ranked last. Thomas had the satisfaction of gaining the most yards of any Washington ball carrier when the Skins beat San Diego, 38–0, in the opener, a modest 30, but that would be his most productive afternoon of the season. He finished the year with 95 yards on 32 carries.

"I thought I did okay," he said, "considering the time I'd been away from football."

Actually his best game had come in a Friday night exhibition in Buffalo, but the thing that got him the national headlines was his going into the stands after a heckler.

"The only time in my life I've ever seen a player climb up into the stands and go after a fan," Redskin guard John Wilbur said.

"A guy threw a Coke bottle at my helmet," Thomas says. "I told Tommy McVean, the trainer, and he said, 'Duane, Duane, don't turn around . . . I'm gonna show you who it is.'

"He pointed him out. Everyone else moved away. It exposed him naked. Some papers say I threw a thermos at him. It wasn't a thermos, it was my helmet. What the hell would I have been doing with a thermos on the sideline? It wasn't a construction site or something. I just took my helmet off and slung it. It didn't hit him, but it shattered right by the guy. I mean I threw it with everything I had. Then I went over the wall, after him. Big Dave Robinson came and grabbed me around my ankles and pulled me back down . . . 'Duane, don't do that' . . . I never made it in.

"Buffalo was mad. They were losing anyway, and I ran a mile on 'em. George Allen told me, 'Just walk off.' All you heard out of the stands was 'Boo! Boo! Booooo!' Screw all you sons of bitches. I'll kick all your asses.

"Back in the locker room after the game everyone was saying, 'All right, don't worry about it.' George said, 'Duane deserves the game ball, especially after all that harassment.' I told him, 'I don't need the game ball, I need that guy.'

"George said the following week, 'You don't have to worry about it. We'll have extra security at every game to protect you.' So after that we had extra security.

"The funny thing is that a week after the incident I saw that guy's picture on the wall in the Redskins' office. I asked George about it and he said, 'It's just a fan.' I wonder."

Actually Thomas did get the game ball for his night's work, which included 16 carries for 70 yards and a TD, plus 3 passes caught for

42 yards. The rest of the season, though, was a blur. He never started a game.

"He'd come and talk to me during the warm-ups before the game," said St. Louis wideout Ahmad Rashad, who had changed his name from Bobby Moore that season. "I think he was fascinated with me because I'd changed my name. Once he came down to our locker room afterward and we kicked it around for a while. I was hoping he'd play well, I really was, but it seems, I don't know, it seems that he just wasn't with it.

"He seemed to be kind of a confused individual. Usually sports is an escape, and when you get on the field, you forget your personal confusion, but he looked just as confused on the field."

Thomas played unsigned in 1974. His salary was $58,500—his 1973 salary of $65,000 minus ten percent for playing out his option. It was a strange kind of year. When Larry Brown was hurt, Thomas would play, occasionally putting decent numbers on the board—96 yards on 26 carries against St. Louis, 65 on 20 against the Eagles. Then Brown would return and he'd go back on the bench.

"I went along with the program," he says. His weight was down close to 200 pounds. He still had the moves and the speed, but somehow the explosion wasn't there.

His wife and two children were still back in Dallas, but she would make frequent trips north to see him.

"We went out looking for apartments a few times," she says. "He seemed to be getting things straightened out. These were our best years together."

Toward the end of the season Brown was limping on a sprained knee and a sore leg. He missed the Philadelphia game, and Thomas was the leading ball carrier in the 26–7 Redskin win. The following Thursday the Skins were going to Dallas for the Thanksgiving Day special. Washington was fighting St. Louis for the division lead. The Cowboys were going nowhere. Thomas would start for the Redskins.

"George had this ritual," Thomas says, "of having a different guy make a speech each week on how to beat the particular team we were playing. He had so many players who'd been on different teams around the league that he could usually find one for every opponent. I was chosen to make the speech for the Dallas game.

"I got up and said, 'The way to beat Dallas is the way to beat anybody. Just get out and flat kick their ass.' Everybody booed. They were expecting something real scientific.

"I enjoyed the game. Charlie Waters yelled, 'Hey, Duane,' as soon as I came on the field. Roger, Rayfield, Jethro Pugh, they all came up to me. I remember Cornell Green said something.

"The game was all defense for a while. On one play, a flare pass to me, I saw Lee Roy Jordan coming up, ninety miles an hour. I saw him out of the corner of my eye, and I saw he had position on me, so I let the pass go. It would have lost yards anyway. He was coming for my head. I ducked.

"In the third quarter we're leading 9–3 and we have the ball on their 9-yard line. In the huddle Charley Taylor said, 'I'll get open, I'll get open.' I said, 'Run the short post.' I knew they'd bite. My route was a sideline and up. We'd run a pick on them.

"Charlie Waters went for the quick post. The ball was still in the air and I heard him yell, 'Jeez!' I caught the pass and scored the TD. Everyone got quiet in Texas Stadium.

"They're leading by a point in the fourth quarter and we have the ball on their 19. I run the three-hole. Ed Jones is sitting right there, Cornell Green is flying in for the force. I backed out and took it around the end. I saw that Cornell couldn't recover. Good-bye. Roy Jefferson ran all the way across the field to meet me in the end zone.

"He was yelling, 'You're bad! You're bad!' "

Thomas scored two touchdowns in the game and was the leading Redskins' ball carrier, but no one will ever remember it, because that was the game in which rookie Clint Longley threw the 50-yard Hail Mary to Drew Pearson that won it for the Cowboys with 28 seconds left.

"George Allen had the best secondary in the league," Thomas says, "but he put in Ken Stone as his nickel back. Ken Stone couldn't cover anybody. Drew ran a post-fly on him and turned him 360 degrees. Stone didn't know what happened. The rest is history."

The following Sunday the Redskins played the Rams in L.A. The midweek speaker was Deacon Jones, who'd been with Thomas in San Diego but had had his all-pro years with the Rams.

"After telling me how great San Diego is," Thomas says, "here's Deke, a Redskin, same as me. He made this speech and talked for about two minutes, and I remember his last words: 'Follow me and I'll take you there.' Everyone cheered.

"Larry's back in at halfback for us, and Brian Salter and I are watching the game from the sidelines. We're watching Deke against big No. 75, their right tackle, John Williams. Deke tries a head slap and No. 75 knocks his hand down. Then he knocks the other hand down. Then he floors Deke.

"We had this thing where if a player raises his hand that means he wants a substitution. Deke raised his hand. I ran out to meet him.

"Deke, baby, we can't follow you like that."

The final game was against Chicago at home. On Monday, Allen told Thomas that Brown was really hurting and Duane would be starting.

"We're coming out of the tunnel and I'm standing in line waiting for the introductions," Thomas says, "and George taps me on the shoulder and says, 'Look, Larry's gonna start, is that all right?' I said, 'Fine.' I was upset but I didn't say anything.

"At halftime Larry's practically out on his feet. He started the third quarter. George came over to me and said, 'Be ready. Anything might happen.' I came in the third quarter and rushed for 102 yards, the only back to go over 100 that year."

Thomas's stats were 102 yards in eight carries. It was the last time he would carry the ball in the National Football League. It ended his season at 347 yards on 95 carries—and six TDs. The Redskins were high on a rookie halfback, Mike Thomas, in 1975. Duane said the team asked him to take a fifteen percent cut in pay. He could see the handwriting on the wall. Calvin Hill had jumped to Hawaii of the World Football League—and then hurt a knee.

"I called Duane from a hospital bed," Hill says. "I told him he could get $5,000 a game down there. He said he'd think about it."

Thomas flew down and signed a contract with the Hawaiians on August 23, 1975. Wallace Fujiama, the owner, gave him $25,000 to sign and $5,000 a game. In his second week there he pulled a muscle. He had never missed a game because of injury since his sophomore year in college. In all, he played five games for the Hawaiians, carried the ball 34 times, and gained 92 yards.

"He'd go to practice, get his treatment, and wouldn't stick around," Hill says. "George Najarian, the general manager, said, 'I don't know about Duane. I thought I was getting a great player who wouldn't talk. Now he talks a lot but doesn't play.'

"I told him, 'Wait till he's well, you'll see,' but I really didn't feel he was the same player. Part of his demise, I think, came when he lost all that weight. At 220 he was a slasher who could run with power and pick a side, never give you a whole shot at him. He became a finesse runner. He changed. I think he lost a little speed, too, when he lost his edge. He was always a smooth but explosive runner. He lost that explosion."

"When he came to practice, he'd already had a full day's workout under his belt," said the Hawaiians' coach, Mike Giddings, who later became an NFL scouting consultant.

"He'd have run eight miles. Maybe he realized he'd lost his burst, so he became a long distance runner type. He had moves and he could catch a pass, but he'd lost his power burst. He weighed less than 200 pounds, too."

"No drugs, I can guarantee that," says John Wilbur, who'd been Thomas's teammate on the Redskins and was a guard and line coach for the Hawaiians. "I saw him every day. I would have known.

"He was clean, but he never did anything for us on the field. He was into his heavy vegetarian phase, plus he'd lost all that weight.

"I had no problems with him at practice, he just couldn't play. He'd play at a jog, he'd put it on cruise control. He wasn't exploding, he was loping, like he'd lost his fast-twitch muscles."

"The hamstring never really felt right," Thomas says. "One of my legs is longer than the other, and I had to go to a chiropractor constantly. The contact in football knocks your joints out of place. It's like driving a car over big holes. You have to constantly realign it. I needed a masseur, too, to actually work out all the kinks."

Hill and Thomas would tour the island together, an odd couple, Hill on crutches, Thomas in a business suit.

"That's all he wore," Hill says, "and you know how the people dress on the islands. He'd take his treatment at practice and Mike would say, 'Where are you guys going now?' and Duane would say, 'Calvin's gonna show me around the island. We're gonna do some goodwill.'

"Duane was really fond of Hawaii, and the people loved him. He was fascinated by them. We'd be driving and he'd say, 'Hey, let's stop,' and we'd get out and talk to some fisherman about what he did. It was a real cultural exchange. He felt a kinship with a lot of those people.

"He did some funny things, too. When the Shreveport Steamer came down to play us, Duane developed a friendship with Warren Capone, one of their linebackers. They hung around together early in the week. On Friday a few hours before the game Capone brought some friends over to meet Duane. Duane said, 'I don't know you.'

"In the warm-ups Duane's pointing to Capone and he's looking at Duane like he's ready to kill him. By kickoff he's really steaming. Then Duane sits out the game with the pulled hamstring. Poor Capone was really deflated. That was the old side of Duane coming out . . . doing things to see how people would react. It was almost like he was watching a show."

"During the week it was fun," Thomas says. "On game day it was business."

The WFL folded before the season was over. Thomas went back to Dallas. He worked out at SMU. One day Pettis Norman, his old Cowboy teammate, said, "Why don't you try Dallas again?"

Norman met with Schramm. He arranged for Thomas to come in and meet with him individually.

"I felt strange," Thomas says. "I had mixed emotions. They were very reserved. They said they'd give it a try. That's when the prodigal son came back."

He was a different Duane Thomas. He submitted to interviews. He was humble—also twenty-nine years old. And he needed money. The Cowboys signed him on April 30, 1976, and cut him during the exhibition season. Tom Landry said his legs were gone.

"We were all pulling for him to make it," Roger Staubach says. "Tom, too. They needed running backs. The strangest thing is that Duane didn't look any different, except lighter. He was in good shape, he just wasn't the same Duane."

"In the preseason opener, each time I'd make a move the crowd would cheer," Thomas says. "I don't know what it was . . . I felt I was in shape . . . the blocking wasn't really that good at the point of attack . . . I don't know.

"Gil Brandt came and told me I was cut. He said, 'Sorry it didn't work out,' and gave me my release.

"I thought, 'That's it. It's over. No more camps.' "

20

LIFE AFTER
FOOTBALL

J&J Numismatics, Inc.
P.O. Box 55254
Riverside, Cal. 92517

July 23, 1987

Dear Sir:

I have just been informed that you are currently writing a
book with Duane Thomas. I purchased his Super Bowl ring
in 1978, and I currently have it for sale. If Mr. Thomas
would like to repurchase it, it is available at $12,500. This
offer is open to him for the next 45 days. If there is any
interest in the above, you may write to me at the above
address or call 714-788-9522.

Sincerely,
Joseph Diehl

I called Duane Thomas in Los Angeles as soon as I got the letter. He took down the address and phone number.

"Are you going to buy it back?" I asked him.

"I might," he said. "It's a lot of money. I'll have to think about it."

I lost a few hours sleep that night thinking about Duane Thomas and his Super Bowl ring. Well, of course he should have it back. My God, yes. It represents the peak of his athletic brilliance. But then again, what did it really represent? Hypocrisy. He should have been named MVP of the game but wasn't, for promotional reasons. Misery. It came during a sad, depressing period of his life, his bitter period, before the disjointed meanderings of his San Diego days. But still—it was his ring and he earned it and he should have it.

Next time I was in his home in Los Angeles I asked him about the ring.

"Yes, I think I'm going to try to buy it back," he said. "I'm saving up. I guess you want to know when and why I sold it." I nodded.

"I pawned it in 1977 at a jewelry and coin shop on Josie Lane and Beltline in Dallas," he said.

"I had gone to W. O. Bankston, the Lincoln Mercury dealer . . . at one time he was going to buy the Cowboys . . . to try to get a job in sales or advertising or something. It took him two months to make a decision that based on what the job paid, it wouldn't be enough for me to live on. I would have taken anything. I had five people to feed.

"I asked him if he wanted to buy my ring. He said he had no interest. I asked him for a loan; I said I'd put the ring up. No interest. You know what came to my mind? Ali, after he won the Olympic gold medal. From his perspective it had no value, based on what he'd expected to gain from winning it. I thought about it. The only value the ring had at that point was whatever I could sell it for.

"The Bankston people were pretty diplomatic. The guy told me, 'The job only pays $20,000. You can't live on that.' I said, 'Look, I'm living on zero now. How can you tell me what I can or can't live on?'

"He said, 'I've got nothing to do with it, Duane.' I said, 'Yes, you do.' He said, 'I'll get back to you.'

"Then this little voice said to me, 'Hey, brother, it's getting close to the end of the month . . . hey, brother, take the ring . . . do what you have to do.'

"Wait a minute, let's talk about it . . .

" 'Hey, brother, you know what you have to do . . . do it.'

"So I sold it. I got $5,000 for it. That's what I asked for. I called the guy and asked him if he had any interest. He was kind of surprised.

He said, 'Yeah, bring it in.' It was just a straight business deal. He did say, 'Are you sure this is what you want to do?' I told him yes.

"I went out and bought some groceries. I was dead broke. There was a big story in the papers about it. He must have called them for the publicity. Yeah, I guess it was sad.

"The ring represents more pride than anything. But in the back of my head something always said I'd go back and get it. I kind of felt it would turn up. Something told me, don't worry about it. But I was kind of hoping I'd hold on to it for a while.

"I realized how hard it would be for me to make a decent living in Dallas. The city was telling me their policy was hands off. So I decided to let go of everything and come out to L.A. and make a new start."

After the Cowboys cut him in 1976, Thomas tried sales, advertising, radio stations, selling pharmaceuticals from his car . . . Cowboy players remember buying stuff from him, "to help him out." He even sold Cowboy novelties for a while.

He went to Los Angeles in 1977 and applied for work through a black business community agency. Within three weeks he'd landed a job for 20th Century-Fox, "legal affairs, accounting, microfilm work, general office work," he says. He stayed there for two years.

"I started baking pies on the side," he says. "Cooking was always a hobby. People in the office who tasted my pies said I should be selling them. So I did. I baked over six hundred pies for the Thanksgiving and Christmas holidays and sold them all. I made all of them at my cousin Wenefrett's house, thirty, forty pies a day. I'd be up all night cooking. I sold them for six to eight dollars apiece. Sweet potato, lemon meringue, apple, and pecan—those were my biggest sellers."

"He spent Christmas of 1977 with my family," Thomas's old friend from West Texas State and San Diego days, George Powell, says. "We were living in the L.A. area then. My wife's parents were elderly. They followed football. They knew of him, the stories I'd told them about how strange he was in San Diego.

"They were scared to death when he came over, but he was great. He baked a pumpkin pie for us. He felt it was up to him to make sure they felt comfortable. He was totally back to normal."

Thomas was still working out, keeping to a training regime. He'd run his miles in the park across from 20th Century at six A.M., take a shower on the studio lot, and go to work. The people in his office were impressed, especially the ones who followed football seriously. As there is in every office, there was a hard core of football followers. They'd keep track of the NFL injury lists, the waiver transactions. One day in 1978 they brought Thomas a list of teams that might need running backs, heading into training camp. They had drafted a letter to every NFL coach and general manager, suggesting that he be given a tryout. They asked him what he thought.

"Send it out," he said. "Might as well."

Green Bay showed interest. They flew him up. He worked out for them and pulled a muscle. Apologies all around. Try us again next year.

In 1979 he was back. The Packers stashed him in a hotel for two days without signing him to a contract, a no-no under NFL rules. Bart Starr, the coach and general manager, was a fair-haired boy in league circles, one of the newer members of its prestigious Competition Committee. The league looked the other way. If it had been the Raiders, they'd have lost a draft choice. Thomas worked out for two days and was released.

"I knew it was over for good now," he says. "I just didn't want to leave any crumbs on the table."

Thomas took a leave of absence from 20th Century and went back to Dallas. He called Tex Schramm in the Cowboys' office. Schramm asked him what he had in mind. Thomas said he was just looking around.

"You want to be in a movie?" Schramm said. Thomas said yes.

They were about to begin filming *Cowboys Cheerleaders II*. Thomas landed the role of Tim, a boyfriend of one of the cheerleaders. "An aspiring young business guy," Thomas says. "A Bernie Casey kind of guy." Thomas was paid $20,000.

The whole thing represented a double irony. He had returned to the city that had turned its back on him, and he had asked for help from a man he'd once regarded as his bitterest enemy. It's an incongruity, a puzzler.

"This is hard to explain," he says, "but I still regarded it as my club, my family. You can fight but it's still your family. Football does that to you. Maybe I felt I earned some of it. I helped win them their first championship. Maybe they felt they owed me something, too. Maybe it was Tex's way of clearing his conscience. It's funny, though, wherever I applied for a job, they'd always call and check with Tex. It was a form of bondage in a way. But I'll say one thing for Tex—he always returned my phone calls."

Calvin Hill ran into Thomas during this period. He found out one thing. Duane hadn't given up on his obsessive training routine.

"The Players Association had a contract with the Labor Department to send athletes down to Job Corps sites to conduct clinics," Hill says. "They were paying $400 a day. I called Duane to see if he was interested. He was. We went to this abandoned air force base in San Marcos, outside Austin.

"After the second session we decided to go out jogging. Myself, Brig Owens, and Jerry Smith of the Redskins, Tommy Nunez, a lot of women athletes, Duane, Rod Milburn, who'd won the Olympic high hurdles in Munich, and Gerald Irons of the Raiders. Milburn was wearing all the latest track gear, and he did these fancy warm-up exercises. Gerald was with me. He was a fitness freak, a good friend of mine.

"I said, 'Gerald, don't run with Duane. Do like I'm doing. Run with the girls.' He said, 'No, I'm running with the leaders.'

"For the first quarter mile we're all together. Then Duane takes the pace. Gerald and Milburn take off after him. We're running on a service road beside the interstate. I could see a mile or so down the road. They were supposed to run to the interchange, then stop. Duane keeps running. First Milburn stops, then Gerald. He's throwing up by the side of the road.

"Duane got to a spot and did his stretches and calisthenics. Finally we all caught up to him. Everyone was in a state of collapse. We're running in that Texas heat, don't forget. Then Duane turns around and runs back and everybody watches him go.

"I really think it's a mind-set with him. He becomes myopic and concentrates and he can do it. He decides he can run a certain distance and not be beaten, and he can't be. Maybe it's his heart rate or something, but he doesn't seem to feel fatigue.

"He used to get in a whirlpool for thirty minutes, and I mean it was scalding. I'd go in for five minutes and almost die."

From 1980 to 1981 Thomas went through what he calls his Nigerian period. He met with Russell Foster, who was prominent in the black business community in Dallas. They talked about the great opportunities for establishing marketing outlets in Nigeria, how it was virgin territory. Thomas says they got $50,000 seed money from the Popeye's Chicken franchises to get a presentation ready for the trade fair in Kaduna in February 1980.

They made a couple of trips, established contacts, traveled deserted roads at midnight despite warnings about hijackers. They found out that the only way to be successful was to run a complete operation, the refrigeration, the food processing, everything. Other companies got interested. A printing company sent a man down to share their booth at the fair. Popeye's sent a representative.

"Our presentation at the fair was a success," Thomas says. "We represented twelve different products at our booth. Food storage, ice factories, a computerized printing press, Popeye's Chicken. I thought Popeye's couldn't miss there, because their chicken was spicy, the way the people in Nigeria liked it. Also they like it hard because their local chicken is tough. They don't like the meat soft. Kentucky Fried went under down there because of that.

"We were ready to go. We told Popeye's we had to have a complete operation, a chicken farm down there and everything. They weren't so sure. They just wanted to send down equipment. It's the American business mentality of going in only where a market exists, rather than creating a market.

"Popeye's was worried about the unstable nature of the government. We were making trips on our own. The seed money had run out. Each trip cost us $12,000.

"Well, the whole thing ended when they had a government coup and everyone had to get out. I left in March 1981. Russell stayed until June and just made it back. He ran out of quinine, got malaria. And I was flat broke."

In the mid-1980s Thomas was invited to join the HBO program— Hyperbaric Oxygen Therapy Appliances. The concept was fine—oxygen administered in a chamber instead of by mouth. No leakage, less chance of infection. Everything was okay except the head of the Dallas office, who used company funds for personal investments and soured the Dallas operation. Another venture had gone bad for Thomas.

"I lost $20,000 through HBO," he says. "I lost my house in Dallas on a wraparound note, a $300,000 house with an acre of land."

He was going through a strange marital period. He and Imani had finally gotten a divorce in 1980, but two months later they were back living together, as if it had never taken place. He was still not sure how he felt about his wife—sometimes love, sometimes the weight of crushing pressure and obligation, sometimes bitterness.

"Our third child was born in 1977," she says. "We were struggling but making it. When Aisha was born, it was a high point. She was a baby we'd really planned for. She was our first child in ten years. Duane was back and forth from L.A. He was trying to get into acting. During that period Jamila was born—1978.

"Duane came back to live here in Dallas in 1979. We picked an apartment out in North Dallas, Village Glen Apartments. Our fifth child, Duane, Jr., actually Duane Jabari in Swahili, was born then. We moved to Parkway Apartments. It was a nice area—with a drug problem. We found out after four months.

"We moved out of Parkway and lived with my mother. By then we were technically divorced, but living together. My mother and Duane didn't get along. He had to leave. We moved back to Parkway, then we moved out. In 1986 we got a house in Wynnewood Hill. By then the baby, Naeemah Elizabeth, had been born.

"We were like a nomadic tribe, the way we kept moving. Right now I'm writing a book. I'm going to call it *Two People Lost in a Storm*."

The house in Wynnewood Hill was repossessed. They were divorced, this time for good, in August 1986. Imani Pamoja was to make two more moves, finally settling in a house in Cedar Hills.

"In 1986 I really felt the effects of the divorce," she says. "Writing the book brings back so many of those moments, the hard moments. My older children were very resentful of Duane at one time. Once Idris, who's twenty-one now, got so mad he took Duane's suitcases with all his newspaper clippings and stuff and threw them in the lake."

The strange relationship that stretched over a twenty-two-year period, the whirlwind moves from house to house, it's almost too much for an outsider to comprehend. Imani Pamoja is a sensible person, a college grad, a teacher of English and creative writing at the high school level. Why did she do it?

"I guess I'm foolish. I guess at heart I'm a romanticist," she says. "We met in high school and I felt we were meant for each other. My mother was married and divorced; her husband was like Duane. I believed in trying to salvage a marriage. When we'd get back together, it just seemed like things would work out. Then when he'd have his angry periods, when he'd leave and go out to the Coast, I felt it wasn't really his fault. Pressure was forcing him to act a certain way. I didn't want to desert him."

She says she gave the children and herself Swahili names when she got into black consciousness in 1970. I asked her what Imani Pamoja meant.

" 'Imani'—faith," she said. " 'Pamoja'—together."

In 1987, Duane returned to the Cowboys' football scene amidst much fanfare by the Dallas press at training camp. But this time he was an observer. He was living in Los Angeles, married to the former Shatemar Benson from western Pennsylvania, a talent agent and business manager who commutes back and forth to a New York office. Thomas had worked with Paragon Sports Inc., a firm that offers financial counseling to professional athletes . . . don't do as I did, do as I say. He had been involved with charity work and children's groups.

On Sunday night, November 22, I met him in the press box at the Cowboys-Miami game in Dallas. It was the fifth Cowboy game he'd seen.

21

THE LOST SEASON, FINALE

This is a bad team, worse than anyone imagined, and it's getting worse by the week. It has no heart. No compelling will to win. No leadership. No character. No pride. The Cowboys quit against Atlanta.

Frank Luska, *The Dallas Times Herald*

I'm looking at my notes on the Dallas-Miami game: offense inconsistent . . . Pelluer great scrambling first half, then stopped running, why? . . . Dolphins D played bump on both corners, removed Cowboys' wideouts from game . . . good pressure on Marino . . . Dolphs ready to topple . . . Cowboys no finishing punch . . . def. collapsed . . . Stradford uncontrollable . . .

And onward, into the football never-never land of jargonese, half of which I usually can't read the next day. I think back now and what do I recall of that 20–14 Miami victory?

Steve Pelluer, a scrambling fool in the first half. Who would have thought? He showed a rather wild and dazzling side to his nature, running for 78 yards, 12 short of Roger Staubach's team record for rushing yardage by a quarterback. And he still had a half to go.

The Dolphins rolled up their cornerbacks in tight bump-and-run coverage on both wideouts, sometimes leaving the safetymen behind in a double zone. Pelluer tried two passes to the split end, Kelvin Edwards, in the first half, both intercepted. He threw none to his flanker, Mike Renfro. He threw no more to either one of them thereafter. A blitzkrieg! The Dolphins, who came into the game as the team with the AFC's worst pass defense, pitched a shutout against the wide receivers.

Now an experienced quarterback would have worked inside against this coverage. He would have had his reads down, he would have gone to checkoffs, but Pelluer hadn't played a down in 1987. And he was working with that primitive game plan. So he did what any red-blooded young Cowboy would have done, he tucked the ball away and hoofed it, mostly up the middle, through the gaps between the pass rushers, the danger zone for QBs. Then he stopped. He carried twice in the second half for six yards. Good-bye record.

Why? After the game I asked him if he had been told to stop running. He said no. I asked the coaches. Head shakes, no. I couldn't believe it. In my mind's eye I saw an arm around his shoulders. Listen, Steve, it's all well and good, but this is, ahem, not Cowboy football. Just go out and execute the game plan, okay?

So he did, and he put together one decent drive, which produced a TD and got the Cowboys within 6 points, down 20–14 . . . with 5:18 to go. At this point the defense said good-evening, and Miami, one of the NFL's weaker rushing teams, ran the clock out—on the ground— with a terrific little rookie halfback named Troy Stradford simply killing the Cowboys with a wildly imaginative assortment of fakes and jukes and quick, darting moves.

Dan Marino, under a bit of a rush, was up and down, and when Marino is not hot all the way, that's when Miami usually loses. Yep, the Dolphins could have been taken that night, but this little halfback kept bailing them out of tough spots, doing a lot on his own, improvising, creating. He'd had a statistically heavy night—17 carries, 169 yards. He had been a fourth-round draft choice. For years the Cowboys had been bitching about their low drafting position, due to their winning record the year before, and how that was crippling the draft. Well, anyone could have had this guy.

I saw sociological implications in all this. One kid has been allowed to do his thing and his team had won. Another had pulled in his horns, either by desire or instruction, and his team had lost. Individual creativity is not part of the Dallas system, never was, never, uh, well, maybe someday it will be. I remember something told to me by Ahmad Rashad, who had spent eleven years in the NFL.

"I hung around with a bunch of players in this apartment in L.A. before I was drafted," he said. "College players, some pros, some Cowboy guys. It seemed that those college guys all lived in fear of being drafted by the Cowboys. I know I always hoped they wouldn't draft me. After I got in the NFL I knew why.

"The Cowboys' system is like the service. You can't be an individual first. They'd break everyone down and then make you a part of the team. It wasn't normal. Their players lived in constant fear.

"Don Shula is different. He's a person, the Cowboys are an institution . . . the fans, the town, you can't escape it. I remember talking to Larry Little of the Dolphins. He said Shula worked 'em to death, and he ran a disciplined system, but he was an individual, too, and he made the players feel like individuals."

And one of Shula's individuals, doing his individual thing, had done in the Cowboy organization on that November night.

Duane Thomas and I had bumped into Stradford outside the stadium, next to the Dolphins' team bus. We talked for a while. I couldn't get over how tiny he was. The program euphemistically listed him at 5-9, 191, but he was hardly that, 5-8 maybe, perhaps even smaller. A bouncy little guy, he couldn't stand still, he kept bouncing up and down on his toes like a fighter waiting for the opening bell. He looked like he was ready to run for another 169. He smiled a lot, his eyes flashed, Walter Payton style . . . oh, he was a live one all right.

Then I thought of the eyes I had seen in the Cowboys' interview room after the game, the sad eyes of Tony Dorsett, who had seen no action . . . "Sooner or later they're gonna make a mistake and give me the ball" . . . the slightly bored, distant-looking eyes of Herschel Walker, who was really the only thing the Cowboys had going for them offensively.

Timmy Newsome, the eighth-year fullback and one of the Cowboys I've always liked to talk to after games because of his logical, analytical way of looking at things, said, "We didn't have a lot of plays tonight. We didn't have many passes. We just went with basic stuff . . ."

"How about your young offensive line?" I asked him, and he shook his head.

"It sounds good . . . Young Offensive Line, big, strong, straight-ahead, zone-blocking offensive line . . . but when you're facing a defensive line that stunts, you've got problems. Zone blocking is great when they just sit there, but Miami stunted a lot. And that's what happens to a young offensive line."

Tom Landry said the team had defeated itself with penalties, etc. He said, "Our goal was to keep them to 20 points or under and our defense did that."

I remembered something Walt Michaels once told me when he was defensive coach of the Jets.

"If you need to hold 'em to 7 to win, you hold 'em to 7 . . . or 27, if that's what it takes."

The Cowboys' defense had collapsed at the end, when Miami ran the clock out for the last five minutes and change. Landry didn't mention that.

At Campisi's that night I asked Duane Thomas what he had thought of the game. He had, after all, seen the Cowboys five times that season. I never expected him to say what he did.

"I thought the Cowboys lost the game in good taste tonight," he said, and I nearly knocked over my glass of wine—and it was good wine, too, a 1984 Brolio Chianti Classico. How's that? Says which?

"I saw young guys who were into the game, who were hustling," he said. "Pelluer, Rohrer, Brooks, Francis, even Ruzek, the kicker. I watched him. He was really into it. I talked to Rohrer. He seemed very down.

"I said, 'Look, home in on your positives and the negatives will work themselves out.' He said, 'Yeah, but the coaches are always harping on the negatives.' I think some of those guys are more worried about the coaches getting on them than winning a game.

"I saw Francis make a mistake and then redeem himself on the same series. I liked that."

The rookie right corner had committed a 35-yard interference penalty on Mark Duper in the second quarter, then he had ended the drive by neatly stepping in front of Duper and picking off a curl pass on the Dallas 19.

I told Thomas he sounded like a fan, and one of those ancient, dying breeds of Dallas fans at that, the kind that looks for the positives, for hope for the future. Even with the Dan Marino passing show coming to town, Texas Stadium had fallen short of a sellout. ESPN had to buy up the remaining 8,500 tickets to keep the game on local TV.

"Look, you try to help people," Thomas said. "Kevin Brooks was complaining how outdated the coaching staff was, how sometimes you ask them a question that's easy to answer, just to make them feel important.

"I told him, 'You've got to do some things on your own. You've got to work with the middle linebacker behind you, get the feel of what he's doing, and vice versa.' A guy like Harry Carson of the Giants helps the people in front of him because he's so smart. He's a student of the game. I guarantee you Lee Roy Jordan was one of the most brilliant students of football who ever lived."

The Cowboys' middle linebacker behind Brooks was Gene (Hittin' Machine) Lockhart, a hitter, as his name implied, but hardly a student, after four years with the Cowboys. Bob Breunig, the middle linebacker who succeeded Jordan, had been a student. That's what got him in the Pro Bowl.

I remember once I was in the Cowboys' locker room and I was looking at their scouting report for the Washington game. Included was a gigantic computer printout of raw data, not a breakdown or summary, but page after page of Redskin plays that had been called that season, hundreds of them.

"Why do they give you all this?" I asked Tony Hill, the wide receiver.

"Because we're the Dallas Cowboys," he said. "If someone else has a two-page scouting report, we've got to have ten."

"What does a guy like Hollywood Henderson do with this stuff?" I asked him.

"Probably throws it under the bed," he said.

"Does anybody read it all?"

"Yeah, Breunig. That's why he's starting."

One of the guys at Campisi's asked Thomas what he thought of Herschel Walker.

"I still go back to what I said in camp," Duane said. "Herschel has to learn the art of running. He's a natural raw talent, but eventually he'll end up like Earl Campbell. He'll take too many blows. You can't be running at those defensive linemen who weigh 280 and bench press 500 pounds and take all those hits.

"They talk about Herschel being built like a Greek god. In a few years he'll be built like Goofy. The guy needs to know the little tricks of the game, like a quarterback looking off his receivers. He's got a few elusive moves, but nothing instinctive.

"That little No. 23 on Miami, Stradford . . . he reminded me of Mercury Morris. Take the pitchout, three steps, boom! One-two-three and gone. He had no doubts as to what he was doing. Shula teaches like that. He coaches techniques, but up to a point. When he feels it's interfering with a guy's performance, he leaves him alone. The Cowboys are overcoached in concept, not technique. The Dolphins are the other way around, except they're not overcoached.

"My rookie year, the coaches would tell me how to run, and I'd get the living hell beat out of me. Then my instinct took over. Tom would say, 'Great run, Duane. Great recognition.' It was okay with him as long as it worked."

Someone asked about Danny White.

"Danny White is gone," he said. "He never should have shown up this year. Actually it wasn't Danny White so much, it was the personnel he had."

Well, he was wrong about that one, about White's being gone. White started the Thanksgiving Day game against the Vikings. The move surprised everybody. It surprised the two people who should have been closest to the situation, the two offensive assistants, Paul Hackett and Jim Erkenbeck. On Monday, Erkenbeck told a couple of writers that, just guessing off the record, he thought White would start. On Wednesday, the day before the game, he had switched to Pelluer.

"I didn't find out White was starting until we came in after the pregame warm-ups and were getting ready to pray," Erkenbeck said.

Hackett said he didn't know White was starting until he was up in the press box and saw White run out on the field when the offense was introduced.

"I was disappointed," Pelluer said. "I'd prepared all week for the game."

Once again Landry found himself with the same kind of problem that has haunted him throughout his whole career in Dallas. Which quarterback? White was physically flawed, but was this worse than an inexperienced quarterback working with a basic game plan, a set of wide receivers who couldn't shake tight coverage, and a short practice week? He didn't know. White would start against the Vikings, then would get benched for Atlanta, then relieve Pelluer, then get benched again. Landry checked White's wrist action carefully in the warm-ups before the Minnesota game and told him he was starting. And he almost pulled it off.

Things went badly at first. White fumbled twice in the first half, each one caused by sacks by Chris Doleman, the right end. Mark Tuinei, the Cowboys' left tackle, had gone down with a knee early in the game, and his place was taken by Daryle Smith, a strike replacement player, who was having a terrible time with the agile Doleman. The interior line wasn't doing much better against Floyd Peters's stunting and looping defensive tackles. And the Cowboys' defense was getting overrun.

With 8:24 left in the game the Vikings had a 38–24 lead, and it looked like curtains for Dallas. Then White got hot. He drove the Cowboys 88 yards for a touchdown, then 52 yards for another. The score was tied, and with 56 seconds left, Dallas got the ball back on its 20. The drive ended on Issiac Holt's diving interception. Overtime.

The Vikings were stopped. Dallas took over on its 37. White hit Renfro, who was having a career night—7 catches, 100 yards, and 3 TDs—for 20. Walker gained 3 to the Viking 40. One first down and they'd be in field goal range. White looked for tight end Doug Cosbie, running a post pattern on the right side. The pass was badly underthrown. It had nothing on it. Middle linebacker Scott Studwell fielded it, returned it to Minnesota's 37, and seven plays later the Vikings had a touchdown against the exhausted Cowboy defense. Final, 44–38 Minnesota. Dallas was 5-6.

White had tears in his eyes as he addressed the media afterward: "There's no question that I cost us the game . . . I got too brave too many times, and the defense can cover up for you for only so long . . ."

Well, what the hell. They had gone down fighting against a playoff-caliber team. There was still hope. They'd have a nine-day layoff for Atlanta, a team with the worst record in the league. That one probably would be a blowout, so they could rest people for the Redskins in Washington. Maybe the Skins would have clinched the division by then and they'd be on cruise control. Then the Rams in L.A., hell, they weren't going anywhere, and the finale against the Cards in Texas Stadium. A 9-6 record was possible. So were the playoffs—barely.

Everything was logical, except for step one. It had a pothole under it. Atlanta, crummy Atlanta, came into Dallas and in front of 40,103 mildly booing fans, the smallest crowd in Texas Stadium history, the Falcons humbled and humiliated the Cowboys, 21–10. It was their third victory of the year.

Frank Luska wrote his scathing piece in the *Times Herald,* which ran a picture of three fans in the stands with bags over their heads. The headline: "Put a Bag on the Cowboys' Season."

Randy Galloway in the *Dallas Morning News*—"That peels the paint off the franchise walls . . . The Cowboys are homeless, helpless, and prideless. Worst of show, as in dog show. Pit city."

Blackie Sherrod in the *Morning News*—"Oh, America's Team lost another? Pass the dip."

Atlanta kicker Mick Luckhurst, the team player rep and a member of the Players Association's Executive Committee, tried to give the game ball to Cosbie and strong safety Bill Bates to take to Tex Schramm.

"Your management gets the game ball for this one," he said.

They refused to take it. Luckhurst ran up the tunnel, waving the ball, yelling, "This one's for Tex!"

Next day Schramm said glumly, "This is the lowest point in my career, which has been thirty-eight years."

Landry's postgame press conference lasted ten minutes. The press just seemed to run out of questions about the dull, lifeless contest.

"I don't think it's like the Detroit game because we weren't flat," he said. "We tried, but we just weren't quick enough up front. Why, I don't know. I just know we were not moving as fast as they were."

Two hours later Steve Pate of the *Dallas Morning News* called Harvey Robert (Bum) Bright, the Cowboys' majority owner, at home. Bum Bright is a native Oklahoman who made his money in oil and gas and banking. In his four years as Cowboys owner he had never said much. He had left the football operation to Landry and Schramm, whom he called his CEO . . . chief executive officer. As a former chairman of the Texas A&M Board of Regents, though, he had gotten involved in Aggie athletic politics, and he did a lot to turn their football program around. He had been a behind-the-scenes backer of right-wing political figures. But like Clint Murchison before him, he preferred to keep his hands off the Cowboys' football operation.

It was a different Bright that Pate talked to that Monday evening.

"I get horrified sometimes at our play-calling," he said. "I've heard that we're not using certain players because they haven't been brought along yet. Maybe the problem is we can't utilize the talent of certain guys because we don't have anybody to direct how to use them.

"It doesn't seem like we've got anybody in charge that knows what they're doing other than Tex. I don't want to do the coaching and I don't want to try to run the team, but I'm not satisfied with the results we get. We can't go along like we are.

"I'd back Tex in anything he wants to do. I've got all the confidence in the world in him. He's a tough person.

"Did you see how many people had left midway in the fourth quarter? I'm afraid it will be worse. People are saying, 'You changed things at A&M, why don't you change things here?' This is not an easy situation.

"I think the aura of the Cowboys is dying. I'm talking about an aura where they were smart, where they were leaders around the league, where they were slick and smooth and had a high caliber of individuals playing for the team. At least the Cowboys had that projection. But they've lost a lot of that image. You can build it back around Herschel Walker and some bright young people, but it's not there now."

Landry's first response, to a group of ten reporters at his Monday press conference, was, "At least he didn't give me a vote of confidence, so I've still got hopes—I guess."

He had felt this kind of heat once before. In 1964 the Cowboy fans got tired of five straight years of losses by their expansion franchise, and they called for Landry's scalp. Murchison responded by calling a news conference and announcing that he had just signed Landry to a ten-year contract. *That* was a vote of confidence. Murchison's next news conference came twenty years later when he sold the club.

"I could step down now if I wanted to and I wouldn't go hungry," Landry said on Monday after the loss to Atlanta.

"But I made a commitment to stay three years and try to get this team back up and then step out of the way. But who knows? I don't have time to think about it right now. I don't know where this thing is going.

"We agreed on what we wanted to do before the season. If losing to Atlanta changes it, it changes it. I know where we're going to go. I knew we would hit a spot like this."

Two days after he had leveled his tirade, I called Bum Bright in Dallas. I had spoken to him once before, when the team was going through its front office reorganization in the spring of 1986. At that time he had told me, "I let my CEO handle things like that." This time his tone was different.

"I saw the game and I was just frustrated," he said. "Every time we tried to run the ball they came powering through. I was horrified. Every play we called, they dumped us. We weren't completing passes. The line was leaking bad. They were rushing our passers."

I asked him if he'd talked to Landry.

"In none of our operations do I talk to the people below the CEO," he said. "I have all my conversations with the CEO so there's no confusion as to where instructions are coming from. I don't try to evaluate how people in the mortgage company are selling mortgages, I look at the bottom line, and the bottom line here . . . well, it's pretty evident that we don't have a good bottom line."

Fair enough. Every time an oil well runs dry, you don't go out to the drilling site and pester the foreman. But how about his overall evaluation of foreman Landry?

"Goodness knows, Tom Landry has a reputation for being a good coach," he said, and in my notebook I underlined the word "reputation."

"I don't say his coaching is good, I don't say it's bad. I just don't have an opinion. I don't know why we're losing . . . the coaching, the strike, the players' attitude. I don't know what it is. I just know we're not winning. We might not have the right leadership on the field or off the field."

Hardly a ringing endorsement for the coach. No, not an endorsement at all. A nagging thought was pushing its way forward. Would Bright ever fire Landry? No, I couldn't ask that. The guy might hang up the phone. But I've got to ask it. I asked it.

"Would you ever fire Tom Landry?"

No slammed phone. No shouts. A pause. Oh-oh.

"That's kind of a harsh word to use," he said. Another pause. Time for reflection on just what he should say to this stranger from New York.

"I don't think that would ever come about," he finally said. "It just wouldn't happen that way. Tom Landry would not be fired. The relationship between Tex and Tom is such . . . well, it wouldn't happen that way."

I thanked Bum Bright and said good-bye and caught a flight to Dallas. I checked the newspapers. Middle linebacker Gene Lockhart had been reserved with a broken leg. His backup, Steve DeOssie, had a sprained ankle. The starter for the Washington game would be Ron Burton, a rookie free agent from North Carolina. Gil Brandt had looked at two films of him and watched him against Duke and liked what he saw. Still, he had not been drafted.

"Keep your fingers crossed, huh?" Burton said about his starting role.

Offensive left tackle Daryle Smith's sore neck was worse. He hadn't practiced for two days. Mark Tuinei, the regular, had been reserved with a knee injury. Who would start against all-pro Dexter Manley—Brian Baldinger, a guard, strike replacement Bob White, strike replacement Steve Cisowski?

"Got any suggestions?" Landry said.

There had been a Legends of Fame dinner at the Fairmont, and a lot of past and present NFL people had shown up, and there were numerous quotes about the Landry and the Cowboys situation in general.

Larry Cole, defensive end on the Super Bowl teams: "If I were the coach, I would have stopped a few weeks ago and had the surgery on Danny White's wrist. They're asking a lot of him to play and put up with all that pressure when he's not 100 percent."

Former Redskins' quarterback Billy Kilmer: "People talk about quarterbacks. They're getting beat in the trenches. I don't care what quarterback they had in there. They could bring in Dan Marino and he'd look bad . . . but I don't mind seeing 'em get beat."

Hall of Fame quarterback and former Redskins' coach Otto Graham: "You're crazy to play football and even crazier to coach it. Look at what's happening with Tom Landry. First his general manager and then his owner question if he knows how to do his job. I can't believe it. There's no way he deserves the abuse he's getting now."

Former Cowboy halfback Preston Pearson: "In the NFL today there is a difference in style and philosophy. Everyone reaches a point where you have to ask: 'Has the game left us in the dust?' If Tom Landry is being honest with himself, and he is honest, he'll look at that."

Schramm was being honored that night. Landry made the award. When Landry was introduced he got the strongest applause of the night. Schramm drew one boo from a distant corner of the ballroom.

"When the Houston paper ran a story of Tex criticizing Tom," said Dicky Maegle, a halfback for the early Cowboys, "I sent a clipping of the story to Tom with a letter expressing my support of him."

The first night I was in town I had dinner with Lee Roy Jordan. I had covered the Cowboys during their five-Super-Bowl run, but I never had much of a chance to spend time with Jordan, their great middle linebacker and defensive leader.

He looked weather-beaten, gray at the temples, a little heavier than I had remembered him. He walked with the slight rolling gait, part limp, part roll, of the old veteran whose knees had seen the surgical knife.

"The Flex defense had its time," he said. "They stayed with it too long. Things could have been done with the same concepts, but different alignments. I talked to people about it my last couple of years.

"Coaches have given up trying to fight Tom. Ditka, Reeves . . . they fought him and left."

He stopped for a moment. This was coming out harsher than he intended, and that wasn't his meaning at all. Not at all.

"It's been Tom's way, offense and defense," he said, "but you have to give him credit. His system was damn good over a twenty-plus-year period. It's not the system now, or the coaching. It's the players. Look back . . . it seems that more free agents made all-pro than number one drafts. The last ten years of number ones . . . I don't know where they are now, but very few of them started. But they all were tall and fast and they could jump high. For years the team complained about its low drafting positions, but I don't believe the twenty-fourth or twenty-fifth best player in the country can't help you—if you really pick the twenty-fourth best.

"Do you really think Tex has gone up one hundred percent as a general manager and Tom has gone down as a coach? I think Tom is as good as he always was. He just doesn't have the personnel. To me the scouting department is the poorest part of the Cowboy organization. There used to be self-motivated people on the team who weren't great athletes. Now you've got athletes who can't play.

"Tom's in a tough situation now, but he's got as much fire as he ever had. But Tom never had to fight within the family and organization before."

I asked him if he meant Tex Schramm, and Jordan's face got hard and his eyes narrowed. I realized what it must have been like, looking at him across the line of scrimmage.

"Tex hired Hackett himself, and he and Hackett decided on the offensive line coach and the kicking team coach," Jordan said. "I think it's a total division of the team. Tom used to be in charge. Now I believe it's Tex, with maybe pressure from the owner. Tex and Hackett and Erkenbeck are over here, and Tom and the old guard are over here.

"It's Tex's baby . . . the radio shows, the magazine. Tex is promoting the Cowboys the way he wants to. It's football according to Tex. I'd say that over the last year and a half management has worked on promoting the image that Tom can't coach anymore. It's not us. It's Tom's fault.

"I called Tom earlier this week. I told him how much I thought of him, how he was getting the short end of the deal on where the blame should be. He thanked me for calling."

I asked Jordan if he actually came out and asked Landry if he thought someone was doing a tunnel job on him.

"I wanted to ask him but I couldn't," Jordan said. "I pussyfooted around it. I said, 'Seems like you've gotten a little divided up there.' He laughed. No comment on that."

Something, obviously, was bugging Jordan about Tex, something personal. The old pro returning to the scene. Was it that?

"You get to feel how little you're welcome," he said, "like you were something out of the past and not welcome now. Once you leave the Cowboys, there's no sense of closeness. You had a job to produce on the field—fine—but there's no sense of warmth coming back.

"Tom's personality . . . well, he doesn't know how. I know he's a warm person inside, but he just doesn't know. Tom's wife, Alicia, once said to me, 'I wish you knew the real Tom Landry when he's not with you, talking football.' God, I wish I could have. We all feel the same way. Tremendous respect, but we couldn't express it. He's not open.

"Tex, well, yes, he's interested in you if you can be a real asset in helping him promote himself and the team right now. I've never met one player who was close to him. I don't know whether he feels players are important or whether management is the only thing important to having a winning football team."

Suddenly it hit me. The Ring of Honor. That was it. Six names on the wall ringing Texas Stadium. Bob Lilly, Don Meredith, Don Perkins, Chuck Howley, Mel Renfro, and Roger Staubach. The immortal six. Hallowed names from the past. Why wasn't Jordan there? Players had told me he deserves it as much as anyone. Staubach had said that, even Duane Thomas, who didn't much care for Jordan off the field.

"No one deserves to be in the Ring of Honor more than Lee Roy Jordan," Thomas said.

I asked Jordan why he wasn't in it.

"People call Tex about it," he said. "It still rankles him. Look, Tex is a one-man committee on that thing. No one else has a say in it. Only Tex."

To get from the airport to the Cowboys' complex at Valley Ranch in northwest Dallas you head east on the LBJ Freeway, cloverleaf left onto MacArthur, make a right on Valley Ranch, and you're there. You'll pass through a couple of miles of development tracts. You'll come over a rise and you'll be stunned by the sight of a vast plain of identical boxlike houses; you'll pass another forest of condos, more stucco, a little fancier; then another, Spanish style; then Tudor, all clad in the same uniforms.

Barrington Court, The Tree Tops Villas, The Hamptons, The Collection Series, Casitas Stone Canyon, Santa Fe Trail, Silverton Village, Canyon Crest, Marble Canyon, Mandolin Collection, Hills of Valley Ranch . . . "Single Family Homes for Every Lifestyle" . . . "Town Houses and Condominiums for Carefree Living." It's dizzying. The American Dream gone haywire.

They expected 25,000 to fill those developers' dream houses, 7,000 live there now. So they promote. A trail of Cowboy lone star signposts leads you to the three-year-old team complex, which is another dream, of sorts. Three grass football fields, locker room, training rooms, meeting rooms, weight and exercise areas, running trails, racquetball, basketball, and tennis courts, video lab, coaching, scouting, and administrative offices, ticket office, souvenir shop, Dallas Cowboys Travel Agency, Cowboys Cheerleaders Dance Academy, editorial offices for the *Cowboys Weekly,* press room with research library, TV studio, lounge areas. Tours are available.

Wait, there's more. I'm reading from the Cowboys' media guide now:

> The crown jewel of Cowboys Center, Cowboys ShowPlace,
> will enable fans to spend an unforgettable day with the
> Cowboys through exhibits utilizing sight, sound, and touch.
> Fans will enter ShowPlace through a seven-story glass star
> and a sculpture garden of ten-foot-high football players in the
> foreground. Laser-disk projection, interactive videos,
> holograms, and a Magic Motion Machine are some of the
> eighty planned attractions. The variety of displays and
> innovative gadgetry will make ShowPlace a must for all
> football fans.

Innovative gadgetry. That's the Cowboys, all right. You wait in the outer lounge and stare at three TVs, promotional material, Super Bowl highlights vs. Miami, Super Bowl highlights vs. Denver. Both games end the same. Dallas wins.

In the midst of all this opulence he has created is the office of Tex Schramm. He is staring out the window.

"Just once I'd like to hear us called arrogant again," he says. I ask him about the thing that's foremost on my mind. Lee Roy Jordan and the Ring of Honor.

"Jesus Christ, did you come all the way from New York to ask me *that?*" he says. "Look, this has been going on for years. I'm trying to make the Ring of Honor a very, very selective thing. It's not like what you see in Washington or Philadelphia stadiums where there's a whole line of names. I'd like it to be more like what the Yankees used to be.

"Look, we have a reunion. I'm very close to a lot of our former players."

I told him there's a feeling afoot that he was trying to dig a tunnel under Tom Landry.

"I don't think that's factual," he said. "This is an emotional game and people say things under stressful circumstances, me, the owner, everybody. I don't think Tom Landry's position has changed one iota."

He said that Landry had final approval of all coaches when I mentioned the feeling that he'd run in Hackett and Erkenbeck and Mike Solari, the special teams coach. We talked of losing and the state of the franchise in general.

"The higher you get, the farther you fall," he said.

"We're the most visible team in football. That's why you're here. The story is the demise of the most visible team in the last twenty years. Everyone's been rooting for our demise since we got to the top, just like they were rooting for the Yankees to fail. Lookit, we've had the good days. If you can't live with the bad days, too, then get out. I've been in the NFL thirty-eight years. I've seen terrible losses, losses that hurt me terribly.

"The media around the country is just as anxious to see us come down as to do well. But there's one thing the media doesn't want of the Dallas Cowboys, and that's to see us go away."

I found Danny White in the locker room. Steve Pelluer had a sore knee, courtesy of the Falcons. White would start against the Redskins. He gave me an anatomy lesson.

"When I broke the wrist," he said, "I split the radius bone. There was a crack up in the wrist. They put it in a cast. Six weeks later they took it out and it looked fine. There are thirteen bones held by ligaments. If the lower bones float . . . well, there's a blockage now. I can bend it ten degrees back and fifteen degrees forward. I can't bend it more than that. It's a matter of learning how to throw this way. Here, look, this is as far as I can bend it.

"If you let a ligament go, it deteriorates. It's too late to repair it now. The only thing to do, and it's been discussed, is a fusion, fuse the three big bones together. It wouldn't help my mobility. It might hurt it. But it would eliminate the pain. But it's silly to discuss it now. They're talking about a nine-month deal.

"It hurts every time I throw. There's a little twinge of pain. It's gotten to the point where I don't even think about it now. I don't bend over in pain every time I throw. The medical opinion is that it'll get worse as the cartilage wears down.

"The bad throws I've made usually come at the end of games, under pressure, moving in the pocket. If I had the snap in my wrist, I could get it there quicker or hold on to it. The one that beat us in overtime against Minnesota . . . I was throwing to Cosbie and I tried to pull it back but couldn't."

I asked him about Landry. Once, during the playoff years, he had sounded almost spiritual when he talked to me about the coach. "He's the light that guides me," he had said, "the wheel that drives everything forward."

This time he just shook his head.

"So much you see and hear," he said. "So many negatives. You can't talk about it. You just pay attention to business and try to struggle through it. But it's tough when everyone's getting hammered from every angle and it's all negative, negative. You've got to dig deep from within."

I had seen Tony Dorsett in the locker room. He had asked me, "You gonna come to Washington and watch my two or three plays?" I asked White about Dorsett.

"It hurts to see him on the sidelines like that," he said. "There should be another way. He still explodes when he gets the ball. He still runs hard, works hard in practice. Okay, you make room for the best player on your team, but does it have to be at the expense of your second-best?"

"He hasn't lost a step," Brian Baldinger, the reserve guard, told me. "He still sees things as quick as any runner in the league. We're changing so many things that the backs aren't on the same page. We're hitting and missing. What Tony did so well is hit it and suck everyone up and then bounce it outside. Now it's all inside the tackles and make one cut, but not outside."

I saw Landry in his office, getting ready for the plane trip north. He was wearing a red-checked shirt and brown slacks. He didn't look like a man under siege. He looked ready for a weekend's work.

"Do the remarks bother me?" he said. "Yes, of course they do. I'm human. The owner? Well, maybe it's a reaction to all the other bad things that have happened to him—the economy around here, for instance. It's just been devastating.

"A quarterback with a bad wrist, an offensive line that keeps getting banged up, our best wide receiver with a broken leg in preseason. Sure the owner is upset.

"As far as Tex . . . well, I can't say what's in his mind. He's an emotional type of guy. Tex and I have been together a long time. We don't communicate about the day-to-day running of the team, but for twenty-eight years we've been compatible.

"As far as their digging a tunnel under me, running in their own coaches and all, that's simply not true. I have final say on all members of the staff and everything to do with football. I always will. No, I don't feel they're trying to undermine me, but I can't speak for every member of the organization.

"I know where we are now and I know where we're going and that it's going to take time to get there. That's why I asked for a three-year contract."

I asked him if his wife, Alicia, had been upset by all the negative comments from Schramm and Bright and for the first time he smiled.

"Sure my wife was upset by those quotes," he said. "That's what a wife is for, support, and I've got a good wife."

That Sunday a 24–20 loss to the Redskins dropped the Cowboys to 5-8 and guaranteed them their second losing season in a row. The Redskins didn't play particularly inspired football. They beat the Cowboys on four plays—three long passes and a fumble return. They didn't run much, even with the Cowboys' free agent, Ron Burton, at middle linebacker.

The Dallas safeties were run-conscious, which left the cornerbacks in single coverage, and Washington's Jay Schroeder, facing little in the way of a pass rush, had plenty of time to go deep. White had to throw 49 times, and his passes gained 359 yards, but they were mostly posts and seam patterns and things over the middle, which didn't put as much strain on the wrist. He had little luck on the sideline routes.

Daryle Smith pulled himself together and started at left tackle and had a creditable day against Dexter Manley. On the other side, Kevin Gogan, the 310-pound rookie, was overrun by Charles Mann. The running game had no punch up front, particularly in short-yardage situations.

"They're not the finesse team they used to be," Mann said afterward. "They have big bulky guys who don't really come off the ball and get after you. I looked at Gogan on film and he doesn't have good feet. They try to wall you off. They were in trouble near the goal line—they couldn't drive-block. I like playing against the bigger guys."

"Their receivers weren't like the old Dallas receivers," Redskin cornerback Barry Wilburn said. "That Edwards is a large guy who isn't very elusive or quick. I could get my hands on him and steer him out of his pattern and run with him when I had to."

Pelluer came back against the Rams and Cardinals and the Cowboys won their final two games to finish the season at 7-8. He completed less than fifty percent of his passes in the pair but suffered no interceptions, which was an achievement. Walker had big days, running and catching the ball; he became the only Cowboy player selected to the Pro Bowl in two years. Dorsett, who had seen some action against the Redskins and the Rams, sat out the Cardinal game with a bad back. Dallas had the honor of knocking St. Louis out of the playoffs, creating an opening for the Vikings, who did surprisingly well. In the home final against St. Louis 36,788 fans showed up, breaking the record for low attendance set three weeks previously.

Schramm said the team would look into "more aggressive" promotions and marketing for 1988. A *Dallas Morning News* poll of 266 fans showed that there were more negative feelings toward the Cowboys than toward the Mavericks, Sidekicks, or Rangers.

Jesse Penn became the third Dallas linebacker to suffer a broken leg—Lockhart vs. Atlanta, Mike Hegman vs. Washington, Penn vs. L.A.

After the Cardinal game Dorsett said he would seriously ask management to trade him. Schramm reminded the writers that any team interested in him would have to pick up the final two years of his annuity, which probably would amount to a total outlay of $1 million a year in real money, counting salary. In June, Dorsett was traded to Denver.

In his postseason press conference Landry said, "My New Year's resolution is to get over .500 next season. If I can get over .500, I'm in business."

With what? The young offensive linemen were a bust. Pelluer was still unproven at quarterback, and in the off-season White said he might retire after twelve seasons of taking abuse . . . "It's the beating you take off the field," he said. No one knows if Mike Sherrard can come back from his broken leg, and how effective he'll be if he does. Without him the receiving corps is punchless. Once you get past Walker, where are their offensive weapons?

The statistics were depressing—counting only the twelve nonstrike games. The new offense, under Hackett, gained slightly fewer yards per game than it did in 1986 when White missed half the games. Unsettled personnel, lack of talent, injuries—it's surprising it even came close. The defense gave up 26 more yards per contest. Pass defense dropped from third in the NFL in 1986 to twenty-sixth, using the twelve games for rating purposes. The defensive backs had problems holding their coverages because the pass rush was weaker. Sacks were down twenty percent. Danny Noonan, the number one draft choice, never became a starter. He finished the season with one sack. Linebacking was average. There are no longer any stars on the team, except for Walker.

Were they dogs, as the papers said after the Atlanta game? Were they quitters? It's too harsh an assessment. They played hard against some of the tougher, physical teams they faced—the Giants, whom they beat twice, the Vikings and Redskins, who beat them. They played worst against the worst—Detroit and Atlanta. That's the mark of an inconsistent team, not a doggy one.

They were an average team with average to less-than-average talent, magnified in the public eye because of what they once were. They were America's Team.

22

THE SYSTEM

JOURNAL: Special effects, Dallas deals with special effects, which is called hype. That's the crux of their organization. That's the complaint, in dealing with the human side. They want everything run like a machine.

This is a tale about a masterpiece of public relations and about my favorite Cowboy of all, through the years. In December 1977, I was on my way down to cover the Dallas-Chicago playoff game. I had to write an advance, a column, a feature, and a game story. I had my column idea all figured out on the plane down. "Why I Hate Dallas," a collection of one-liners—Dallas is run by computer and the computer always messes up my phone bills; that up-down herky jerk of the offensive line reminds me of the East German Olympic soccer team doing calisthenics; their team colors look like a jewelry store, not a football team—you know, hilarious stuff like that. I was sitting there on the plane, writing them down as they came to me.

When I got to Dallas, George Heddleston, the assistant PR man, said I could go out to practice. No problem. The locker room was open. I sat there talking to the players, they offered me hot chocolate that was bubbling in a glass pot. It was a cold day. The hot chocolate hit the spot. I talked to Tom Landry—surprisingly candid, I thought. I got my feature story, I got my advance.

Heddleston came by and said that Cliff Harris, the free safety, had a new restaurant in Addison and he wanted to know if I'd like to have dinner with him that night. Sure, why not? Every time the Cowboys played the Giants, Gene Roswell of my paper, the *New York Post,* would always work Harris quotes into his story. I wondered why he leaned on this guy so much. I found out that night.

First we talked about wines. Harris was laying in a serious list, and he wanted to know about the '76 vintage in Germany. I also wrote the wine column for the *Post* at the time. I thought it strange that this young guy from Fayetteville, Arkansas, who'd come into the league as a free agent out of Ouachita Baptist College, would be a wine buff, but there it was.

Then we started talking football, the hitting part of it. Texas coach Darrell Royal once called Harris "a rolling ball of butcher knives," a very apt description. He had made all-pro because of his hitting, his almost maniacal frenzy when closing in on a ball carrier.

We talked of hitting and the science of hitting. His eyes sparkled. That's the definitive part of Harris's features, the bright, almost diabolical-looking eyes. He told me he'd made a study of hitting, and he drew diagrams for me on a large, legal pad—maximum-impact point when the ball carrier is most vulnerable, the idea is to get a receiver out of the backfield not when he first catches the ball and turns upfield, but when he starts to gather momentum—that kind of thing. We closed the place at two A.M. My column for the *Post* was "Cliff Harris and the Science of Hitting."

I covered the game, did another feature on Too Tall Jones's emergence as a serious force, and caught my plane home. On the way back it dawned on me: Whatever happened to my piece on "Why I Hate the Cowboys"? It had been driven clear out of my head. That, to me, was PR. In that department the Cowboys excelled.

Through the years I became friendly with Harris. We set up wine tastings, ate out a lot. I agonized with him when it became apparent to him that he no longer figured in the team's future plans, when he felt like an outcast. I learned what it was like to go back to the games as an ex-player and face the backslappers and handshakers. This was at a Bears game a few years ago. His wife wanted them to go early and spend some time in the Stadium Club. He didn't want to but said he would.

"The Stadium Club," he said, launching into a monologue. " 'Hey, Cliff, what do you think about William Perry?'

" 'Well, as long as he doesn't fall on you.'

" 'Ha, ha . . . hey, that's a good one, Cliff . . . as long as he doesn't fall on you . . . Hey, you guys hear what Cliff said . . . ?' "

At the tail end of the Cowboys' 1987 season we had dinner in the Old Warsaw, which is where we always go. I'd first gone there in 1969 when I was covering the Notre Dame–Texas Cotton Bowl . . . Woo Woo Worster and the goal line stand, you remember. A miserable, sleety night before the game, a dim light . . . La Vieille Varsovie . . . hmmm, French name, Polish restaurant, and in Dallas yet? Why not?

I was the only person in the place. The old Polish sommelier came over and sat down and we talked for a while, and he sold me a bottle of 1960 Château Petrus for twelve dollars—and he helped me drink it. It was the first time I'd ever tasted this king of all Bordeaux. I've loved the place ever since, even though it's changed now, gotten a lot fancier and bigger, and the old sommelier is dead.

So we sat there in the Old Warsaw, Cliff Harris and I, and I wanted to know what had happened to the Cowboy team. What really was The System, the Landry system, and why had it failed? I didn't care about the offensive line and the rookies and all that. I knew about that. It was the system itself I was trying to learn about.

"Tom Landry creates the box of gears," he said. "He turns the handle and generates tremendous energy. He has created a machine that now thinks it can operate without Tom Landry. But Tom knows how to make that machine work, and only Tom, not Tex Schramm, not Gil Brandt.

"Gil can line up people who look like the proper parts to the machine, but Tom is the only one who can look deeply at them and tell if they're going to make it work. When Tom's out of the system, when you leave out that one vital ingredient, then it doesn't generate energy."

Why not?

"Because he's created a machine that's too overwhelming."

I must have looked a little puzzled. Harris majored in physics in college. I got a D in it. So he simplified for me.

"When I came in, Tom was a drill sergeant," he said. "He was tight jawed. There was no slack in the system. It was totally and completely single-minded. There was not one degree of looseness that would allow any sidetracking of the job at hand. Coach Landry was a man possessed with proving to the world that the Cowboys could win the big one.

"Where are the leaders now? They're me, me, me guys. But you can look at those teams of the early seventies and see a maturing group of individuals, with one great leader, Lee Roy Jordan. Lee Roy was the one who stood up when he saw something wrong with the scheme. He was the players' spokesman. Bob Lilly would say the right thing at the right time. When he'd talk, you knew you had to stand up. In later years Charlie Waters and I stood up for our positions, but we did it more subtly, through the levels of command.

"One thing about the Cowboys' system. To perform at championship level you need to stand up, you need to have a player's input into the system. Theoretically it operates independently of any individual players, and all you need to make it work on a certain level is talent and not personalities. But that's only up to a certain level, the over-.500 level or even the playoff level, not the championship level."

I mentioned what Lee Roy Jordan had told me. He had said, "Tom is not going to motivate you to be aggressive. You have to build that little extra toughness into yourself. But he motivated by creating situations where toughness is appreciated. And in order to channel that toughness you have to have knowledge, in order to be able to take liberties with the system you have to have knowledge of how it works.

"I studied films, studied, studied. If the other team lined up two inches differently, I could call it. I could see all the linemen, the two backs, and the quarterback in one frame. If a guy moved just a fraction, it meant something to me.

"I'd call 'Draw!' before they'd run it. Lilly or Jethro would say, 'How'd you see that?' I just knew. It was only when I got to that point that I could make my own adjustments to the system."

I told Harris all that and he nodded.

"They used to say that, when we were rookies, Charlie Waters and I followed Lee Roy around like puppy dogs," he said. "Well, Lee Roy Jordan is the reason why Cliff Harris was allowed to play with his instincts—once he learned the system.

"Lee Roy worked within it, but once he understood it he exercised a certain amount of freedom. Say Jethro looped the wrong way. Well, Lee Roy filled. He made the tackle, but he'd grade out badly on the play when the assistants graded the films because he'd broken his original assignment.

"To be able to play at championship level you have to have people able to do that. There's going to be human error on every play, and when the system breaks down, and it will sometimes because it doesn't allow for that human error, you need to have people willing to make up for it. That's where heart comes in, and the willingness to take a chance. We had people like that."

I told him what Duane Thomas had said, that he got to the point where he'd let his instincts take over and Landry would tell him, "Good adjustment."

"Exactly," Harris said. "Coach Landry understood that, and he expected the superior player to do it. But you either had to ask for it or take it on our own. I believe in the system, but it takes knowledge of the weaknesses within it, the human frailty involved.

"Sometimes I'd see a physically impossible situation. I'd talk to Coach Landry about it. I'd have logic on my side, I'd done my homework. Sometimes it was real difficult to get through. I'd pound my fist on the desk. Charlie Waters was more subtle, but coming from both of us, he'd listen.

"I fought the system throughout my career, but first I had to understand it, and I was committed to winning, the same as Coach Landry was. And he knew it. He was in my corner. He put me in a position where I could perform or fail. He gave me a chance . . . a free agent out of Ouachita Baptist. But I knew what he wanted of a player. I wanted the pressure to be on me to perform.

"And there was pressure, always pressure. We didn't know whether we'd be back the next year. Do you know what he said one time, and I'll never forget it? My second year we were playing L.A. There was a pass to Margene Adkins and he missed it. He came back to the bench and said, 'That pass was a tough pass to catch.'

"Coach Landry said, 'We don't pay you to do the ordinary. When the time comes to make the play, you'd better make it.' "

How about now? I wanted to know, what had happened to the system now?

"A guy's making $300,000 a year," he said. "If he takes the safe route on a play and grades one hundred percent on the films, how can they cut him or trade him? The guy grades out by not taking a chance, by lining up exactly in the right place, by forgetting about his instinct.

"A guy like me will grade out seventy-five percent. If I smelled a run, maybe I came flying up there and filled, and if a pass was completed, I'd grade out zero. But I guessed right a whole lot more often than not, I assure you. My record for interceptions was not great. A receiver would come across the middle. I wasn't going to intercept the ball, I was going to knock him out. You get everyone to hit like that, you've got the makings of a championship team. I gave up TDs, but we played in five Super Bowls.

"When we played against quarterbacks who were technicians, well, I had their number, the Ken Andersons, the quarterbacks from the Denver system, or New York—except for Tarkenton, he dealt in personalities. So did Terry Bradshaw. Billy Kilmer was the best at it.

"I had the most trouble with him because he relied on instinct and feel. I used to love to play against him because he'd challenge your mind. He'd put you in a position where you had to make a decision. He'd force you by your personality to make a decision he expected you to make.

"But there aren't many quarterbacks like that around now. And the Cowboy players are different, too. Tom can't afford to have exactly the kind of players he needs to make his system work because the talent is thinner. They belong to an organization that's got all this glitter, all this promotion, they start believing it. They feel they have to play up to it.

"Tex has created this image of the Cowboys, the new facility, the cheerleaders, etc. And it rubs off on the team. I sincerely believe that. The thing to understand is that Tex Schramm is going to be around after Tom Landry. He's a businessman and businessmen don't deal in personal friendships. It's cold-blooded business."

Well, the cold-bloodedness of it had destroyed one major talent of the past, Duane Thomas. What was it that Harris had said . . . personalities were not built into the system, but if a man understood it, he could take liberties with it, and if that kind of energy were generated, then you've got a championship team.

Maybe the subtlety of all that had been too much for someone like Thomas. He certainly came equipped with the football intelligence necessary to allow him to work within, and outside, the system on the field. But maybe he was looking for more, for something deeper.

I mentioned this to Harris and he let out his breath slowly.

"Duane Thomas represented rebellion," he said, "the rebellion of youth in the post-Vietnam period. They tolerated it for a while and then didn't tolerate it anymore. He arrived too soon. It's sad."

There was a lot more, of course. The system might have been successful as a modus operandi on the football field, but as a way of life? Well, it left one very talented body in its wake. And now, on the field itself, it was just a shell, a gearbox without parts.

23

★

EPILOGUE

JOURNAL: The world's tragedies can be summed up in two words: Too Late.

February 1988. Duane Thomas and I took a drive up to Thousand Oaks, to the Cowboys' summer training camp at California Lutheran College. We hadn't been there since August. It was a warm morning, but you could feel a little nip behind it. Woody Hayes, the Ohio State coach, once said that your blood thins when you're in California and you feel the cold more acutely. I think he was right.

The pace was hurried, students on their way to classes, a contrast to the leisurely atmosphere around the Cowboys' camp. We walked over to the practice field, where we had watched the team work out. Tex Schramm had come over one day in July, and he and Thomas had stood side by side, staring at the field without speaking.

"What happened?" Schramm finally said, looking straight ahead. "Duane, can you tell me what happened?"

Thomas shook his head. Schramm didn't sound like the cold-blooded businessman at that point, like the "closet racist" that Thomas had so bitterly denounced in his journal. He sounded, well, puzzled and a bit wistful.

I caught Schramm in that same reflective mood later in the day, and I asked him how he felt about spending time with Thomas again after all these years.

"Well, he still talks funny," he said, just so I wouldn't forget I was talking to Tex Schramm, "but at least he isn't bringing around that guy with the robes anymore."

Then he thought for a moment.

"Duane said to me, 'You know, I feel a lot more relaxed now than I did as a player,' " Schramm said. "I said, 'I feel a lot more relaxed than I did, too.'

"Two great years are what he had . . . then it ended in ruins. We gave him a chance to come back . . . don't forget that . . . it was a big decision for Tom. Of course Duane had lost it by then."

Thomas had told me of a strange conversation he once had with Schramm in a restaurant in L.A.

"He started telling me about all the problems he had with his parents when he was growing up," Thomas said. "He said he went into football because it was accepted. He was forced into it, and it was demoralizing for him."

But now, in my conversation with Schramm, the mood had passed. He was the general manager again.

"I was happy to see Duane," he was saying, "but I wouldn't want him here every day. We've got enough philosophers around here."

Tom Landry was genuinely glad to see Thomas. So was Gil Brandt, who had negotiated his first contract with him.

"I think Duane always had a good feeling about me; he trusted me," Brandt said. "He went through a period when he would call me every two or three weeks. I got him endorsements. I negotiated a Penguin Shoe contract for him. To me Duane is like a son."

I told him what Thomas had written about him in his journal . . . "the mentality of a street pimp." Brandt put on a castor-oil face and waved his hand.

"Ah, well . . . ," he said. "Then why would he call so much? Sometimes he'd call just to chat . . . 'How does the draft look?' That kind of thing.

"I think there's one key to the whole thing. Right now Duane Thomas loves the Dallas Cowboys."

I couldn't argue with that. "They lost in good taste," was what Thomas said after the Miami game. He had tried to find something upbeat about the loss, anything. I watched him during the rookie scrimmages in camp, standing on the sidelines near the offense, occasionally pulling a rookie running back aside to offer some advice. Once I even saw him snapping remarks at opposing players. A Cowboy PR man had to tell him to calm down.

"Why don't you get yourself a skirt and pom-poms if you want to lead cheers?" I'd said afterward.

"I can't help it," he said. "You don't know what it's like when you get near it again. It's . . . well, it's football, man."

I remember talking to Rayfield Wright, about the bitterness he'd felt when the Cowboys cut him after thirteen years, eight of them as offensive captain, and how he went up to the Eagles, who had put together a Super Bowl team in 1980, and how he was going to help them get over the top, help them beat his old team.

"I passed my physical there," he said. "They were really happy to get me. I wanted to help them. And then it was like a balloon with all the air let out. It just wasn't there. I said, 'My God, Rayfield, after thirteen years in Dallas what are you doing in Philadelphia?' So I retired.

"You know, it's really deep, deeper than a lot of people can understand. It had been, well, it had been my team."

And it had been Thomas's team, too. For only two years, granted, but they were two Super Bowl years. Football played at its highest level, with himself as a focal figure. And then it collapsed.

During the 1987 season I ran into Berkeley's Dr. Harry Edwards in the 49ers' locker room, and I asked him how he, as a person active in black causes, viewed the tragedy of Duane Thomas.

"Tragedy? What tragedy?" he said. "Here was a guy on the professional level . . . he was on Front Street, in front of all those people . . . and he simply blew it. It was brought to everybody's attention because he was a great athlete. So what? I've seen hundreds of Duane Thomases who were great athletes who never made it out of the ghetto.

"Okay, so he took on the establishment, but on behalf of what, for what cause? Was it to reemphasize human dignity? I say prove it. Prove it to me."

Harsh, uncaring, the feelings of a person who has seen too much misery, too much misfortune. No, I could understand Dr. Edwards, but I couldn't agree with him. To me the fact that the world was full of tragedies didn't make Duane Thomas's story any less sad or compelling. He had been a purist in a way, a purist in football, in running, conditioning; actually an idealist, but there was a dark side, too. Rebellion, an irrational streak . . . his father sitting in front of the TV set in silent rage. He was a finely tuned instrument that needed delicate handling. Even the blunt, tough Joe Kerbel at West Texas State had understood that, but in the Cowboys, Thomas was confronting a system that no one had beaten. Or as the Raiders' all-pro tight end Todd Christensen once put it, when his battles with the Cowboy management resulted in his being cut—"I was going up against a monolith."

But here was Thomas back again talking with me about how "Tom has to talk to those young running backs and get them to lift their knees when they're running" and "Tom has to get them believing in themselves."

I reminded him of what he'd once written in his journal about Landry—"used Christianity for his own vanity, greed, and power . . . a John Birch mentality"—and the change was striking. All of a sudden the old defiance was back.

"I'll never forgive him," he said. "A man who's supposed to be a Christian gentleman and he destroys the life of someone who wanted nothing more than to make a decent living for his family."

We walked in silence for a while, past the locker rooms and the training facility.

"You know what he said to me back in July?" Thomas said. "I was working out in the weight area and he said, 'You know, Duane, Eric Dickerson would have a hard time with his rushing record if you were playing right now, with the kind of system defenses are playing today.' "

I've thought about that many times since then, about the strange duality in this person, how the bitterness can be overwhelmed by an even more powerful force. The game. Football. The love of it. Is this too trite? But I had seen it. I had seen football bringing these two divergent parties together again. I had seen a man lifted from one level to another within the space of minutes, by what? Sounds from a locker room. A scrimmage. The smell of sweat.

Thomas said another thing when we were at camp during the summer that I thought was particularly interesting.

"Do you know what player in this camp I can most relate to?" he said.

"Tony Dorsett," I said. He shook his head no.

"Johnny Lam Jones," he said.

I would never have guessed that. Jones had been a $2-million bonus baby for the Jets, and that was before the USFL war jacked up the salaries. They'd given up on him. So had the 49ers. Injuries, not enough production. Now he was a Cowboy.

"He came in glorified," Thomas said. "Red carpet treatment, never had to struggle. Now he's struggling. It's hard to have to let your pride down. I went in there and talked to him about it. I told him why I quit in 1972 . . . I just didn't want to be hurt anymore."

"You know," I said to Thomas, "I think you'd like nothing better in this world than to join the Dallas Cowboys as a running back coach."

"Well," he said, "I think I might be able to help some of those young guys."

I asked him how he could explain this duality in himself, love and hate crowded together in the same frame, how he could hate Schramm and Landry and Brandt one moment, and be on the phone the next. We were walking in the dormitory courtyard now, where he had looked out his window as a rookie and seen Lance Rentzel kissing Joey Heatherton good-bye.

"It's the truth and the honesty and the purity of the game away from all the corruption," he said. "It's the power of it.

"Isn't it amazing how when you break that huddle and start walking toward the ball it all dissipates, all the envy and hatred? Then after the game is over, we all go our separate ways, back to our own problems. You're together, then you're apart. That was the worst part of it. After you left the field your pain was your own."

So in 1987 they had come back together again, the Cowboys and their most notorious rebel. The weak one was becoming strong, the strong one was on the verge of a great slide: it was on the way down. They passed each other in transit. An organization so powerful that it could change a man's destiny had consumed itself, had become a cripple. And the individual who should have rejoiced at its downfall, who should have pointed the mocking finger, felt . . . what? Only compassion, a wistful kind of sadness, a longing for what could have been.